International Management Practice

An Insider's View

International Management Practice

An Insider's View

Gunnar Beeth
Cartoons by Wilhelm Noll

amacom

A Division of American Management Associations

© 1973 AMACOM
A division of American Management Associations,
New York. All rights reserved. Printed in the
United States of America.

International standard book number: 0-8144-5321-X
Library of Congress catalog card number: 73-75669

First printing

Preface, Introduction, Acknowledgments, and All That

THIS is a book of practical guidelines for international executives of American corporations. It is a "how to" book for generalists. It gives a brief overview of international business without becoming involved in the many important details that concern the specialists in different aspects of international business.

I am not a writer of books by trade, but an international operating manager and a management consultant. Here you will find only my personal opinions and some rules of thumb that have worked. Many of these rules have never before been presented in print, or even been expressed clearly. I have made my rules as brief as possible, even at the risk of oversimplification, and it is up to you to judge when to apply or not to apply them.

One subject, however, has been treated more thoroughly than the others and has been discussed from different viewpoints in various chapters. This is the subject of cultural differences as barriers to communication and business, a subject that is little understood, even by many businessmen with years of international experience. I hope that this book can help them appreciate how many of their difficulties come from an inability to truly cross the cultural barriers.

Although this book is about the simplest fundamentals of international business, it is addressed more to experienced managers than to beginners. To experienced managers many of my statements will ring a bell of recognition, and some may ignite new fires. To beginners the same statements may be meaningless or even controversial.

This book was completed despite eloquent opposition from my dear wife, who urged me to devote my few leisure hours to the family. I hope you don't agree with her after you've read it.

GUNNAR BEETH

Brussels

Contents

International Management Practice

An Insider's View

1

What Does It Take
to Go Global?

THERE are six main reasons for venturing into international markets. The first reason given below is by far the most important one for most companies.

1. *To harvest the profits.* With your company's know-how, you can harvest the profits not only from your domestic market, but also from the whole world.

Part of the additional profits harvested outside the home market can be reinvested in additional research and product development, giving your company more know-how, which in turn can be applied around the world—yielding additional profits, which in turn can be reinvested in additional research . . . and so on.

2. *To be close to new technical developments and trends in customer desires.* Because many new technical developments originate in Europe and Japan, your being on the scene, in close contact with your customers, will enable you to send back and exploit these new ideas much sooner than a purely domestic company can.

Suppose your domestic company, exporting abroad, uses foreign distributors or importers to reach your ultimate foreign customers. Do these independent intermediaries pass on to you as much market information on trends and developments as a subsidiary would?

And if the independent is a licensee, he may purposely stop information from flowing back to you, the licensor, for such reasons as we shall see in later chapters. The ingeniously devised clauses in licensing and distributorship contracts about feedback of information are totally un-enforceable and widely ignored, except when they suit the licensees or distributors.

3. *To avoid giving foreign competitors the edge.* Suppose your company has a strong position only in the United States and leaves the remainder of the world market uncovered. That gives a foreign competitor the opportunity to grow so strong abroad in the vacuum you have left him that he may later open up shop in the United States and challenge you.

4. *To utilize lower labor costs in manufacturing.* This reason for going global will be further discussed in the chapter on location of manufacturing.

5. *To get manufacturing inside certain customs duty or import license barriers or into a preferred country of origin or a low tax area, or to meet local, chauvinistic safety requirements.* Take, as an example, the U.S. safety requirements for compressed-air pressure vessels. They are a needless, chauvinistic import barrier. German, Swiss, and Swedish electrical safety codes also are often difficult for non-European manufacturers to comply with. These safety requirements are not always intended as barriers to foreign manufacturers, but that becomes one of their main practical effects. Were all the safety codes equal, the manufacturers could comply with them all using a single design and a larger series of manufacturing, to the subsequent benefit of the ultimate customers.

But the above barriers are those of industrialized countries, and they are child's play compared to the import licensing requirements, high customs duties, red tape, and many other barriers restricting international traders in the less industrialized countries, usually to the detriment of these countries themselves.

6. *To locate near the sources of supply.* This applies especially to extractive industries, of course. There is a new fear among less industrialized nations that some companies may want to locate there to be able to do the opposite and dump pollutants; but I doubt that there is much basis for this fear now.

Of course, there are many other reasons why companies expand abroad—for example, to get away from trust-busters at home who don't allow them expansion there; but generally these reasons are valid for only a few companies.

Does Your Company Have the Qualifications?

Only two qualifications are necessary to begin with; the others can come later. The two are an outstanding product or service and an outstanding international executive.

AN OUTSTANDING PRODUCT OR SERVICE

This qualification is so simple and self-evident that it is often overlooked. Yet it is by far the most important qualification for success in global markets.

Even a company that has capable international executives, excellent international advertising, hard-hitting sales forces, modern manufacturing plants, solid financing, and excellent international connections will fail internationally if it does not have a product or service that is outstandingly good or outstandingly inexpensive. Hundreds of American overseas subsidiaries lose money year after year because their products are mediocre—or good, but not outstanding.

Furthermore, a product that is outstanding in Kentucky may not be outstanding in West Germany.

A product that is outstanding in Kentucky
may not be outstanding in Germany.

You might feel that some products sold in the home market are too good and therefore too expensive for the global market; but I have not seen such a product, and I doubt that it exists. On the contrary, I have found that

> *In international business, he who makes a product a little better usually has a greater chance of success than he who makes it a little cheaper.*

Let's examine two examples from the automotive field that might seem at first glance to refute that statement: Cadillac sales in Europe are small, not so much because of the cost of the product as because of the high taxes on gasoline and heavy cars and the narrowness of streets and parking spaces. In fact, the European luxury cars, which are more suitably sized for Europe, are often more expensive, less comfortable, less powerful, and require more service than Cadillacs.

The Volkswagen "beetle" earned its international success because it was an outstandingly good car in its class, not because it was cheap. There used to be other European cars on the international market which were cheaper; where are they today?

How much better or cheaper must the product be? Exporting is expensive, and it is usually a laborious task to determine exactly how expensive it will be to export a new product. It is not at all enough to add up specific costs, such as freight and customs duty, because so many other more abstruse and less easily obtainable costs enter into the picture. Therefore, I find the following simple rule of thumb useful, even though it can be highly inaccurate in many cases:

> *To carry the costs of international trade among industrialized countries, a product must usually have at least a 25-percent advantage in the form of lower price, better quality, or more desirability of features.*

This rule is, of course, oversimplified. Two of its conditions must be carefully considered.

The rule applies only to trade between *industrialized countries.* The cost of exporting into less industrialized countries is usually much higher, frequently far above 100 percent of the value of the product.

The rule states *"at least* 25 percent." It is often necessary to have a bigger advantage. For example, if you are trying to sell a finished product to Australia and a competitor assembles a similar product there, then he can try to get the local customs authorities to clobber you with some 50-percent customs duty. (That once had a sobering effect on one of my competitors, who was hit with a 55-percent duty.)

If you plan to import to the United States a product on which you compare retail prices here and abroad, you must add to the 25 percent base the differential of distribution costs in the United States over those in the product's home country.

One exception to my rule of thumb is a product outside a company's main line. For such a product, you might accept an advantage much lower than 25 percent. Low-volume side products necessary to complete the line can sometimes be carried at lower profit or at no profit at all, barring antitrust, customs, and tax complications.

The percentage by which a product must be cheaper or better is, of course, much lower when the volume is sufficient for local manufacturing in the market where it is sold, because then the product need not carry the full international trading costs. (Also, there are fewer fingers in the pie.)

Sometimes the percentage is lower for trade between neighboring countries, especially within the same trading bloc. But even in this case, there are costs involved.

For example, if freight were the only consideration, it would be much cheaper to truck a product from Stuttgart in Germany to Strasbourg in France than to truck it the much longer distance from Stuttgart to Hamburg, although both are in Germany. There are no customs duties between Germany and France, but even this export transaction must carry the weight of international trade costs, which involves much more than handling red tape, trying to communicate between the two widely different cultures, and translating instruction books. In this particular case, French buyers might be prejudiced against the German product, whether it is a consumer product or industrial capital goods.

For many products, such as electrical control cabinets, this prejudice alone may create a disadvantage equal to more than 25 percent of the value of the goods. For some goods, the additional time required for an international transaction may warrant a substantial part of the 25-percent advantage.

Thus, each case must be studied on its own merits, and there is much more to consider than the figures you can obtain from forwarding agents and customs authorities. In any case, you will need a simplified starting point; 25 percent is mine.

Is the product really suitable? We are all well aware that the sale of consumer goods can often be attributed to local tastes, but many think that industrial equipment is purchased on a more rational, dollars-and-cents basis. This is usually not true. Local tastes and ideas may be as important in the sale of industrial products. Furthermore, preferences vary widely from country to country. A successful international manager works *with* these variations, develops sensitivity to them, and uses them to work in his company's favor. An experienced international manager never tries to hammer through a "logical approach," disregarding local emotional preferences.

Here are a couple of examples of the power of industrial customer tastes.

Several years ago, a leading international manufacturer of rock drills had developed a small, lightweight hand-held pneumatic drill for drilling vertical holes downward. It was an excellent drill and sold successfully in most of the world, but not in the United States, where it was not accepted, even though cost advantages could be shown easily in black and white on a small piece of paper. Why did the drill fail to sell in the United States? American contractors *preferred* much heavier and more expensive crawler-mounted machines, despite the additional cost per cubic foot of rock blasted. This seemed illogical to the European

The more dials and blinking lights, the better.

engineers involved. But nevertheless, the preference was there and just as formidable as if it had been logical.

Turning now to an example in the opposite direction, American engineers in industrial indoor plants want automatic equipment that works, is reliable, and has small, simple, functional control cabinets. They pay little attention to the looks of the control cabinets. But West European industrial engineers attach a great deal of importance to the appearance of the control cabinets. Generally speaking, the more dials and blinking lights, the better. A big, sloping control console with a hand-brushed stainless steel top that surrounds the operator on three sides is very attractive to European engineers, and they will pay well for this eyewash. American engineers are more likely to ask, "Now, wait a minute. What does this big thing do?"

In summary, we can say that before a company attempts to go global, it should determine whether its products or services are sufficiently outstanding to carry the costs of international trade and whether they are desirable in the import markets in terms of local competition as well as from the viewpoint of unusual or illogical local tastes and preferences, including any local emotional preferences or prejudices concerning the country of origin. Naturally, other potential barriers, such as local electrical codes, safety regulations, and union objections must also be investigated.

AN OUTSTANDING INTERNATIONAL EXECUTIVE

Assume that you have found your product outstanding in comparison with its international competitors, and potentially satisfying to the tastes of overseas buyers. Now you must have the second qualification: an outstanding international executive.

Apart from the usual qualities you would seek in a domestic executive, you must also look for evidence that your international man is able to understand, influence, and motivate people of different continents. Does he *really* know what makes them tick? In how many countries and in which ones does he know the people this well?

Other specific qualifications, such as knowledge of foreign languages, will be discussed in the chapter on international staffing. It is important at this point, however, to emphasize the vital nature of selecting an outstanding man for this position. All the remaining qualifications necessary for successful global business—from creating an international distribution system to hiring a good shipping clerk—can be developed by the international executive, if he is capable.

Some people think that to go global a company must have two additional qualifications: (1) it must be big, and (2) it must invest much money in the effort.

They are totally wrong on both scores. If the company has an outstanding product and an outstanding international executive, it can expand its operations around the world without using much money from the United States, and using only part of the international profits generated in the process.

2

Where to Use:
Combination Export Managers, Distributors, Licensees, Subsidiaries, and Joint Ventures

MUCH confusion exists on the subject of this chapter. So many otherwise well-run companies have made such obviously bum decisions that it is about time to strip away the multitude of secondary considerations and side issues that obscure the prime reason for working with, say, a distributor in one country and a subsidiary in another.

I will therefore simplify drastically by disregarding most of the interesting side issues and staying with only the main considerations in the hope of clarifying the fundamentals that have been unclear to many international executives.

Terms

Before going any further, I should clarify the way in which I am defining certain terms that will be used in this chapter.

An *agent* is the same as commission agent: a foreign company that promotes the sale of products directly from the manufacturer to customers in his country. The agent does not take title to the products. His customers normally carry out the work of importing them. For his services, the agent receives a commission from the manufacturer. (In domestic trade, the agent is often referred to as a manufacturers' representative or simply a rep.) For industrial goods, the agent's customers are the ultimate users. For consumer goods, his customers are wholesalers and mass merchandisers.

In contrast, a *distributor* buys for his own account, carries out the importation, maintains stock, and resells in his country. Although a distributor is very different from an agent, I often use the word "distributors" loosely to cover both distributors and agents. Neither of them performs manufacturing.

The term *importer* generally belongs in the consumer goods field. If an importer acts as an agent, he is sometimes called an import agent; if he acts as a distributor, he may be called an import wholesaler. Mass merchandisers often function also as their own importers.

I have used the term *licensee* narrowly to denote only an independent foreign company that performs manufacturing or processing in his country under license from the *licensor*. Usually, the licensee acts also as a distributor in his country, and sometimes also in some other countries of the same trade bloc.

I have used *manufacturer* to indicate the domestic company that originates the international business.

An *independent* is a foreign company in which the manufacturer has no capital, or only insignificant amounts of capital. Agents, distributors, importers, and licensees are all independents in this text.

A *subsidiary* is a wholly owned, or almost wholly owned, foreign company, whereas a *joint venture* is a company in which ownership is shared to a significant degree with one or more independent companies, usually foreign.

A *combination export manager* is an independent firm that functions as export agent for several manufacturers (hence the term "combination"), usually located in his home country. Such a firm is sometimes called an "export management company," which means exactly the same thing.

The relationships between manufacturers and importers in the consumer goods field are not usually as formalized, firm, and long-lasting as the relationships between manufacturers and distributors in the field of industrial goods.

Main Considerations

When you are choosing among all the different types of organizations, both at home and abroad,

> *The one overriding factor to consider is the potential size of the market for your products.*

In deciding on an organization abroad,

> *The second factor to consider is the legal and political climate for subsidiaries.*

As we shall see in more detail later in this chapter,

> *Distributors are chosen for smaller markets, subsidiaries for larger and politically secure markets or in cases when you need to manufacture in the foreign markets.*

> *Licensees are sometimes chosen when the legal and political climate prevents you from establishing a subsidiary, or when the foreign market size or the exportable know-how does not justify one, or when the capital investment in a subsidiary would be burdensome.*

> *Joint ventures are used where you would prefer subsidiaries but are prevented from establishing them by local laws or attitudes.*

In this chapter and in a few that follow, I am assuming that the American company is the manufacturer or the licensor and the foreign company is the distributor, licensee, subsidiary, or joint venture. Many of my statements also apply when the reverse is true. There may, of course, be some differences introduced by the large size of the U.S. market.

Combination Export Managers

The decision to use a combination export manager instead of having an inside employee in your company in charge of your exports deal directly with the foreign importers depends on a consideration of two main conditions.

A company uses an outside combination export manager:

1. *When the potential export volume warrants neither the employment of a capable inside export manager and all the foreign travel expense necessary for understanding foreign importers, nor the establishment of separate distributors for this particular company; and*

2. *When the product line of the company lends itself well to combination with exports of other companies.*

These are the two main conditions for preferring such a manager. There are also two secondary conditions that make it easier to work with such a firm:

When no great amount of technical knowledge is required to understand the product and its application, and

When high-speed communications are not of the essence. (Such speed is required for trading in items like fresh fruit or teenage apparel.)

Now let's get back to the main consideration, the one of potential export volume. At what volume do you abandon the combination export manager in favor of handling the exports yourself?

The answer may be determined after a weighing of the combined factors. For example, an industrial equipment manufacturer in a very specialized and complex field might dispense with the services of the combination export manager at less than $50,000 annual export volume, especially if he has employees who know how to handle the exports. On the other hand, a manufacturer of an item such as rubber shoe heels might do well to stay with his combination export manager for an export volume of hundreds of thousands of dollars a year, if the manager also represents manufacturers in closely allied fields, such as shoestrings or soles. He may also keep the combination export manager if the latter has just the right overseas distributors and manufacturing customers tied up.

The importance of volume in the choice between outside and inside export managers points up the dilemma of most combination export managers: If they do a bad job for a client, he lets them go for that reason. On the other hand, if the export managers do a good job for him, he lets them go because his export volume has grown so big that it is better for him to handle his exports himself.

Therefore, enlightened combination export managers view their jobs for each manufacturer as temporary. The business continuity for these capable managers comes from having a flow of new clients continually replacing those who leave.

Piggyback exporting is a program recommended by the United States Department of Commerce. Under this program, successful exporting manufacturers function similarly to combination export managers for smaller manufacturers in related, complementary fields.

Successful exporting manufacturers are classified under this program according to products and are matched to smaller manufacturers of exportable related products who lack knowledge in exporting. In theory it should be possible to sell the smaller companies' products through the established worldwide networks of the larger companies. Through this program, the U.S. government wants to increase exports, but I don't know whether in practice the program has had much impact.

Independents: Distributors vs. Licensees

We noted that independent companies such as distributors and licensees are usually chosen in countries where the potential sales volume and potential profit do not justify establishing subsidiaries. There are some additional considerations in the choice between independents and subsidiaries, but they will be discussed in the next section. Here we will concentrate on the differences between the two types of independents, distributors and licensees, because these differences go far beyond a definition of terms, and I have never seen them described in print.

Internationally experienced men know the real reason why there are often strong pressures from distributors to become licensees. The distributors will give only superficial reasons for these pressures and never mention the actual ones. It is important that you know the real reasons, because these pressures should often be strongly resisted. They can be much more against the interests of the manufacturer than is apparent on the surface.

Let's assume that a foreign distributor of yours is beginning to raise his voice about wanting a license to manufacture in his country because "the import duties are too high" or "the import licenses are too difficult to get" or "I could use local labor for assembly operations and perform them much more cheaply than you could." It is up to you to study his reasons. You may find that it would be even more difficult to import the many different components and parts needed to make your product in his country than it is to import your finished product.

You may also find that the lower hourly labor rate there is more than offset by lower productivity caused by a smaller scale of manufacturing, lower skill, less willingness to work, lower sense of responsibility, more government interference, or just the unfortunate instability of the country.

Why is the distributor then so eager to manufacture locally and become a licensee? Because he then gains control of the second one of the three main parts of the total business. The total business cycle can be pictured as in Figure 1. A distributor controls only one part (sales), whereas a licensee controls two out of the three areas in the total business cycle (sales and manufacturing). Furthermore, it is often logical for a licensee to add his own product development over the years, so that he then controls the whole business cycle.

In the case of a split in the international business relationship between a manufacturer or licensor in one country and a distributor or licensee in another country, the party that needs the other party least has control.

It might be even more difficult to import the many components to make your product in the foreign country than it is to import the finished product.

Figure 1

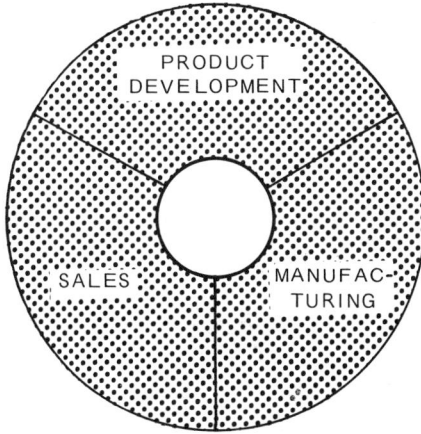

If there is no split, the party that has control can in the long run take the largest part of the total profits. If the overseas party has control of two of the three parts of the total business cycle shown above, he can usually take the lion's share of the total profits.

Don't believe the person who tells you that he can write a license contract in such a way that the licensor maintains control. He can't—not unless the licensor has unusually good patents and is known for his willingness to defend them strongly, or he is in a rapidly changing technical field in which today's know-how becomes obsolete quickly, so that the licensee continues to need the flow of new know-how from him.

Thus, apart from these two exceptional cases (strong patents or rapidly changing know-how), the difference between a distributor and a licensee goes far beyond the difference between importing and manufacturing. It reaches to the heart of the questions "Who controls the business in the foreign country?" and "Who gets the main profits?"

That does not mean, though, that all arguments from distributors who want to assemble or manufacture locally are wrong. Freight may be very expensive. New local customs duties may be prohibitive. (In some countries, however, you may want to find out who recommended the new duties and whether they really will be adopted.)

To summarize, I recommend the following rules of thumb for most businesses:

> *Examine with much suspicion the arguments of distributors in favor of local manufacturing.*

(Amazingly, the same should be done with subsidiary managers' arguments for local manufacturing. Often they underrate or ignore the reasons against it.)

If the distributor's arguments for local manufacturing are valid and carry enough weight, and if the potential market is large enough to warrant it, consider instead starting a subsidiary or a joint venture rather than letting an independent company gain your manufacturing know-how.

If you find yourself with manufacturing licensees where it does not make sense for you to manufacture locally, here is an additional rule:

Keep such manufacturing licensees from manufacturing your new products as they are launched.

Thus you can eventually gain back some of the control you have lost. This will arouse very strong resistance from the licensees, but it should, nevertheless, be done with a firm hand for the sake of your control over the business and your future profits.

Control of foreign operations is an elusive, indefinable matter seldom discussed in print (maybe because nobody wants to seem Machiavellian). Yet, you must consider it squarely. Therefore, I repeat:

Ultimately, the party that needs the other party least has control.

Even when discussions are not carried to the extreme of threatening to split up a business relationship, he who has control can tell the other party how the business shall be conducted and how the total profits shall be split, because both parties know that he can add "or else."

In the relationship between a manufacturer and a distributor, it is usually the manufacturer who can say "or else we will find another distributor." But in the relationship between a licensor and a licensee (except for well-patented or fast-changing products), it is usually the licensee who can tell the licensor "or else we will go it alone." This is one of the main weaknesses of licensing.

A licensee for a nonpatented product that is not changed rapidly typically spends the first few years absorbing all the know-how he can, the following few years finding reasons why his royalty payments should be lowered, and the remaining years figuring out how he can break loose and go it alone as a competitor of his former licensor. Thus, we conclude in many cases:

> *Do not use licensing when manufacturing of your products involves much secret know-how.*

Subsidiaries vs. Independents

Subsidiaries are the first choice of experienced international managers, provided that: (1) the potential volume of business in the specific foreign country justifies it; (2) the potential profitability of the business is good; (3) the political stability, laws, and attitudes of the country permit it; and (4) financing of the subsidiary is not an insurmountable obstacle, or too risky. Let's briefly examine each of these points.

POTENTIAL VOLUME OF BUSINESS

The potential volume of a subsidiary cannot be judged by what an independent has achieved, but only from what carefully calculated statistics show to be possible, as we shall see in a later chapter. The potential sales volume must in any case be sufficient for a company of minimum size.

Suppose the potential volume in a country is big enough for only two full-time employees. Don't get involved in a subsidiary there. A great deal of the work with lawyers, tax authorities, import authorities, auditors, the parent company, and others is approximately equal in volume, whether the company has two or ten employees. Translation of company literature, participation in trade shows, and many other expenses are also somewhat independent of company size.

If one of the company's two employees is ill, the work load becomes impossible for the remaining one. Furthermore, bookkeeping, mailing, telephone answering, and similar necessary but unproductive tasks are too large a burden if the company consists of only two highly qualified employees, because they will have to spend most of their time on work beneath the qualifications for which they are being paid. In this case, a subsidiary should not be used.

POTENTIAL PROFITABILITY

If the distribution of your line has good profitability in a country, then you want to be able to take *all* the profits instead of giving away part of them to an independent. This should usually be the main consideration in the choice between subsidiary and independent companies, yet this fundamental point is sometimes forgotten among the many lesser considerations.

The world is only a finite market. It will always be there for you to cover. Rather than rushing in and handling all of it halfway, concentrate on exploiting the major parts of the world as fully as circumstances permit. For this reason, it is important to get the whole profit from the major countries wherever possible.

If, on the other hand, the potential profitability in a country is not high, you might as well let independents struggle with it. Often a distributor can make good profits where you cannot, because only a small part of his overhead is charged to your line, or because his salesmen sell other goods along with yours at many of their calls.

Sometimes a distributor will take on a line only for its prestige value, to use it as a door-opener for the sale of his remaining products, or to complete his other lines.

If the potential profit is too low in a specific country even for a distributor, forget that country entirely and sit back and watch with glee when competitors struggle with it. Be firm against those of your colleagues who invariably argue, "We must cover Country X because Competitor Y is trying to land some orders there."

When your colleagues tell you that you must manufacture in less industrialized Country W, because Competitor Z intends to start manufacturing there, and Country W will, therefore, establish prohibitive customs duties, then you must be even more adamant in examining critically the profit potential before plunging in.

Many sophisticated international managers can sit back quietly in a situation like this, forget Country W for a few years, and watch Competitor Z lose lots of money and valuable central management time there. It is even better if Competitor Y also starts manufacturing there. They will both lose twice as much.

POLITICAL CONSIDERATIONS

If the political stability of the country is low, the profitability, including the part of the profits that you can take out of the country, must be correspondingly much higher before you can invest in a subsidiary there. If they are not, you should choose an independent instead. If, on the other hand, everything points to a subsidiary in the country, and yet the laws don't permit it, then you should choose a joint venture.

FINANCIAL CONSIDERATIONS

If your company wants to set up operations in an industrialized country, financing will not usually be an important barrier against establishing a subsidiary. Exceptions include heavy industries and certain mining operations, where financing becomes one of the major considerations; and high-risk ventures, where financing can be burdensome in relation to the risk.

Now let's review some of the *advantages* of the independent company. We noted that an independent can operate more economically, partly because he can split his overhead on more than one line of business, and partly for other reasons. He generally has more local knowledge and connections. And the benefit of the financial incentive to the owner–manager to do a good job may outweigh the benefit of the incentive derived from the commissions and bonuses given to executives of subsidiaries.

On the other hand, foreign licensees and distributors are more fleeting or transient than subsidiaries. They are subject to serious changes beyond the control of the manufacturer or licensor. They are frequently hampered by the manufacturer's or licensor's necessary hesitation in giving them all the confidential know-how they need to operate well.

Thus, we conclude that foreign subsidiaries constitute the really solid part of a company's foreign operations.

Joint Ventures

In terms of capital investment and legal position, joint ventures are the intermediate solution between independents and subsidiaries; but do not let that mislead you into thinking that a joint venture is the answer if you are sitting on the fence trying to decide between a subsidiary or an independent company. On the contrary, in these borderline cases, you must get off the fence and choose either an independent or a subsidiary.

> *Choose joint ventures in those cases where potential volume and profit point squarely to the choice of a subsidiary, but the laws of the country make it impossible or very difficult to have a subsidiary there.*

Examples might be Japan and Mexico. (And yet, Japan may change the rules to allow more subsidiaries that are foreign-owned.)

In the same way, if the attitudes of the local people and government are too strongly against subsidiaries, you may prefer a joint venture. Your decision in favor of a joint venture over a subsidiary is further reinforced if the country is politically unstable, as are most of the less industrialized countries.

At the time this is being written, there is vociferous antagonism against American subsidiaries in some West European countries, especially within certain industries. This antagonism may well increase. Yet it should not prevent many companies from establishing subsidiaries in most of Western Europe, including France. Forget it. Close your ears and do whatever your market figures show to be best.

If the prospective profit figures for Italy, however, show that country to be just above the size for which you would normally choose a distributing subsidiary, then you might choose instead an independent distributor for Italy.* The reasons are that Italian sales methods are often "colorful," and local methods of tax avoidance are "effective" but of a kind no American subsidiary can long engage in.

If you want to set up a subsidiary in a country, but there is some legal barrier against it, investigate this barrier thoroughly. A good corporate advisor may well find ways around it. For years this has been possible in Spain; and even Japan is not as closed to subsidiaries as it may appear at first glance.

My own preference for subsidiaries over joint ventures is by no means shared by everyone. The vice-president of one of the largest international corporations stated that he strongly favored the joint company concept in foreign ventures. In my opinion,

> When the conditions in the country are right, subsidiaries are preferable, foremost, to get the whole profit; second (and much less important), to get more freedom of action for global optimization of the locations of manufacturing, research, etc.; and third, to get more freedom in intercompany pricing—within legal limits—leading toward minimization of the global sum of taxes and customs duties.

I would use joint ventures instead of subsidiaries in the following three cases:

1. When forced into it by local discrimination against foreign-owned subsidiaries.
2. When the capital investment is unusually burdensome. For example:

* The above comments cover only an Italian distributing company. They do not apply to a tax-exempt Italian manufacturing company in the Mezzogiorno (an area in southern Italy within which special aid is available to industry).

—With unusually large capital requirements, such as for heavy industries like steel.

—With unusually risky capital investment, such as drilling for oil in a new part of Algeria.

—With unusually low availability of capital from the U.S. parent—for instance, if the necessary borrowing power is unavailable or needed for other purposes. In some such cases, it might be better to have one-third of a big, strong joint venture than 100 percent of a small, weak subsidiary.

3. When having a minority of an independent company can give you important U.S. income tax benefits that are not obtainable if you control the foreign company. (Such cases are unusual.) The tax benefits may include capital-gains treatment of the sale of substantial assets, such as patents (but not know-how). (Of course, such a sale can be made only if the independent company can be convinced of the high value of the assets.)

I stated earlier that the main consideration in favor of a subsidiary—gaining the whole profit—is often obscured by many secondary considerations in favor of a joint venture or some other arrangement. Now let's briefly review a few of these secondary considerations. Boosters of joint ventures say that, in comparison to subsidiaries, joint ventures provide:

Access to good management with knowledge of local conditions.

My comment: Usually you can hire excellent local management for a subsidiary for much less than the amount you would have to pay foreign partners as a share of the profits.

Good connections.

My comment: Often you can hire a subsidiary manager, an assistant manager, or a chairman with the good connections.

Access to scarce labor and other employees.

My comment: If you have hired good local managers, they can hire better-than-average employees in any industrialized country at little or no premium and at any time, as explained in the chapter on subsidiaries.

A good way to overcome U.S. limitations on foreign direct investments when such limitations exist.

My comment: If the profitability of the venture is high, there are good ways of investing in an overseas subsidiary without sending money abroad. If, on the other hand, the profitability is not good enough for this, then you should choose an independent company anyway.

3

Distributors:
Finding and Keeping
the Excellent Ones

IN this chapter, I have used the word *distributor* loosely to denote "sole distributors," one for each country, or sole agents, or sole importer–wholesalers. (The antitrust section of the chapter on legal and tax matters further describes the "sole distributor" concept.)

The Importance of Having the Right Distributor

Most international companies looking at the actual performance of their foreign distributors find that it does not fall within, say, 80 to 120 percent of their expectations based on carefully determined market-potential figures. Instead, they find actual performance varies from 0 to more than 200 percent. Thus, the difference in performance of distributors is enormous. Finding the excellent distributors is, therefore, all-important.

But even with your best efforts, you will never have a collection of only excellent distributors. With hard and careful work, you can have a few excellent, many adequate, some mediocre distributors, and a few worthless ones whom you are always trying to replace. There is no way to hit 100 percent.

According to my rule of thumb, in most countries with only *small* markets you will find in each field zero or one excellent distributor, zero or one adequate distributor, and one or two mediocre distributors; all the remaining distributors will be worthless to you.

In most countries with somewhat *larger* markets, yet not so large that they warrant a subsidiary, there often are a few more distributors in each of the above categories.

This severe limitation in the availability of excellent and even adequate distributors is one of the basic factors in determining how to organize sales through distributors and, in turn, how to cultivate the few excellent ones.

How to Find the Excellent Distributors

Although one or two distributors may have contacted you, the statistical chance that they happen to be best is small. Lists of distributors, broken down by fields of activity, are available for each country from the U.S. Department of Commerce (a good source), from local chambers of commerce (usually not good), from local classified directories of various kinds (often too inclusive), and from other sources. But you don't want a list; you want the name of one distributor in each country—the best one.

To begin with, don't waste your time contacting them all by mail and sending them forms to complete. This is worthless, as we shall see shortly. Here is a three-step procedure I have developed to find a good distributor:

1. Go in person to the country, allowing ample time to talk to the people who will buy from your future distributor, and find out from them which distributors they prefer and why. Two or three names will keep popping up in the replies you get.
2. Then go to those two or three distributors and see which one or ones you would be able to sign up.
3. But before making the final choice, look for the distributor who has the key man for your line, as explained below.

Long ago, I used to travel around with a list on which I rated each distributor on a scale from one to ten in each of 24 different categories, such as sales force, coverage of the market, management ability, capability of service personnel, financial strength, connections, warehouse and service facilities, stocks of spare parts, performance in related lines, and technical ability to understand the equipment. Then I weighed these different matters in accordance with the importance of each and arrived arithmetically at a single overall rating figure for each distributor.

Unfortunately, the final rating figure for the distributors I was supervising showed no correlation at all to their actual performance.

So I threw away the list and looked for what was common to the few excellent distributors I had the privilege to be working with. In this way, I discovered a single new factor to replace my 24-point list, and this new factor bore 100 percent correlation to success. I started to

> *Look for a distributor who has one capable man who would take the new line of equipment to his heart and make it his personal objective to make the sale of that line a success in his country.*

In some small distributorships, this key man was the owner. In others, he was the sales manager or a salesman. In one company, he was the service manager. In one case, there were two such men instead of one, but that was a rare distributor who somehow did three times what we considered the volume possible for his country.

In fact, often it is not as easy as indicated above to find a good distributor in a country, especially not in a very small, less industrialized country. As stated earlier, there you might find no excellent distributors, no adequate distributors, and only one or two mediocre distributors, firmly tied to your competitors; the remaining distributors will be worthless to your business. Suppose none of them shows any sign of having or getting the key man you are looking for. What do you do?

First, you can try to find a local businessman in a different field, who wants to fill the obviously crying need for a good distributor in your field and related fields. Failing that, you can try to get one of the mediocre distributors to switch from the competitor to you. Occasionally you may get to him just when he is disgruntled with your competitor for some reason or other.

If that falls through, you had better forget about appointing any distributor at all in that country, because having a worthless one will cost you time and money every year and possibly prevent a good newcomer in that country from requesting to sell your line.

In such a case, however, you may want to consider attending a local industrial exhibition in that country and ask further advice from the prospective ultimate users of your products in the area. If there should be a nearby U.S. Trade Center, they can help you mount a small exhibition of your products for the specific purpose of finding a distributor.

If you do find a number of distributors worth investigating, listen closely to what they tell you when you interview them, because they often reveal more about themselves than they realize. Here is an example: I used to sell compressors and call on distributors in the heavy construction field. The prime line of some of them was Caterpillar tractors and of others, International Harvester tractors. When asked how their business was, some would answer "great," while others would say that it was impossible to compete against International Harvester or Caterpillar, whichever line they did not have.

Those who said it was impossible to compete raised one warning signal: Are these distributors going downhill? What has happened to them? Why can't they compete?

But those who said that the tractor business was great raised another, equally important warning signal. Do they concentrate all their efforts on their tractor line? Are they great at selling tractors and rotten at selling everything else? Latching onto distributors who are excellent for another manufacturer in an allied field does not always produce excellent results. Here, as elsewhere, the availability of the key man for your line can easily make the difference between the excellent and the worthless distributor.

How to Keep the Excellent Distributors

The only way to keep a good distributor is to work closely with him so that he can make money with your line.

Look at your business from the distributor's side: First of all, he must make money for himself. If that automatically makes him earn money for you, too, then fine. But if he does not make money for himself with your line, any really good distributor will quickly drop it. Or worse, he may put your line away where he has it available should one of his customers ask for it, but otherwise he will ignore your products.

Thus, you must not only keep the good distributor but also keep the distributor good. And the last part is not always easy, because there are many demands on his time from other lines of equipment and from customers with interests and problems outside your field. Somehow, through direct mail and visits, you must arrange to keep your line constantly in front of your distributor, among his daily duties and thoughts.

It is best, of course, if you can require that he have one or more full-time people handling your line; but if the potential sales volume is not high enough to warrant this extra effort, do not ask for it. If you cause the distributor losses through excessive demands on him, your efforts may backfire.

Above all, you must not be stingy in matters such as paying for the training of your distributor's men and going beyond your legal warranty obligations to him. He goes beyond his legal obligations to his customers, and he expects the same from you.

It is important to spell out the rules concerning when the distributor or agent is paid a commission, and to make sure that he understands these rules in advance, especially the ones about when he is *not* paid a commission.

Nevertheless when an unclear, borderline case occurs, you should rule in favor of your distributor. In the long run, the distributor's goodwill toward your company is more valuable than the commissions paid in borderline cases. The quickest way to destroy a distributor's goodwill is to make him feel cheated, even on a small matter.

Unless your sales volume with each distributor is very large, you cannot afford to run his business or to try to remake a mediocre distributor into a good one. One American company has an outstanding record of going against this rule: Caterpillar Tractor Company works so closely and well with a distributor that it can make him good in many cases. But for most other companies, this method is too costly.

Instead, if a good distributor changes into a mediocre or bad one, the sooner you can find an excellent replacement for him, the better off you are. Unfortunately, you will never know in advance if your new one is excellent. But try anyway, and if he is the same or worse, switch again, as soon as you have found a third (hopefully) excellent prospect.

Some people argue that this switching around shows a lack of stability and seriousness toward the customers of the distributors. Don't worry. They are probably better aware of the shortcomings of your former distributors than you are. They appreciate your trying to find a good one. And your sales figures show it quickly when you succeed.

The list of distributors of any aggressive, worldwide company is constantly changing, because the distributors themselves rapidly undergo changes. It might be that the key man for your line has left a distributor, and your sales drop forthwith by 90 percent. Unless you can get the distributor to replace the former man with an equally good key man, or switch the responsibility for your line to another of his best men, don't keep that distributor. Don't just hope that things will improve, as some people will advise.

How to Get Rid of the Mediocre Distributors

When you do change distributors, do it totally, quickly, cleanly, and thoroughly, without worrying about being called ruthless by your old distributor. He will always feel your cancellation as a personal affront anyway. He will say that you are not loyal. Forget it. An active, aggressive, changing distributor list produces more sales.

In addition, your aggressive policies tend to keep your merely adequate distributors on their toes and doing their best.

The lengthy distributor contract has only one important clause: the cancellation clause. Most of the remainder is a listing of who does what, written in legalese. In most light industrial equipment businesses, it should be possible for either party to cancel at any time after the first year, after 60 days' notice to the other party. Other industries may have longer cancellation periods, but beware that you are not trapped into an *overly* long cancellation period—which is common with sloppily managed companies.

What happens to the distributor's stock in case of cancellation by the manufacturer? The answer varies considerably from country to country because of local laws, but never should the manufacturer be required to take back any obsolete or otherwise unsalable merchandise. If the manufacturer must agree to take anything back, it should be at the net f.o.b., factory price, less a hefty restocking charge, unless local laws force the manufacturer to do otherwise.

Of course, some distributors may object to a strong cancellation clause, but it is well worth fighting for, although you naturally hope that you will never need to use it.

Before you sign a distributorship contract, the cancellation clause should be checked by a local lawyer to minimize any local indemnification requirements to distributors upon cancellation. In some countries, the amount of indemnification to distributors upon cancellation depends on just how the business is conducted. In France, if the distributor has certain reporting obligations, the indemnification risk increases. In Germany, there is no indemnification to a true stocking distributor, or *Eigenhändler,* but there is one to a commission agent, at least if he has certain reporting obligations.

Since the laws governing distributorship contracts vary widely from country to country, their impact on cancellation of distributors must be taken into account when you are choosing the country *from* which you want to service and supervise distributors in an area such as Europe. You may prefer a country with favorable laws that you can utilize in governing the distributorship contracts.

To illustrate, assume that an American subsidiary in France supervises and supplies a distributor for Italy. In this case, the contract must be written so that either French or Italian law applies. Neither is particularly favorable, but Italian law will serve you somewhat better than French law if the distributor has to be cancelled.

But if the same Italian distributor is to be supplied from an American subsidiary in Denmark, the contract should specify Danish law to apply instead, to lower the risk of indemnification upon cancellation, because Danish law is usually more favorable to the manufacturer than Italian law.

The cancellation of a distributor or licensee can be a delicate transaction, and it must be handled well. If the cancelled distributor was ineffective, then the remaining distributors in neighboring countries will understand and support the cancellation. If, on the other hand, the matter is not as clear-cut, yet for some business reason it should become necessary to cancel an adequate distributor, then the action must be thoroughly explained to the remaining distributors, customers, and others. An excellent distributor is never cancelled. Any cancellation must, of course, always be thoroughly prepared under the applicable law.

Contrary to what distributors seem to feel, there is nothing morally wrong in cancelling a distributor who doesn't work out. This is usually the only economical way to change from an ineffective independent company to an effective one.

Had it been your subsidiary instead, you could have remedied the specific cause for the company's ineffectiveness. As mentioned, this is usually too difficult to do in an independent company, because you don't control it. In a subsidiary, if the sales manager becomes an alcoholic, you can try sending him to clinics or—if everything else fails—fire him. But in a distributorship, the sales manager might also be the owner's son, for instance. You have no control over this, so you are forced to change to another distributor.

4

Licensees:
Their Care and Feeding

MUCH of what has been said about distributors applies also to licensees, except that licensees cannot be changed as readily as distributors. Therefore, they must be selected even more carefully. The requirements on a licensee are somewhat similar to those placed on a joint venture partner, as described in a later chapter.

The Delicately Balanced Relationship

We saw earlier that in the relationship between licensor and licensee, the party who can most easily get along alone has control; and the one who has control takes the majority of the profit. So we conclude:

> *To protect his profit, a licensor is forced to try to maintain a licensee in a state of dependence.*

When the licensee gains independence and takes control in his country, the whole relationship changes. Many manufacturers have found that their relationship with some licensees is like holding a tiger by the tail: The licensor is holding on only because he would be in even worse trouble if he were to let go. As mentioned earlier, many have let go, only to find that their former licensee has become a formidable competitor.

When much secret know-how has already been given to the licensee, other manufacturers have found that their only alternative is to acquire all or part of the licensee, often at far too high a cost. The capable international executive plans ahead far enough to avoid getting his company into such an awkward position.

Below we will consider three types of licensing in which these unfortunate situations can sometimes be avoided.

LICENSING OF PATENT-PROTECTED ITEMS

Licensing is not dangerous if the goods or processes are well protected by patents running far into the future, especially if the licensor is known for willingness to protect his patents through years of expensive litigation.

LICENSING OF RAPIDLY CHANGING KNOW-HOW

Licensing is not dangerous if technical development in the specific field progresses so rapidly that the licensee can gain more by staying with the licensor than by going it alone. In this case, the licensor keeps feeding the licensee more and more new, secret know-how. This is good "feeding" of licensees and keeps them tame—if the technical know-how becomes obsolete fairly quickly.

Know-how that is not changed rapidly—static know-how—cannot be licensed. The basic difference between licensing a patent and licensing static know-how is that the patent is on a string and can be pulled back to the licensor, but once the know-how is delivered, it is gone. This is why static know-how can be sold outright (perhaps even on long-term credit and with payments subject to future sales volume), but it cannot be licensed or rented. Many companies that make the mistake of trying to license it find themselves holding onto that dreaded tiger's tail.

LICENSING OF TRADEMARKS

In contrast to patents, trademarks can maintain their value for many years. If trademarks are licensed for a reasonable fee, maintained well in the market, and protected through various means, including advertising, closely supervised quality control, and engineering standards, then it is often better for the licensee to stay with the trademark-owner than to strike out on his own.

However, remember that in order to maintain this situation, the trademark and the licensee must constantly be well cared for by the licensor.

Never sell your trademarks in any country if you intend to continue using them in your home country. Those who bought them might misuse them and cause the trademarks to lose value in the rest of the world.

Some trademark licensing, with the accompanying quality control and other requirements, comes quite close to franchising. Undoubtedly, we will see international franchising come of age in the near future and bring much profit to franchisors, franchisees, and the many lawyers who will settle their disagreements and complex antitrust matters. But only those franchisors who adapt to local tastes will have a chance to be successful in their international operations.

Antitrust Barriers to Licensing

As if the natural business barriers to licensing were not enough, in 1970 the U.S. Department of Justice added to the already high legal barrier against licensing by bringing suits against a number of well-known multinational companies headquartered in the United States, Japan, and Germany.

The government attacked allocation of markets for goods made with patented processes, and for extending rights available for patented products to unpatented allied products. These suits already make it dangerous to license many patented processes (as opposed to patented products) to independent foreign firms.

This new, sharper antitrust attitude will have serious negative effects on U.S. licensing of independent foreign companies for years to come, putting U.S. licensors in an unfavorable position in relation to their foreign competitors. Whatever the outcome of these suits, the new attitude certainly does not help the U.S. balance of payments.

Japanese antitrust regulations on the books since the late 1960s have now become activated. Just how troublesome these new rules will be in the future is not yet known, but they have some paragraphs that may restrict even necessary quality control. In general, these Japanese regulations take a dim view of:

Restricting the licensee's right to export to other countries, or forcing the licensee to export only at fixed prices, or restricting resale prices in Japan.

Restricting the licensee's sources of purchasing, channels of distribution, or the quality of purchased materials and finished goods.

Restricting the licensee's right to use similar, nonlicensed technology or deal in similar, nonlicensed goods or processes, or requiring him to pay license fees on similar but nonlicensed goods or technology.

Tax Barriers to Licensing

The tax situation should be carefully investigated before a license agreement is entered into. Taxes on royalties vary from 0 to 80 percent in different countries.

Generally there are no royalty taxes, or they are low, in industrialized countries (except Australia), and high in the less industrialized ones. (This is ironic, because the less industrialized countries need the licenses most.) Often the taxes are higher on royalties between related companies than between independent firms. Some companies establish a Swiss "paper" company to receive and hold license royalties from several countries. It is sometimes a tax advantage if the American parent company does not own more than 50 percent of this Swiss company.

In addition to the main taxation of royalties, there may be turnover taxes, value-added-type taxes, and municipal, cantonal, or other local taxes, which are not always minimal.

Keeping the Licensee Up to Date

Good luck to the licensor who must transfer enough technical know-how to his licensee to enable him to work satisfactorily without passing on so much of that know-how as to enable the licensee to become a full-fledged competitor in the future.

Sometimes these two opposing requirements are not as conflicting as they seem on the surface, however. For example, the licensor might hold on to all new secret manufacturing know-how and transmit only know-how regarding the sale and application of the product. He might insist on *exporting* the newest and best equipment made with secret manufacturing know-how, rather than licensing it for manufacture overseas.

Transferring the applications know-how to a licensee can be quite a problem, as we shall discuss in the chapter on barriers to communication.

Maintaining Quality Control and Engineering Standards

It is of the utmost importance for a licensor to establish from the beginning strict quality control—and engineering standards, if the products are of a technical nature—and to police its licensees. Neglecting these responsibilities is a major error that is very difficult to correct once the bad habits have gained a foothold.

In the industrial equipment field, you should have equipment that is interchangeable between countries. Consumer goods should usually be required to meet equally high quality-control standards everywhere. Otherwise, international customers who have bought products of lower quality in one country may think that your products are equally bad elsewhere.

Some Tips About the Licensing Agreement

The list of recommended information sources at the end of this book includes works itemizing the many points to be remembered in drawing up a licensing agreement, as well as sample contracts and other helpful information. Here I will just mention some of the main points included in most contracts, so that the nonlawyer or layman, the executive who initially negotiates the main points, can remember some of the matters to cover:

Definition of the parties to the agreement (if there can be any doubt).

Specification of the products or processes to be licensed.

Specification of exclusive or nonexclusive license. Specification of whether sublicensing is permitted or required and how it must be conducted.

Assignment of territories. (Be careful with antitrust regulations!)

Definition of patents, existing know-how, future know-how, and trademarks subject to the license.

Detailed description of the role each party should play in the agreement as regards disclosure of know-how (and obligation of the licensee and his employees to keep it confidential), technical assistance, travel, quality control and policing by the licensor, and quality maintenance by the licensee (and recourse of the licensor in case of quality failure).

Cross-licensing of new know-how or patents developed by the licensee.

License fees and who pays local taxes on them.

Legal action against third-party infringement of any patent.

Duration, termination, and the parties' rights after termination.

Assignability; purchase options of any share of ownership in the licensee.

Arbitration and applicable law.

It is best to seek legal advice and to arrange a briefing on the many pitfalls to avoid *prior* to starting the negotiations for any major licensing agreement. Then go, unaccompanied by a lawyer, to the top executives of the licensee, concentrate on the main points during the initial phase, write them down, exchange drafts, and celebrate together the basic agreement prior to legal refinements. Finally, get together with lawyers from both sides (after having both sides instruct their lawyers to keep it all simple and brief) and push the lawyers to come to an agreement on all the details before the atmosphere between the two companies goes sour over dickering.

In addition, some recommend obtaining the prospective licensee's estimates of future sales and including them in letters between the parties, so that they can be referred to in the future.

We saw that simple licensing of straight know-how can be unwise for the licensor in the long run. There are often better alternatives to this type of licensing. Here are just a couple of combinations that can be considered:

Combination of know-how and trademark licensing. (Be careful, though, to avoid subjecting yourself to the possible future accusation of having used trademarks only for the purpose of dividing territories. This is taboo!)

Combination of the initial sale of current secret know-how for a substantial lump sum with a licensing agreement (with moderate fees) for transferring future know-how on a continuing basis.

5

Subsidiaries: Building Them Strong

OVER the last 15 years among international companies, there has been a trend from licensing toward joint ventures and from joint ventures toward subsidiaries, in those countries where the laws and attitudes permit them. We have discussed the advantages of subsidiaries over other forms of organization. This chapter deals with developing strong subsidiary operations.

Some of the later chapters in this book cover other aspects of subsidiary operations, especially the chapters on staffing, crossing barriers to international understanding, financing and pricing, statistics for monitoring operations, legal and tax matters, and Operation Europe.

Acquisition vs. Starting from Scratch

Once you have decided that you should have your own company in a country, the first question is whether to acquire a going company or start a brand new one from scratch.

Your move is usually obvious when the owner of a suitable company wants to sell out to you. It might even be your own distributor or licensee that is offered. But even then, it is in your interests to consider the alternative of starting from the beginning. What would a brand new company cost you? That figure should be weighed against the price of the company offered you, while also taking into account the advantages and disadvantages of acquiring a going concern.

A foreign owner's ideas about the value of his company's obsolete inventory, unsalable assets, and goodwill are often inflated. You will be in a better position if you can show him, for comparison, what you have actually spent on start-up expenses in a brand new company in another country of similar size.

The licensee, however, might demand more than this figure, stating that he has a chance to sell out to your competitor. To fight such a sale in the courts might be messy, costly, and time-consuming. Therefore, such a threat might increase the price of acquisition to a cost somewhat greater than that of starting from scratch. Practically all licensees are familiar with this method of increasing the price of their companies, so it is useless to hope that they will not consider it.

The time-saving factor in acquiring a going company instead of starting from the beginning must also be considered. But if the licensee has too much, too old, or otherwise unsuitable personnel or facilities, the value of his company can be drastically decreased. As a matter of fact, unsuitable or surplus personnel often change the total value of a company from a positive to a negative figure, especially in countries where it is costly to lay off surplus personnel.

Some people tend to exaggerate the cost, difficulties, and time required for starting a subsidiary from scratch. All these factors depend to some extent on how good the company's product is. If the product is outstanding, it is often possible to break even in a brand new operation as early as the second year. The average length of time it takes to break even for all new U.S.-owned foreign subsidiaries is five years. But that is far too long, and the average in companies with excellent international managers is much shorter.

Difficulties in finding personnel have also been vastly exaggerated— for example, in West Germany during times of overemployment. This difficulty has been given as an argument for going the acquisition route. Usually, this argument is pure nonsense. Capable management and personnel are always available in a country such as West Germany for the right price and in the right company atmosphere.

I can even go one step further and state that with capable, imaginative management, good personnel is available at little or no premium over what well-established local companies pay. Your company's attractiveness to personnel should not be in the form of higher salaries but in the opportunity they will have to work for a good company, under fair and capable managers who charge them with responsible and interesting work. Often the locally owned companies are not particularly well run, so it can be comparatively easy to do better.

If you are considering acquiring a going concern, beware of sick foreign companies offered for sale at low prices. Before acquiring such a company, make sure that you know *all* the reasons why it is sick. Many such companies are bought by American firms who think the companies are only lacking capital. So they pump in lots of fresh capital, only to find that their companies are still ailing. In many cases the mistake is not acknowledged early, so that losses cannot be cut and the companies dumped. Instead, more and more good money is thrown in, but the companies continue losing money for one or more fundamental reasons. Even if the reasons are finally discovered, it can be difficult to change bad habits in a company that has been mismanaged for years; and it can be ruinous in a country where it is expensive to lay off personnel.

As we all know, the relative profitability of an operation is often due to many small things. Nearly everything in a company has to be right for it to produce high profits, and a sick company usually has more than one problem. To go into such a company and cure all its diseases is often a larger, more expensive, and more time-consuming job than to start a new company from scratch with energetic young management and an optimistic, enthusiastic staff.

Establishing a new company can be an exhilarating experience. You can optimize everything, from the location of the firm to hiring the right management and employees—or at least you can attempt to do so.

Let's look for a minute at a detail such as location. Many older foreign companies are hopelessly tied either to a countryside location far away from communications and customers, or to a central, congested city location that used to be good before everyone had automobiles, or that is still a prestige location in the minds of the old guard but is, nevertheless, hopelessly hampering company operations.

In contrast, a new company can be located, from the beginning, in the open suburban spaces, near superhighways and airports. It can have excellent communications and acres of free parking space and be situated just a short distance from the pleasant suburban living areas where you are most likely to find the best employees.

Future expansion can be thoroughly planned from the start. When considering building space, the most common error is being too timid in planning for expansion.

It is much easier in a brand new company than in an acquired one to get the management and staff to consider themselves part of the worldwide group. In an acquired old company, it can be virtually impossible to eliminate the "we" and "they" attitude toward "their" company and the "other" companies in your group.

In an acquired company, it often takes a long time to get the local managers to understand, let alone implement, the global company's philosophies and policies. Some older executives will refuse to make the turn-around, and therefore, after some time, they have to be "de-hired" or, alternatively, shunted into positions where they will not do any harm.

Another argument for starting a subsidiary from scratch is that public attitudes and regulations in some countries are hostile toward foreign acquisition of existing companies but welcome brand new foreign ventures.

Furthermore, for a company that is already dominating its field, it is difficult to acquire a competitor in the European Economic Community. In fact, in the future it may become as impossible to do so there as it is in the United States.

Building Strong Subsidiaries

From the very moment you start a foreign subsidiary, your goal must be to make it a strong, flexible unit, certainly a much more self-contained one than a domestic branch office. On the other hand, the subsidiary must not be so self-contained that expensive facilities and efforts are duplicated needlessly.

This question of how self-contained a subsidiary should be is the subject of constant arguments between subsidiary managements and central management. The answer should not depend on who controls what and who is strongest, but on how the whole organization, including the subsidiaries, can become strongest, most effective, and most profitable. In actual business practice, these obvious goals are sometimes the last ones to be considered when headstrong executives are fighting about who gets to do what.

Suppose that the parent company has an excellent engineering staff in a highly specialized field in which the subsidiary alone could not justify a full-time man; in that case, the subsidiary will be stronger and more efficient if it depends on help from the parent company in this field, rather than dabbling in it by itself. Although this conclusion seems self-evident, you may receive lots of heated arguments against it from strong-willed subsidiary managers.

If, on the other hand, this field justifies a couple of full-time experts at the subsidiary, and if many on-the-spot decisions in this field must be made in the course of daily work, then the entire organization is, of course, better off if the subsidiary has its own specialists. The parent-company engineering manager may not agree, though.

Between these two clear-cut cases, however, there are many less obvious cases to be decided one way or the other by the executives involved.

According to the same principle of making the total organization strong, efficient, and profitable, it must also be decided where each component or product should be made and to what design. This question is often a source of deep conflict among companies in the same group.

Americans sometimes have the impression that Europeans consider manufacturing to be much more wholesome than just trading, and that they vastly underestimate costs of purchasing from outside sources, costs of overhead, and other necessary expenses that must be added to the net manufacturing costs. Against this, Europeans often accuse American parent companies of hogging manufacturing operations and not giving sufficient consideration to strengthening the subsidiaries by letting them integrate vertically and control a larger part of the product-development–manufacturing–marketing cycle. The Europeans have a point here: Only through controlling a large part of this cycle is a subsidiary company truly strong. In this way, those heavy international trade costs can also be avoided.

Local vs. Central Direction of Foreign Subsidiaries

Several years ago, the Ford Motor Company found that Ford of England and Ford of Germany were in many respects going in different and conflicting directions. To correct this, they formed a top management steering committee, "Ford of Europe," by carefully balancing a collection of British and German managers. Ford of Europe then was supposed to tell the English and German companies the directions in which they should go.

This scheme sounded good on paper, but Ford people later reported that it did not work as intended, at least not in the beginning. Let's consider this type of problem in a general context.

It is extremely difficult to achieve *all* the following goals:

1. Have top managements of local nationalities.
2. Delegate authority to the subsidiary managers to run their companies for maximum present and future profitability.
3. Get subsidiary managers to coordinate their efforts and share facilities and services, and get them all to pull in the same direction.

Goal 3 is inherently in conflict with goals 1 and 2, which are more important than goal 3. In other words, it is better to fall short of goal 3 than to be deficient in the first two areas. Of course, you should still try to come as close as possible to achieving goal 3, in addition to achieving goals 1 and 2 completely.

An exaggerated way to formulate the same dilemma could be to ask whether foreign subsidiaries should operate as separate companies or as different departments in the same worldwide organization. This is one of the most difficult problems in international management. No across-the-board solution can be given. Each business policy must be decided in favor of the highest profitability of the total organization at the present and in the future.

Each strong subsidiary manager has the tendency to go in a different direction and run his company as his personal fief. The central management of the parent company has the tendency to want to usurp power and run the subsidiaries as if they were different departments of the same organization. Both extremes are wrong, but the second one is worse.

A flexible middle way has to be found that leans toward giving as much authority as possible to local managers, especially in day-to-day operating matters that should be decided on quickly, without taking time for consultation, and in matters requiring understanding of local attitudes, tastes, and the personalities of individual customers. Central managers from the parent company, especially those who have little international experience, must exercise great self-control and leave such decisions to their local managers, even when the central managers do not agree with them.

An example of what can happen in the case of strong American direction of a foreign subsidiary occurred in 1969 to the 850-man Italian subsidiary of a large, well-known, and highly respected American engineering firm. The Italian manager tried to get the subsidiary out from under American headquarters' control. He was promptly fired. But then the whole company immediately went out on strike in his support, demanding local managerial control and threatening to form their own competing firm, leaving the subsidiary an empty shell—quite a threat in an engineering firm, where the only substantial asset is the personnel.

Obviously, this was a very serious situation. But such divergent developments can be avoided by good international top management possessing deep sensitivity to different foreign desires and attitudes. Lack of such sensitivity and too strong central direction cause many less publicized daily incidents in lots of companies.

There are a couple of exceptions to the general rule of giving as free rein as possible to local managers. One exception involves adherence to central quality control and uniform engineering standards. Another exception is the case of the local manager who has not yet learned to use modern management methods.

Modern management techniques first appeared in the United States. In Europe, they have reached only the most advanced companies. How can I be so certain that these American methods are suitable in Europe, when they have gained so little acceptance there?

Well, the proof of the pudding is in the eating, and a European pointed it out more dramatically than anyone else: J. J. Servan-Schreiber said in *The American Challenge* that American companies in Europe were more successful than European-owned companies, even though the American-owned firms used borrowed European capital, European employees, and mostly European managers. The Americans added only some know-how and—above all—modern American management methods, including delegation of authority, open channels of communication, practically no secrecy, and emphasis on modern marketing concepts.

Thus, even though most other matters in the overseas subsidiaries are conducted in the local manner, management must be conducted in accordance with these proven modern principles. The best methods are barely good enough.

The main difficulty is to find local managers who can inspire their employees and are capable of learning and practicing modern manage-

The main difficulty is to find local managers who can inspire their employees.

ment methods. Those foreign managers who don't must be moved aside to staff duties, in favor of local executives who are able to use modern management methods in line positions. Otherwise the subsidiaries will not progress as much as they should.

On the other hand, the good international manager at headquarters will constantly remind himself that he is not necessarily in the right, and that the quaint approach he meets overseas may not necessarily produce worse results—especially considering that his local top executives also have to be personally convinced that the methods they use are, in fact, best for the company.

It is a very difficult task to introduce better and more modern procedures overseas and yet not do it so quickly and adamantly that you lose the cooperation and enthusiasm of otherwise excellent foreign top executives. On this point, all parties generally end up having to compromise.

Quality Control and Engineering Standards

It is impossible to make a general statement that will be valid for all global companies regarding the necessity for maintaining rigid quality control and engineering standards. Three examples will illustrate the situation.

1. Caterpillar claims that all of its machines are built to the same engineering standards and quality, regardless of where they are built. Parts are interchangeable between Caterpillar machines built in different countries.
2. In contrast, Singer builds sewing machines in different countries adapted to the taste of the local population.
3. An executive of one of the world's two leading abrasives firms stated that if his company were to build certain grinding wheels in Europe to American quality standards, these wheels would be so expensive in relation to the European competition that they would not sell in satisfactory quantities. For this reason, they are forced to build wheels in Europe to European quality standards.

Each of these three companies has chosen the policy that is right for it, and yet the policies are different. Thus, no single policy on engineering standardization is right for all companies; perhaps it is even true that no single policy is the right one for all products of any single company.

Yet, as we saw in the chapter on licensing, it pays to try to maintain as uniform a quality as possible throughout the world, and, if the goods are of a technical nature, to try to maintain as uniform engineering standards as possible, especially if the products are sold to international customers.

Local safety requirements, local variations of measurement, local thread standards, and locally available subcomponents will invariably force deviations from uniform designs; but each of these deviations should be submitted from overseas for approval by the company's central engineering staff. That staff, in turn, should be highly knowledgeable regarding the requirements of all countries concerned and sensitive to the different desires of these countries.

> *The duty of the central engineering staff is to maintain maximum interchangeability and reasonably uniform quality standards within the limits of what competitive price pressures allow, as well as to meet diverse national desires to the greatest extent practicable.*

This seems simple, yet the execution of these simple rules can be complex. The central engineering staff is constantly under heavy pressures from different countries to allow variations. If these pressures are not resisted when it is appropriate to do so, each plant will end up going its own way; interchangeability of parts will disappear, and quality will suffer in many locations.

If this happens, it will be very difficult, expensive, and time-consuming to introduce worldwide uniform improvements whenever a better method, material, or adaptation is discovered. Thus, I repeat:

> *Responsibility and authority for setting and meeting engineering standards and quality control requirements must be assumed centrally. Such decisions should never be left up to the local plant managements.*

6

Joint Ventures: Keeping Them Joint

AS you remember from Chapter 2, joint ventures are chosen not as the middle ground between independents and subsidiaries but as a less attractive alternative to subsidiaries, an alternative to consider whenever laws or attitudes put substantial obstacles in the way of subsidiaries.

Types of Joint Ventures

In the following discussions (unless otherwise stated), we shall be concerned with what I call the *common joint venture,* which is formed by an American partner with know-how and/or patents and one or more partners of Nationality X who have the necessary local market knowledge. Their common joint venture is the local sole distributor or sole licensee for Country X and possibly also for neighboring smaller countries. See Figure 2.

The foreign partner might be:

In the same industry. (Caution with antitrust!)
A landowner or a concession-right holder.
A major distributor.
A major customer.

In the last situation, remember that you should join a customer only if he is larger than all the other prospective customers put together, because the other customers may hesitate to buy from a company partly owned by one of their competitors.

Also, if the customer–partner is going to buy the major part of the output of the joint venture, be very careful not to let him get too big a hand in the venture. Otherwise, you may later find yourself at his mercy.

Figure 2

```
┌──────────────────────────┐   ┌──────────────────────────┐
│                          │   │   One or more partners   │
│  American partner with   │   │     of Nationality X     │
│  know-how and/or patents │   │  with knowledge of the   │
│                          │   │     local market and     │
│                          │   │     local conditions     │
└──────────────────────────┘   └──────────────────────────┘
             ┌──────────────────────────────┐
             │   "Common Joint Venture,"     │
             │   appointed sole licensee     │
             │   or distributor for Country X │
             └──────────────────────────────┘
```

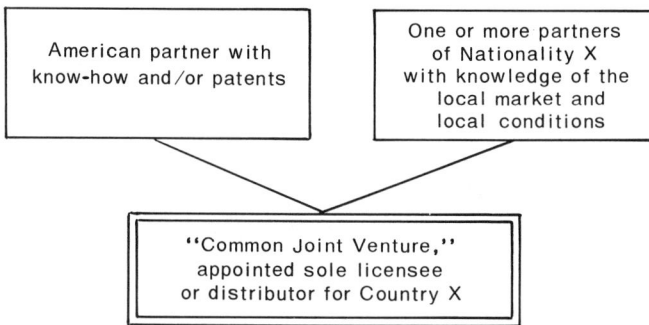

In another type of situation, an American company first forms a joint venture with an ailing foreign competitor, rescuing the competitor, and later offers to buy his partner out of the joint venture, as in Figure 3. The last step in this development, the step into a sole venture, causes too much political opposition in some countries, so it should be done with caution (if at all), especially by any well-known corporation.

Figures 4 and 5 illustrate a few quite different types of international joint ventures. The one shown in Figure 4 seems quite simple and logical, and yet is very difficult to make work in the long run, unless the product or service of the joint venture is different from the normal product or service of each partner. Otherwise, both partners may start keeping new know-how secret from the joint venture. Without an open, free flow of new know-how, the venture will fail.

Figure 5 shows three types of joint ventures. The last is really the reverse of the "common joint venture"; it will probably not be used to any great extent, because the United States does not discriminate against foreign investors. Nevertheless, this kind of joint venture may be advantageous to the foreign principal who is unable to transfer the necessary capital to gain a strong foothold quickly in the big U.S. market.

Figure 3

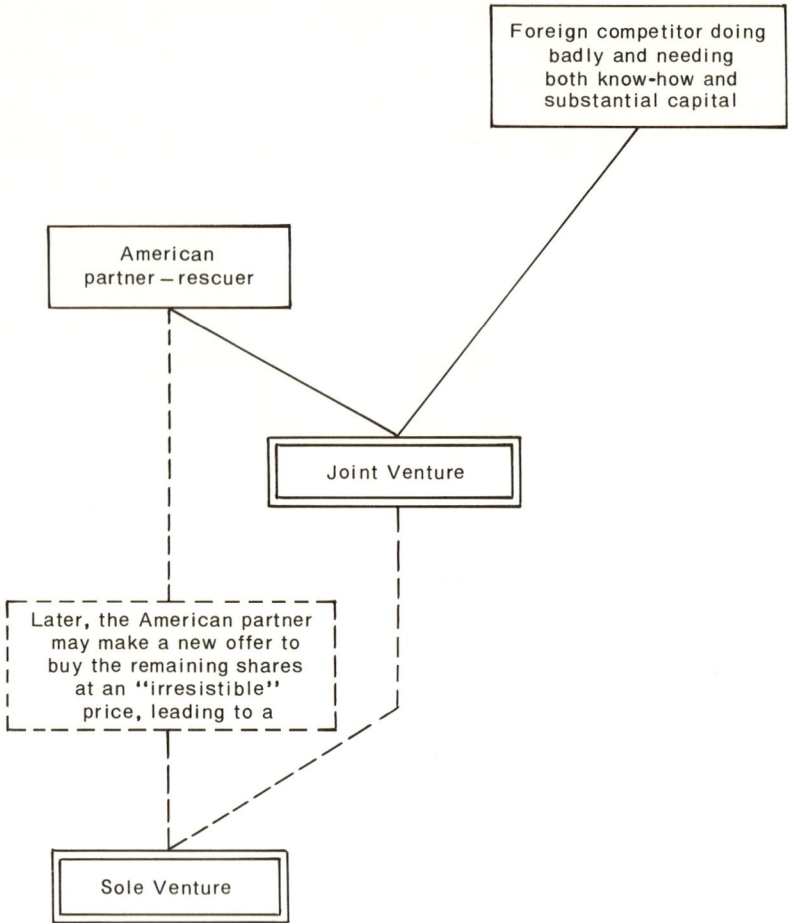

Figure 4

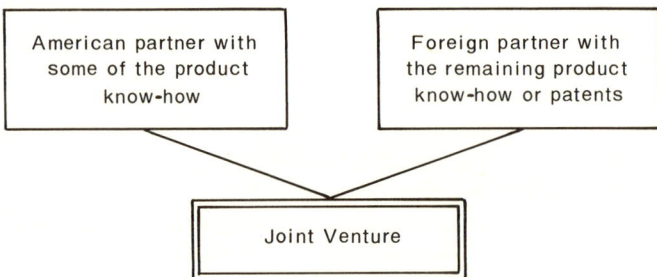

INDIVIDUALITY OF JOINT VENTURES

Even among "common joint ventures," each international joint venture proposal seems at first glance totally individual, entirely different from all others. When considering such a joint venture—often under pressure from capable foreign persuaders—it is easy to get lost in the individuality and complexity of each one.

In these cases, I have found that I have to step back to see the forest rather than the trees. I must consider the general principles for joint ventures and then see how they fit the specific case on hand. I must analyze what is common among successful ventures.

Figure 5

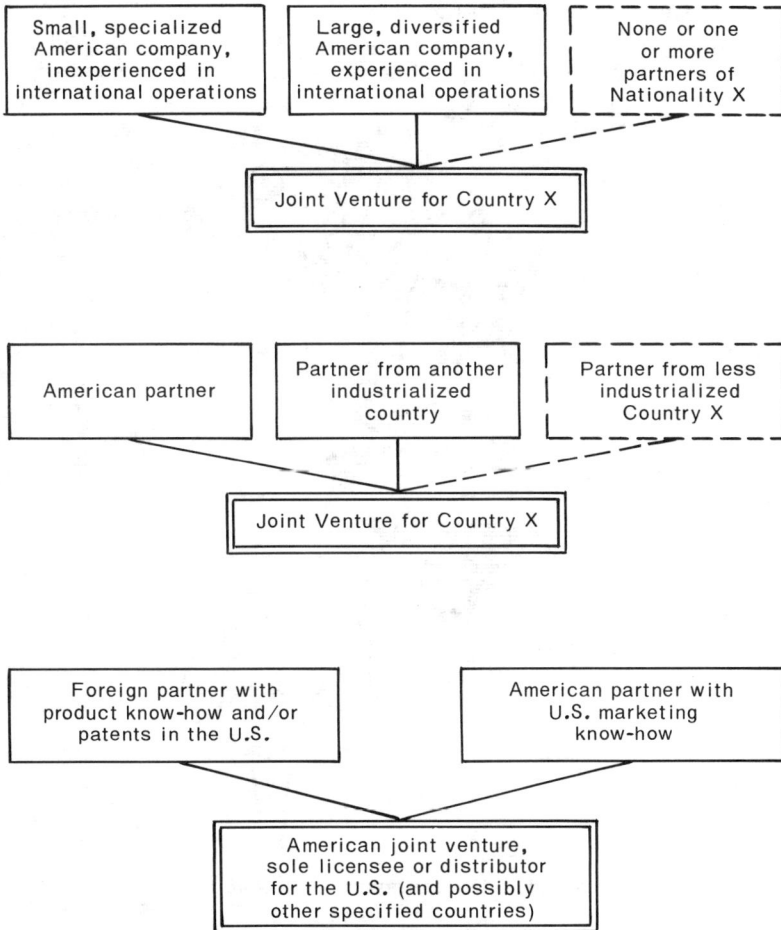

Below are some of these general guidelines. I hope they will also be useful to you.

Development of the Common Joint Venture

Sometimes you may find it possible to transform an independent operation into a joint venture. When this is done, you should usually try to get an option, valid for some future date, to purchase the remaining portion of the company on certain agreed terms, so that later you can transform the operation into a subsidiary. Such an option may become very valuable when the joint venture prospers far beyond the dreams of the foreign partners.

A new joint venture must always be formed with built-in divorce machinery spelling out how a partner can retire from it. Usually the agreement will include clauses on first refusal between partners on shares

Joint ventures often start out in perfect harmony.
Then, as the years go by . . .

offered for sale and on how to determine share prices, and cancellation clauses for any licenses held by the joint venture.

In theory, a joint venture should combine the advantages of independents—local knowledge, connections, good incentives to local partners—with the advantages of subsidiaries—complete access to the know-how and support of the worldwide group. In actual practice, joint ventures too often combine the disadvantages of both types of operations instead.

Let's explore two goals of a joint venture partner: (1) looking after his own interests in the joint venture, and (2) keeping it joint, in an effort to combine the advantages of independents and subsidiaries.

Ironically, the two goals are conflicting, because when both partners are concerned with looking after their own private interests, the joint venture will automatically lose some of its advantages. It will be less "joint."

Nevertheless, both partners might as well realize from the beginning that they are in the venture together, and that what they get out of the arrangement depends on what they both put into it. The joint venture that prospers is the one into which both partners are determined to put more care, thought, and effort than is their legal obligation. It is a venture in which both parties work selflessly to achieve the second goal listed above and let their individual interests fall where they may.

Joint ventures often start out in perfect harmony about the goals to be achieved. Then, as the years go by, the partners change, and their goals change and become more and more divergent. Severe conflicts can then arise. Often these conflicts become unsolvable, even though both partners may sincerely wish to solve them.

Intercompany pricing (discussed in Chapter 10) and decisions on dividend pay-outs vs. plow-back of profits are matters that cause some of the most bitter arguments. To one partner, the joint venture may be his single concern and single source of income, whereas to the other partner it may be a small, working wheel in a large, global machine. Frequently, no matter how much both partners try, they cannot change these basic differences.

Degree of Control

WHY HAVE CONTROL?

This may be a needless question, but I have seen European prospective partners convincing experienced Americans that they were better off letting the Europeans have all the trouble and heavy responsibility of control. As a counterweight, I will list three simple reasons for trying to get control:

To assure that the company is run in such a manner that it produces profits.

To avoid being cheated out of your fair share of the profits.

To incorporate the venture in an orderly, logical, and economically sensible manner into your global operations for maximization of global profits.

WHAT PERCENTAGE SHOULD YOU HAVE?

In the general case of a profitable venture in which the capital amount, cost, or risk is not unusually great, my general rule of thumb is:

Take as large a percentage as possible.

You will have most of the trouble anyway, so you might as well earn as big a part of the profits as you can.

There are some exceptions, however:

1. In some countries, not only the laws but also the local attitudes are strongly against a foreign majority.
2. For certain prestige industries in some less developed countries, many local partners can hopefully provide some insurance against confiscation by the government. For this purpose, some American companies have sold shares in the local company to the general public there. This is usually very difficult to do, though, because of the absence in many such countries of a decent capital market in equity shares.
3. Occasionally it is desirable to involve an unusually good foreign partner to a higher level by giving the control to him.
4. On rare occasions you can get tax advantages from having less than 50 percent of the capital, as mentioned earlier.

WHICH PERCENTAGE GIVES WHAT DEGREE OF CONTROL?

This point must always be checked carefully with local lawyers, since it varies widely from country to country. Here are a few examples.

In Germany, a share of more than 25 percent gives *Anspruchsrecht,* meaning that a 26-percent partner can challenge decisions made by the majority partner.

In France, more than $33\frac{1}{3}$ percent gives a stockholder certain privileges.

In some countries, a share of more than 25 percent is enough to prevent unwanted changes in the articles of association.

Therefore, if you are forced into a position of less than 50 percent ownership, try at least to own the minimum percentage that gives you some rights.

There are many ways for an American partner owning less than 50 percent to maintain a considerable degree of control. Here are a few of them:

Have a very capable resident executive of your own.

Spread the remaining stock over several local partners, each of whom owns less than 25 percent (or whatever percentage gives an individual partner few rights). Try to select the local partners so that they are unlikely to combine forces against you.

Establish a strong management contract with the joint venture. (In many countries, however, such a contract will not hold water in case of severe conflict.)

The 50–50 Venture

To my amazement, several experienced and knowledgeable people have voiced preferences for 50–50 joint ventures, stating that these are the true partnerships, promoting good cooperation and true international understanding, and that they are devoid of the majority–minority problems.

I would prefer the 50–50 venture *only if:*

1. The company I represent cannot own more than 50 percent, and
2. I cannot find more than one local partner.

Suppose you are nevertheless forced into the 50–50 venture. The obvious danger to avoid is a deadlock. The promoters of 50–50 ventures say that the way to prevent deadlocks is to share 50–50 not only the capital but also the control, and to get together in a true spirit of real cooperation. This is, of course, ideal if it can be done; but it is very seldom possible in reality, at least not over a period of many years with changing casts of characters.

What many executives forget is that corporate forms should not be so organized that they work smoothly only with the executives currently in their own and their partners' companies. Executive offices change hands, and the new men may not be able to work together well. The true corporate builder creates enduring organizations for the long-range future.

There are many ways to control a 50–50 venture, or at least to attempt to; and your local adviser can probably devise a formula that fits your case. If you add to his formula the best man you can find as your own representative in the joint venture, then you have at least made the best you can out of the difficult 50–50 venture.

Exercise the Control Sparingly!

While you should try your best to get control, once you have it, you should exercise it as sparingly as possible. The partner who has 51 percent can speak much more softly than the one with 49 percent, and yet, in effect, be much more persuasive. (Exercising control sparingly and unobtrusively is particularly important in Japan.)

For example, you can gain much cooperation in important matters if you have been backing down on some of the unimportant ones. You should, of course, leave the unimportant matters in the hands of the local manager anyway, even though you would have dealt with them quite differently yourself. In international operations this must be done to a much larger extent than in domestic operations.

When you must go against the local management, do it only after explaining your reasons thoroughly and after trying hard to make the local management agree or at least understand. Again, it is necessary to put much more time and effort into such explanations for a foreign operation than for a domestic one.

Nevertheless, in a couple of areas, such as quality control and engineering standardization, strong control will have to be exercised, as we have seen in the chapters on other types of foreign operations.

Requirements for the Foreign Partner

If the prospective foreign partner approaches you, rather than you him, then you might ask yourself why. Is he a competitor who just wants your know-how? Is he a competitor on his way downhill? If so, will he be cheaper after he has slipped further? If you establish a joint venture with him, would the new venture perpetuate this present downhill slide? Many joint ventures have done just that, because they have had the wrong foreign partners.

In most cases (except when capital is unusually important), you would do well to seek out a foreign partner who contributes much more than capital. (Here we return to the side advantages of having a joint venture mentioned in Chapter 2.)

You may want your foreign partner to be able to provide local connections, a knowledge of the local market, and sometimes an excellent top manager for the joint venture. The American partner should attempt to choose the top manager from among available local men. This is most important and very difficult. (I will comment on the top man's nationality in the chapter on staffing.)

> *When seeking the right partner, I would also look for one with the inner resources and resiliency that the venture may need when the chips are down, when the unforeseen economic crisis arrives, when a government coup occurs or a sudden competitive activity springs up. At those times, you will really need your solid foreign partner.*

I emphasize these human qualities in a foreign partner rather than some other human qualities that you would require in a partner in the United States, such as aggressiveness and integrity. Honesty, for example, means one thing in Pakistan, another thing in Finland, and something quite different in Japan, where it is modified by Japanese etiquette. (Japanese businessmen may never say no, but only what you want to hear. They are not being dishonest and cagey, only polite.)

Requirements for the American company as a good partner for the joint venture are covered in the chapter on organizing the corporate headquarters for international work.

Joint Ventures in Some Specific Countries

JAPAN

As you know, Japan is now the third largest industrial country in the world and growing faster than most others. Today, there are still only a few instances in which foreigners own more than 50 percent of Japanese ventures. However, Japan is flourishing with joint ventures, and while many of them are giving American executives prematurely gray hair, others are exceeding the wildest expectations of profit.

Doing business in Japan is so different that anyone who attempts it for the first time had better read up on it in advance. (See the recommended information sources at the end of this book.) Of course, once you are in Japan, it is necessary to get the best advisors you can find and invite them to join you on your time-consuming rounds.

More comments on Japan are given in the chapters on staffing, crossing cultural barriers, financing, and future trends.

INDIA

My personal simple guideline is to shy away from any venture in India, despite all the splendid "risk free" proposals you receive from that country—unless your product is of special importance to India.

If one were to measure the number of Western executive and technical man-years spent on India during the last 25 years against the hard-currency profits taken out, the hourly pay would be dismal.

Saddest of all is that India herself has benefited so little from all this work by Westerners and from very much more work by millions of educated, progressive, conscientious Indians. There are several fundamental reasons for this, but I shall mention only one of them here: the wet-blanket effect caused by the Indian government's constant and pervasive interference in private business.

A couple of the other reasons and more comments on India are given in the chapter on underdevelopment.

EAST BLOC

There are no joint (or sole) venture possibilities in the Soviet Union, but other East European countries seem to be opening up what they call joint ventures, even though we would sometimes prefer to call them licensing or coproduction arrangements. So far, Yugoslavia, and recently Rumania also, have opened up their borders for some foreign capital participation.

As this book is being written, it is too early to state any experience that has been gained from these arrangements. *Business International* magazine from time to time lists new ventures initiated in the East Bloc with international participation.

Over a period of a couple of years, I was in touch with a Hungarian outfit in regard to a proposal of theirs. Once, at a very long and pleasant dinner in Budapest, with Gypsy music, I asked the Hungarians how our company would be paid. They replied that they had just explained for a couple of hours all the advantages we would receive. I said very quietly that we were not interested only in advantages. They asked what we wanted, and I told them quietly, "We like money."

At that time they could not give us anything we could convert to hard currency at a reasonable expense, and you will find that convertibility is the point on which joint venture discussions with the East Bloc often fail even today. So you can probably save yourself much time and slivovitz if you come to this point quickly in your East Bloc negotiations. (This situation may be changing, though.)

The East Bloc is now getting into another kind of joint venture in the West, namely, the joint venture for the purpose of marketing their products in the West.

OTHER COUNTRIES

American joint ventures are being established with the *governments* of several countries, including communist countries such as Algeria and social democratic countries such as Sweden.

Italy has a state-owned company, EFIM (Ente Participazioni e Finanziamento Industria Manifatturiera), for joint venture partnership with foreign firms in manufacturing enterprises located in the Mezzogiorno. EFIM has several joint venture operations with some of the best known American, German, and French companies, with the non-Italian partner acting as the supplier of know-how. In past years, EFIM proved itself to be a flexible partner, able to cut through some of the Italian red tape. Whether the company will remain efficient, time will tell.

In some black African countries, there is growing discrimination against white-owned subsidiaries—for example, in Ghana. In Kenya this is probably going to come, too, though later. At the time of this writing, Idi Amin's Uganda is, of course, at the bottom of the list of African investment locations.

In Spain it is necessary to have local partners, but in all of the remainder of Western Europe, including France, wholly owned American ventures are treated well if they conform to local standards of behavior. You hear much noise to the contrary, but little action when the new ventures are started from scratch in an intelligent manner. Acquisition of existing local companies, particularly well-known ones, has met resistance, especially in France and in industries of special national interest.

France offers, in addition to the normal legal form of a joint venture, another form that is looser and less permanent. It is called a *groupement d'intérêts économiques,* GIE for short. A GIE is halfway between a simple association and a joint venture. It is based on a formal contract between the partners, and that contract is registered with the government. Corporate taxes are levied directly on the partners, not on the GIE.

If you are starting in Mexico, you must plan for a joint venture (unless you are just putting a manufacturing operation in the special border areas).

In Colombia, Ecuador, Peru, and Bolivia, the "fade out" formula for foreign majority holdings is now politically popular. This is a requirement by which majority ownership must pass into local hands. Therefore, the joint venture approach seems to be the only one—if you have to invest there at all. The decisions made in these Andean Group countries in recent years make investment less and less attractive there. You are not likely to invest in Chile at this time. Brazil and some other Latin American countries welcome foreign investments, including wholly owned subsidiaries. The big question is, however, how long each of these countries will remain stable. There is, perhaps, a better question still: How stable is the country right now underneath the surface, and what would happen if control of the army shifted to others?

7

Organizing the Corporate Headquarters for International Work

THIS chapter is concerned only with truly organizational aspects; it does not deal with tax aspects, such as the Western Hemisphere Trade Corporation and the Domestic International Sales Corporation (D.I.S.C.). Once you have found the best organizational structure, you can usually superimpose on it whatever is desirable from tax and legal viewpoints.

As you read this chapter, it may strike you as all too theoretical, somewhat like a school textbook, far removed from the management we practice from day to day. We work with people—real, living people with some good points and some faults—and it is their limitations and their capabilities that determine the actual organization of a company, not some theoretical diagrams put down in a book. The alternatives described in this chapter, then, are presented so that you can see what you might want to shoot for, if you have the people to go with them.

Top Management

The perennial question is whether you should integrate international work with domestic work in the headquarters operations of the parent company or keep international work separate in an international division.

In the industrial equipment field, and in any technically complex field, I am strongly biased toward integrating international work with domestic work at corporate headquarters, especially if the international operations represent a substantial part of the whole company. I lean toward this alternative because of the many over-all corporate decisions that should be made from a global rather than a domestic viewpoint.

However, as just mentioned, it is not possible to ignore the people you work with, and if the top corporate officers of the company are uninformed about international aspects, it is, of course, impossible to integrate international operations at headquarters. Similarly, if the domestic corporation is divided into different product categories all the way to the president, a separate international division is sometimes more logical.

If the international products or services are substantially different from the domestic ones, then a separate international division can also make more sense. In such a case, the organizational structure might be represented by the example in Figure 6. While this organization may be the only one possible, it easily leads to strained relations between the domestic product divisions and the product managers in the international division and in the foreign subsidiaries.

If the international activities are similar to the domestic ones, if the company is not divided by product categories right to the top, and if the top corporate officers have a good international background, or at least take the advice of their international experts, then you can have the better organization shown in Figure 7.

This top organization is much better adapted to a company in which international operations are a substantial part of the whole corporation. It is used often in the consumer goods field by companies that are not diversified.

For the organization diagramed in Figure 7, it is assumed that all the officers shown are concerned with the global aspects of each phase of the business. Thus, the international vice-president is not the only officer concerned with international aspects, but he is the one others consult for his international expertise, and the man with the line responsibility for international profit and loss.

If all the other corporate officers were knowledgeable in international matters, it would be possible, in theory, to do without the international vice-president; but that is strictly theory, not only because it is unlikely that all the officers will have the knowledge required, but also because the foreign subsidiaries, joint ventures, and licensees must report to a single corporate officer. The handling of all the international work would also become too burdensome to the other officers, who should be able

Figure 6

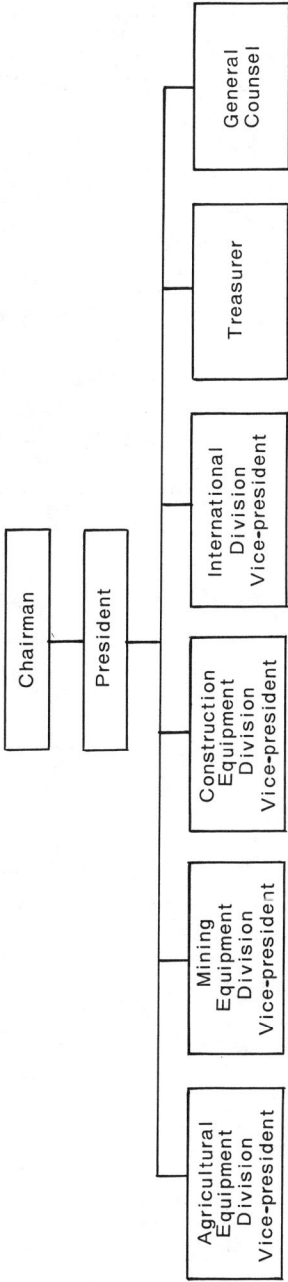

Figure 7

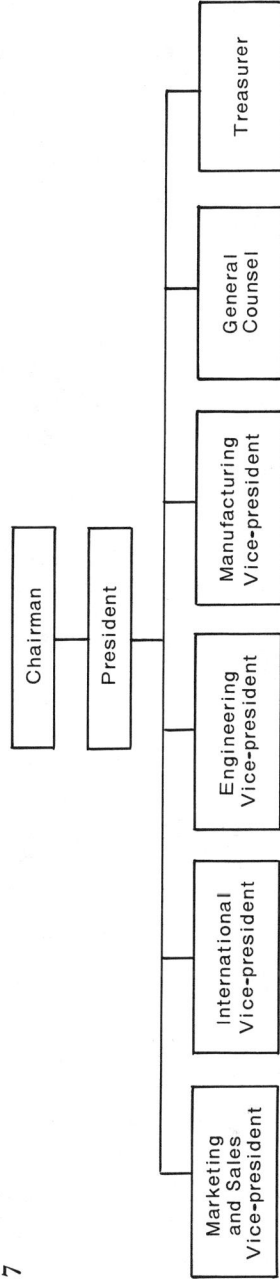

to concentrate on their own fields of activity and expertise. Without the international vice-president, international aspects would not be given the concentrated top management attention they deserve. Without a knowledgeable top officer specializing in international work, overseas subsidiary managers would probably be given less understanding treatment of their problems and less knowledgeable handling of their questions.

Those corporate officers who are not personally knowledgeable in international matters must take the advice of their international experts, even when the actions they suggest for Karachi or Kyoto sound strange in Kenosha or Kalamazoo.

In large, widely diversified, multinational companies, experiments have been made for some years with dividing the companies right to the top into different product divisions, with the vice-president of each given responsibility for worldwide profit and loss within his field. Figure 8 represents such a company headquartered in Europe.

Figure 8

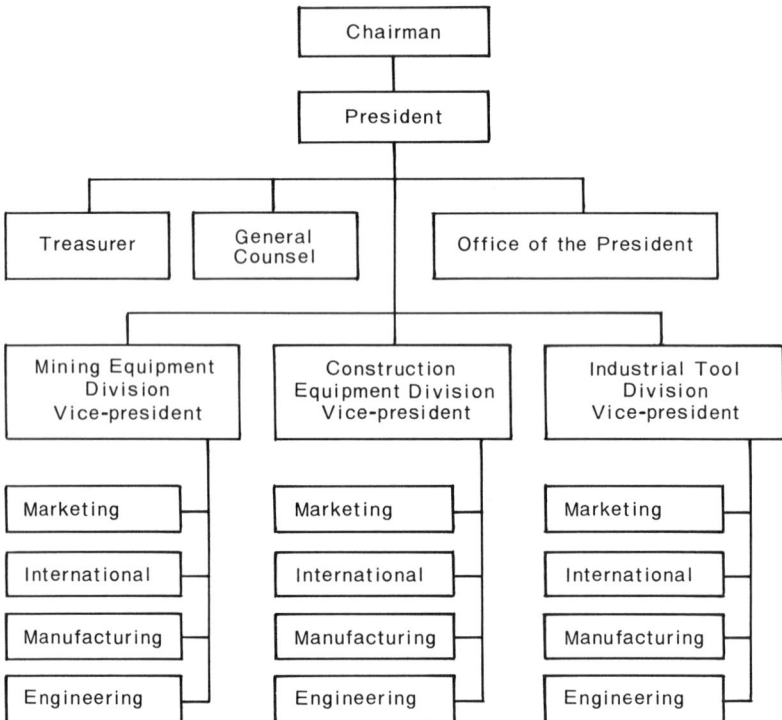

This organization has obvious advantages when the customer groups, engineering, and manufacturing of the different divisions are entirely different. Obviously, it applies better to a large corporation than to a medium-sized or small one.

However, in a foreign country where such a large company has only one subsidiary, the manager of that subsidiary is subjected to conflicting demands on his limited resources and time from the three parent divisions. Furthermore, to whom does he really report?

This divisional organization makes it indispensable to have internationally qualified personnel in each division of the parent company. Some of the requirements on such international personnel are described in the chapters on staffing and crossing the barriers to international understanding.

This structural division is in effect somewhat similar to having three separate domestic corporations under one holding company. In Northern Europe, such a split-up of the parent company has indeed become the next step. Each divisional vice-president has, thereby, become the president* of a separate corporation.

In some high-tax countries, such a structural division can have some advantages, one of which is to make it a little easier to attract and keep qualified top executives. Whereas in the United States you can often attract a good man by offering him $15,000 more than he is earning, in the high-tax countries of Northern Europe the governments will take most of the extra $15,000. So instead you attract the man by calling him president (or managing director) in lieu of vice-president, and you change the division into a separate corporation. (In some countries, this will give you other advantages as well.)

Middle Management and Staff

KEEP THE INTERNATIONAL STAFF IN THE UNITED STATES SMALL

A company must constantly guard against creating a needlessly large international department that removes all international work from the product specialists in the domestic company.

Here is one example of how small the international department at headquarters can be: In a company with hundreds of overseas employees in subsidiaries, joint ventures, and licensees around the world, in addition to distributors in some 40 countries, the total international department at the headquarters consists of only five people, including the secretary.

---

* Or managing director, which is the British equivalent of the term "president."

One or two of these people are usually overseas, so the total staff actually present at the head office consists normally of only three or four, and yet the department probably runs more efficiently than if it had twice or four times as many people. (In fact, staffs several times larger are often found in companies with less international work.) Every person in the efficient international department is a jack-of-all-trades, and everyone can act as a stand-in for the others whenever necessary.

Of course, most of the support functions from technical, accounting, shipping, and other departments are in this case handled by those specialized departments. Furthermore, they can do most of this support work more efficiently than the international department.

If you add needless international department employees at the corporate headquarters, they will have a tendency to get in the way of direct communications between the real technical specialists at headquarters and the corresponding overseas technical specialists. The international headquarters staff rapidly starts to function as message-carriers, thereby impairing instead of improving two-way communication. This area will be discussed in the chapter on overcoming barriers to communication.

One of the main functions of the international headquarters staff in any company is to improve the distribution of parent company know-how to overseas subsidiaries and to improve the return of good new product and business ideas from the overseas fronts to the research, engineering, quality control, and other departments of the parent company. But the international department personnel must act as catalysts, not as message-carriers. Whenever possible, they should shorten the lines of communication by cutting themselves out of the communication chain and having information transmitted directly to the appropriate headquarters personnel.

This work requires tact and ingenuity. Not all domestic product managers are going to part with their know-how voluntarily to "those foreigners," whom they might resent unless good international managers set the stage right.

Another benefit of a *small* headquarters staff is that it stays busy doing the necessary daily jobs rather than usurping decision-making power from overseas subsidiary managers. As we noted in the chapter on subsidiaries, most decisions should be made as close to the front lines as possible.

THE LARGER INTERNATIONAL DEPARTMENT AT HEADQUARTERS

For a company with an international department that is larger than that discussed above, the international department can be organized as in Figure 9. In this plan, the various geographical area managers are direct-line managers with profit responsibility. There are three advantages to this organization:

1. Each geographical area manager can travel frequently to his area.
2. While it is difficult to find people who speak many languages, it is comparatively easy to find someone who speaks Spanish and Portuguese for the Western Hemisphere work, at least German and French for European work, and at least Japanese for work in Asia's biggest market.
3. In times of trouble in an overseas area, or during the establishment of new overseas operations, or at other times when heavy temporary demands are placed on management, the area manager can move to his area for half a year, a year, or whatever time is required.

For many companies, this organization, or some organization like it, works out best; but let's consider an alternative organization for a company operating globally with subsidiaries, joint ventures, licensees, and distributors, as shown in Figure 10.

The advantage of this organization is obvious: Each different group of overseas operations can be under a man who is highly qualified for just that type of operation. A man who is handling both subsidiaries and distributors may slide into the trap of favoring subsidiary operations and be biased against distributor operations. He may not give the distributors the attention, respect, and understanding they deserve. If you seek a man to handle only distributors, you might find one who has worked for a distributor for several years so that he has the viewpoints of distributors well instilled in him. Such a man might handle this side of the operations more expertly.

This organization has its disadvantages, however:

1. It is very difficult to find managers with both the knowledge of several languages and the knowledge of all major areas of the world and their people and attitudes.
2. More travel is involved than with the preceding organization.
3. Some of the subsidiaries may have joint ventures, licensees, and distributors in neighboring smaller countries. When these independent firms report to the subsidiaries rather than to the parent company, this organization becomes messy.

Figure 9

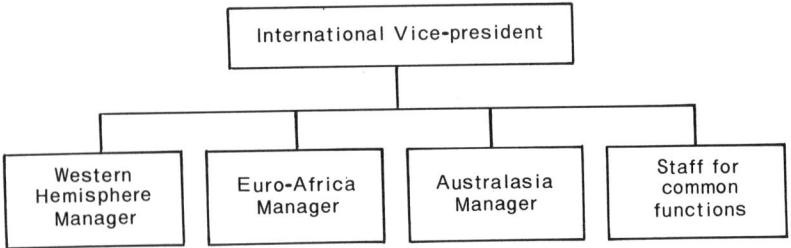

Figure 10

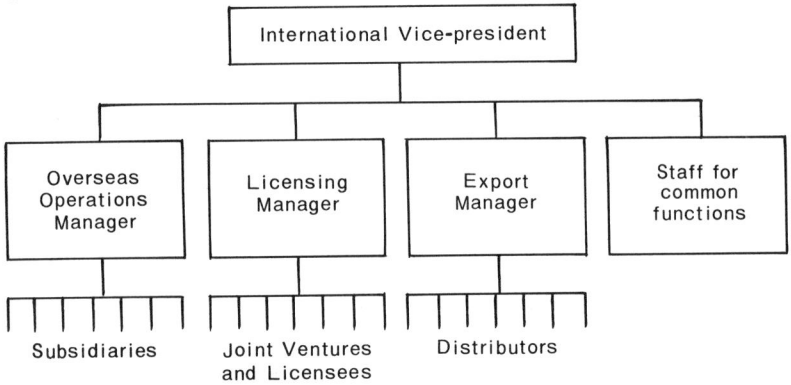

Figure 11

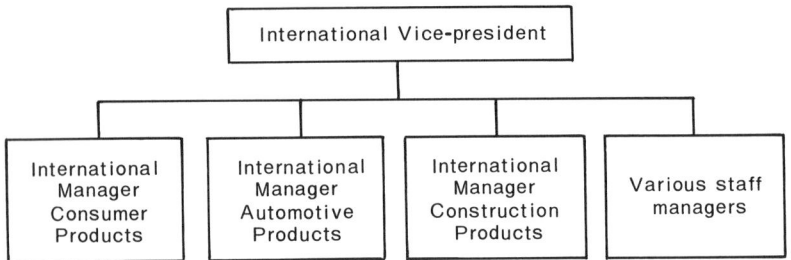

In either of the last two organizations, the staff for common functions may include product specialists, shipping specialists, and manufacturing specialists. The last group may be needed to counterbalance line managers who are too strongly oriented to marketing alone.

A third alternative organization of the international department at headquarters is according to product categories, as in Figure 11. This organization is preferred when widely different marketing channels are used for the different product categories, and these products are sold to entirely different customer groups; and when complex product expertise and worldwide communication of very complex technical material are essential in each field. In most other cases, this alternative organization is rejected.

FILLING STAFF POSITIONS WITH FOREIGNERS

Many companies fill staff positions at headquarters with men from their foreign operations in order to increase headquarters' sensitivity to foreign managers and understanding of field conditions.

If this is done, these foreign men must be chosen very carefully for their personal qualifications, so that they will be able to work well with Americans in other departments. Many foreigners never learn the subtleties involved in such interaction. Their American colleagues consequently find them strange and leave them to form a "foreign ghetto" within the headquarters, a most undesirable consequence.

8

How to Build an Excellent International Staff

STAFF excellence is one of the two most important requirements for achieving exceptional international business success. (The other is an outstanding product.)

Building an excellent international staff is, in my opinion, the single most fascinating job in international business; but setting down definite methods for doing it is difficult, because it is an art more than a science. However, this chapter gives a few hints.

Insisting on Excellence

When seeking international managers, you must settle for nothing less than the best. But those people who may have outstanding qualities in one field often are weak in others, so you must build on their strengths and build around their weak spots.

If, for example, for a subsidiary handling engineering products, you have found a manager who excels in many respects but not in engineering, then you can alter the normal organizational setup and give him a capable engineering assistant.

Another possibility is to have an executive whose judgment in one field is lacking submit decisions in that area to someone whose judgment has proved better.

In this way, instead of building the organization on people who are average in all respects but have no real weak spots, you can build on those who are truly outstanding in some respects and provide others to cover their weak areas—preferably with excellence as well.

You cannot employ such "geniuses" without also making some spectacular mistakes; but these you can quickly replace.

Furthermore, the managers with certain excellent qualities are not always the easiest people to get along with, and they often cause more than their share of friction. These situations may require top management action, yet it is worth putting up with trouble of this kind in order to have people who are outstanding in their fields.

Thus, if you want exceptional results from the managers, you must aim very high and find the real fireballs.

> *When seeking managers, look for proof of excellent past results, evidence of motivation far beyond the norm, and proven ability to inspire strong, capable people to work for them with enthusiasm.*

Once you have secured these leaders, spend much time and effort training them thoroughly for all aspects of their job and making sure they are motivated to do it well.

The Weaknesses in Some Styles of Management

In this book, I present some simple rules of thumb that I have found useful. And yet rules are made to be broken, and this applies here, too. Actual practice in business is complex and fascinating and requires consideration of many more factors than can be described in any book.

Some executives scoff at all rules, saying that management must be *pragmatic*. Unfortunately, some of these executives don't know the primary rules, and the mistakes they make when they "fly by the seats of their pants" are glaring and all too visible in financial statements later.

Other executives go to the opposite extreme and become *dogmatic*. They know and constantly follow the rules they have learned in books like this one—or even worse. Their management techniques may not produce such obviously glaring mistakes, but they are nearly always mediocre, doctrinaire, and unimaginative.

Great, creative management is practiced by those who know the rules as well as when and why to go against them, the risks involved, the chances of success, and the benefits to be derived from doing so.

Far too often, business is conducted on an emotional basis rather than according to facts and figures. Decisions are made with comments such as "Let's help this poor distributor, so that he'll think well of us." I am not implying that this is bad in all cases; certainly human friendship is extremely valuable in business and often very sincere among businessmen. But business friendships are much more solid if there are concrete, mutually profitable, factual business reasons behind them. Whenever these reasons are not there, watch out! The friendship of the licensee in the country where you have good patents is much more solid than the friendship of the licensee in the country where you have only a trademark. The executive who now gets along principally through oozing goodwill and friendship will not survive the demands of the future.

At the other extreme, the calculating cold fish who is always attempting to get the absolute maximum advantage for his company out of each deal will also have serious difficulties. The man who runs his business like a machine without trying to make it prosperous and satisfying for his customers and employees will not go far. Neither will the man who lacks heart, enthusiasm, and a feeling of goodwill toward others.

So we come to this conclusion: Only a well-rounded person who knows the rules yet can act pragmatically, who can calculate his company's best interests and at the same time add sincere human warmth, is able to be a great business leader.

Some International Considerations in Seeking Foreign Staff

Compared with American companies, many foreign firms do not use delegation of authority, and they often surround each department with a wall of misplaced secrecy. So don't be surprised if foreign managers who apply for a position have had no real management experience, at least none outside their specialized field of activity. Such men will usually need substantial training before they can be given true management jobs. Even among foreign top managers, many have never had any formal management training whatsoever—not even a one-week seminar. They may have been managers for years, yet they may need to learn the very fundamentals of management.

For instance, I know one such top manager of a moderately successful Latin American company. He thinks that his job is to go through his mail daily, supervise engineering, hire personnel, and hold down expenses. To him, production, sales, personal relations with middle managers and employees, planning for the future, and organization are unimportant matters and therefore receive only a negligible amount of his attention and thought. The company is successful despite him, not because of any direction or guidance or enthusiasm he has given it. But it certainly would have been much more successful with an outstanding manager at the helm.

ABOUT JAPANESE STAFFING

Apart from this section, most of the remainder of this chapter is not directly applicable to Japan, where personnel and management matters differ a lot from those in the remainder of the world.

A Japanese man often joins his company right after he finishes school and stays until retirement. Labor is a fixed charge in Japan. Japanese are more often paid according to seniority than according to personal effectiveness.

Seeking good personnel is thus quite a different job in Japan. When you find excellent prospective Japanese employees, your main job is to convince them how solidly established your company will be in Japan during the remainder of their lifetime. In Japan it really counts to own a nice, big Japanese headquarters building and to give other outward signs of permanence in Japan, in order to attract good people.*

Japanese top managers (and sometimes other employees) for joint ventures are often obtained from the Japanese parent company on the *shukko* basis. That means that these men retain their seniority status in the Japanese parent company while working for the joint venture. *Shukko* employees know that they can always go back to the Japanese parent company if things should not pan out in the joint venture. The American partner should insist that most *shukko* employees be rather young, since they should have flexible minds, be able to accept new directives from abroad, and be able to instill enthusiasm in their colleagues.

On the whole, the company loyalty of Japanese employees is tops in the world. Nevertheless, when they first come aboard the joint venture, the *shukko* employees are bound to have dual loyalties: toward the company they left—possibly temporarily—and toward the joint venture.

---

* During the past 25 years, it has been virtually impossible not to profit from real estate investments in Japan. Incredible as it may seem when you see current real estate prices in Japan, the outlook is for still higher prices in the future. So if you want to be along for the ride, such investments are a good idea—and they also make it easier for you to attract good Japanese employees.

It is up to the joint venture management to nurture the *shukko* employees' attitudes toward the joint venture so that after a few years their loyalty is fairly undivided.

As mentioned in Chapter 6, the American partner must be especially careful when selecting the best possible top man for the joint venture from the men proposed by the Japanese partners.

Where to Look for Excellent Managers

You can often get results by going outside the established routes. Ingenuity in finding good managers is invaluable.

Have you heard of an excellent manager with outstanding success in an allied field? It doesn't hurt to call him. However, if he works for a competitor, you are not allowed to initiate the proposal, according to the laws of several countries. But you are allowed to hire him if he asks you on his own initiative. In most countries you are also allowed to advertise the opening in the papers he reads.

If you are founding a new subsidiary, you can use imaginative advertising in trade magazines, thus alerting prospective customers and at the same time attracting employees with initiative and ambition.

Once I was involved in attracting excellent clerical personnel, accounting personnel, and mechanics to a brand new European subsidiary in a suburban location. After unsatisfactory results from ads, we simply sent a mimeographed letter by third class mail to the households on the mail route going by our building.

In that letter we introduced ourselves, stated where we were located, and said what we were going to do and that we hoped to be a good citizen of the community. We added that if they knew of any good bookkeeper, secretary, or service mechanic who would like to come in on the ground floor in a fast-growing company, they might ask this person to contact our Mr. X.

Not only did the letter produce some very good employees for us, but also we suddenly found ourselves well known in the community. When prospective customers drove to the town and could not find us, every person in the street knew immediately where our company was located and explained it gladly, sometimes volunteering that "It is a fine, new, growing company," or something to that effect. Some customers were in an excellent frame of mind by the time they found our building.

One of the best ways to hire managers is through executive recruiters or management consultants, provided you choose a good one. If you choose to advertise directly for managers, there is, of course, a huge variation in the effectiveness of different newspapers. Some that I would select at present are listed below:

GERMANY
Frankfurter Allgemeine Zeitung
Postfach 3463
D-6000 Frankfurt am Main 1

Die Welt
Kaiser-Wilhelm Str. 1
D-6000 Hamburg 36

Die Zeit (weekly)
Pressehaus, Speersort 1
D-2000 Hamburg 1

ALL GERMAN-SPEAKING COUNTRIES
IN CENTRAL EUROPE
Neue Zürcher Zeitung
Falkenstrasse 11
CH-8000 Zurich, Switzerland

FRANCE
Le Monde
5, rue des Italiens
F-75 Paris 9e

Le Figaro
14, rond-point des Champs-Elysées
F-75 Paris 8e

ENGLAND
The Daily Telegraph
135 Fleet Street
London E.C. 4

The Times
Printing House Square
London EC4P 4DE

ITALY
La Stampa
Via Marenco 32
I-10126 Turin

BELGIUM
Le Soir
Place de Louvain, 21
B-1000 Brussels

SWEDEN
Svenska Dagbladet
Rålambsvägen 7
S-112 59 Stockholm K

*Göteborgs Handels- och
Sjöfarts-Tidning*
Köpmansgatan 10
S-405 01 Gothenburg

DENMARK
Berlingske Tidende
Pilestraede 34
DK-Copenhagen K

MEXICO
Excelsior
Paseo de la Reforma No. 18
Mexico City

BRAZIL
O Estado de São Paulo
Rua Major Quedinho, 28
São Paulo
(not distributed elsewhere)

ARGENTINA
La Prensa
Avenida de Mayo 567/75
Buenos Aires

For expatriate Americans and third-country expatriates (citizens of countries other than the United States or the country where the operations are), but not for local, foreign nationals, I would select the following papers:

ALL OF EUROPE
International Herald Tribune
21, rue de Berri
F-75380 Paris

JAPAN
The Mainichi Daily News
1-1 Hitotsubashi 1-chome
Chiyoda-ku, Tokyo

UNITED STATES
The New York Times (Sundays)
229 West 43rd Street
New York, N.Y. 10036

The Wall Street Journal
30 Broad Street
New York, N.Y. 10004

For younger personnel, printouts from a computerized list of foreign students who have studied in the United States are available from:

Exchange Records Division
Institute of International Education
809 United Nations Plaza
New York, N.Y. 10017

Their list has about half a million names with 48 items of statistical information on each student.

Keeping Your Excellent Managers

Because of the gap between the quality of management of many locally owned overseas companies (not all, by far) and some U.S.-owned subsidiaries, the best way to keep capable and ambitious people of the local nationality where you operate is to create the right company atmosphere, including proper delegation of authority and absence of needless secrecy, and to provide thorough on-the-job training of your best employees so that they can be advanced.

> *You can motivate capable people strongly by giving them authority, a challenging job, backing and assistance when needed, and the opportunity for advancement after they have proven their capability. In keeping good employees, these factors rate higher than the amount of salary they receive.*

Nevertheless, compensation must still be in line with the local pay scales in the country where you operate, or slightly above them if you have unusually capable local people.

To instill the best modern management methods into the subsidiaries, thereby lifting their methods above the currently practiced local management methods, requires considerable attention, work, and expense. It is a long and arduous process, although a necessary one, for various reasons. One of these is that the major differences that remain between the overseas and the U.S. approaches lead sometimes to heavy criticism from the parent company and often to needless resignations or firings of subsidiary managers.

The situation becomes especially bad if domestic product-division people without international training should be allowed to interfere with international policies beyond their understanding, especially in the field of marketing, including advertising, public relations, and pricing. The negative effects of such interference on foreign personnel can be disastrous.

Personnel policies must also follow local habits and attitudes.

For example, a major American subsidiary in Germany suffered a strike because the American manager refused the workers beer at lunch—until a good German advisor told him that he was out of his mind and got the beer flowing again.

Most of the normal perquisites for managers for each country must be maintained, especially in the countries where the income tax rate is high. Some of the countries where this is particularly important are Japan, England, Sweden, Denmark, and the Netherlands; but there are many others. In many countries the income tax is nearly confiscatory for any income above $30,000 per year.

To alleviate the effects of high taxes, executives are given whatever is tax-free in the particular country. In Japan, the main perquisite is the large entertainment allowance. In other countries, perquisites might include clubs, meals, a car, an interest-free loan, a house, or a part-time chauffeur, gardener, or maid.

Workers and other employees in various countries receive a range of generally accepted or compulsory benefits, including profit sharing (e.g., in France), pay increases tied to cost-of-living increases, bonuses, insurance, pensions, and, in several countries, ample compulsory severance pay. In Italy, for instance, the total direct cost of a worker to a company is roughly twice the wage he is paid.

In many countries, including some in Southern Europe and Latin America, it is extremely expensive to fire employees because of laws giving them huge severance indemnifications, particularly if they have been employed for a long time. Such laws make it necessary to plan differently for enterprises in these countries and set aside reserves for severance pay. Of course you must be doubly careful about whom you employ for a trial period in these countries and whom you retain beyond the trial period.

Nationality of Subsidiary Top Managers

Suppose you are starting a subsidiary in an industrialized country, a country where you have had no prior organization. If you send an American over to start the company, it should be perfectly clear to him and to all the new local employees that the American is there only for a specified, limited time, say one, two, or three years, until the company is running well with local staff and local management, including a local top manager.

If the company is of substantial size and in a complex technical field that requires keeping an experienced American permanently on the spot, then it is important that this American be a technical specialist, not the top manager of the company. The reason for this is that you cannot attract the best local middle managers in an industrialized country if you give the impression that the top position in the company is reserved for an American. A job-hunting, ambitious middle manager will shy away from a company where he knows that he can never reach the pinnacle.

This is the main reason for having a local national hold the top position. A second reason is that the local national will probably be a better manager there because of his thorough knowledge of the people and the cultural environment.

It is just as important in a foreign country as in the United States that the top manager be familiar with the local mores and laws. It is usually as big a mistake to send an American to head up an Italian subsidiary as it would be for an Italian parent company to send an Italian to the United States to head up an American subsidiary (unless the Italian happens to have had many years of experience in America and is a permanent resident immigrant). This applies to all industrialized countries.

In less industrialized countries with a temperate climate, the choice of the nationality of the top manager must be considered case by case. You might prefer a local national in these countries also, if a really good man is available.

In hot, tropical, less industrialized countries, on the other hand, you would normally try to have an American or third-country national as your top manager. There are exceptions, of course: You might find a local man who can give the venture the aggressive leadership you want. Or, companies in extractive industries might prefer the good government relations of a local national to the more aggressive leadership of an expatriate.

Some Difficulties with Expatriates

An American executive who makes a substantial number of quick business trips to many parts of the world notices how well he seems to get along without knowledge of foreign languages and without thorough preparation in the history, habits, attitudes, and mores of the peoples he visits. He therefore draws the conclusion that it would be quite easy for him or for another American employee to live as a permanent resident, an expatriate, among any of these foreign peoples without going through a thorough preparation. Wrong!

Foreigners do not expect the traveling American to know much about each country he visits, but the moment he comes there to stay, they become much more demanding and critical. Usually the local nationals will not accept an expatriate who does not make a serious effort to learn their history, culture, habits, and attitudes.

Unless their language is one that is spoken by relatively few, such as Danish, the locals will also have little patience with an expatriate who does not make a serious effort to learn their language well enough to converse and work freely in it.

Even more importantly, the expatriate will have to make a conscious effort to enjoy the same things people around him enjoy and give up some of the things that he used to enjoy at home. He will have to identify with his adopted home and develop sensitivity to the people.

These requirements are very demanding on a man and even more so on his wife. Many expatriate businessmen or technical experts sent out by American companies fail because their wives cannot adjust to, or do not make an honest effort to enjoy, their new life and their different surroundings. By the time this is discovered, the company may have over $100,000 invested in the man, and invaluable time has been lost.

Therefore,

> *The selection of men to go overseas must be made with the utmost care, and their wives must be taken into serious consideration.*

Usually, the younger a man and his wife are, the more easily they adapt to new, foreign surroundings, and the more easily they learn a new language. Therefore, this consideration must outweigh the desirability of sending a thoroughly experienced man with mature judgment, a man who may have a wife who resists such a change in her life.

Too often the American experts sent overseas are those who were too cantankerous for a domestic product division, or the marginal performers whom a domestic division was considering putting out to pasture.

As we shall see in the chapter on Operation Europe, it is often beneficial to temporarily interchange key men among European subsidiaries; but this can be done only if the men and their families have the necessary adaptability and knowledge of languages. Sophisticated international companies carefully consider such adaptability and knowledge of languages when they hire managers in Europe, even though no immediate plans for exchange between countries exist at the time when the managers are hired.

What has been said about American expatriates applies also to third-country expatriates, as well as to foreigners brought to the United States permanently or for extended periods.

To many foreigners, immigration to the United States is a bigger transition than most Americans realize, and not everyone is able to cope with the new environment. Many a Frenchman misses his wine, bread, and cheese; many an Englishman misses his evenings with the boys in the pub; many a Latin American misses his upper-class life; many a wife misses her parents and relatives; and hardly any foreigners understand even half the American jokes. Thus, you must be especially cautious about bringing foreigners here who are no longer young and easily adaptable.

The American who is sent overseas does not find only the habits and living conditions unusual; his work is naturally quite different and often more difficult than at home.

He often finds himself caught up in details because authority is not traditionally delegated to others down the line. From domestic product divisions he gets little understanding for the need to make product changes according to local market requirements. Domestic colleagues laugh at his promotional programs because they don't understand the local tastes the programs were created for.

Sometimes he feels that he reports to an armchair general at headquarters who second-guesses him on all important decisions with a seemingly total lack of understanding for the front-line needs.

Finally, the expatriate American must struggle with the gnawing thought that he might be passed over for promotion at the parent company because he is so far away and is making such "strange" decisions.

THE HIGH COST OF EXPATRIATES

Typically, a $25,000-a-year middle management American on a two-year foreign assignment will cost a company about $50,000 a year in Western

Europe, more in most of the less industrialized countries, and easily $75,000 a year in Japan.

By comparison, if the same man lives and works in the United States and makes six trips a year to Europe, spending three weeks there each time (over one third of his working time), his time in Europe will cost only about $17,000 a year, or about one third of what it costs to have him permanently in Europe. This figure of $17,000 for a three-week trip every second month typically comprises:

Salary for 18 weeks		$ 9,500
Air travel	$3,500	
Other expenses	4,000	
Total expenses		7,500
Total direct cost		$17,000

Foreign travel has become inexpensive, while by comparison the cost of having permanent American expatriates overseas has remained high. This cost includes the expenses of moving both ways, a cost-of-living allowance, a housing allowance, an income tax differential allowance, a schooling allowance, an allowance for long home vacations for the employee and his family, and in many locations a hardship allowance. It should also include the cost of bringing the expatriate to the home office fairly frequently and not for too short a period each time. This may be necessary to keep him from going stale at his foreign location and to keep him up to date on new developments at home.

For these reasons, many sophisticated companies that would formerly have had a resident American living at a foreign subsidiary now try to get along with exclusively local personnel. They partly compensate for this by having various specialists and executives visit the subsidiary more frequently and for longer stays.

In this way the subsidiaries gain the benefit of having specialists in several fields contributing their knowledge to the subsidiaries on the spot, instead of having one generalist stationed there permanently. Similarly, more people at headquarters will gain firsthand knowledge of the subsidiaries' activities and needs. This greatly helps the flow of good ideas back to headquarters.

An American who is sent abroad only to give temporary assistance for a few weeks or a few months must also be selected carefully. To your foreign customers and affiliates, this man *is* the company, but far too often his selection is left to the domestic division, which sends either the person "most deserving" of a foreign trip—sometimes the one with the most seniority—or the person who can be spared most easily at the time. Both these considerations are totally wrong. Instead, the most capable, adaptable person should make the trip, the one who will leave the foreign customers and affiliates with the best impression of the American parent company.

The worst mistake made by less experienced companies is being too stingy with the amount of time spent by headquarters personnel visiting the foreign subsidiaries. I have only encountered one case of a company dedicating too much travel to its foreign subsidiaries. (This was a British company that always visited its tiny South African subsidiary in January.)

American companies often employ a third-country national instead of an American as their resident manager, especially in some of the less industrialized countries. The cost may sometimes be a little less than the cost of an American expatriate, but the main reason for using him is usually that a capable third-country national can be found more easily.

Compensation policies for third-country expatriates vary widely. One particularly difficult item to resolve is their pension. It is often impossible to include them in the American pension plan, and the security of any pension plan in many of the less industrialized countries is often questionable, to put it mildly. Some companies solve this difficulty by setting up an offshore trust pension plan exclusively for one or more third-country nationals.

Several advisory services for overseas compensation are available to companies that have a number of expatriates abroad. (Some of these services are too expensive for the company that has only one or two expatriates.) Organizations that furnish such services include:

American Management Associations
Business International Corporation
National Foreign Trade Council
Organization Resources Counselors
International Compensation, Inc.
Associates for International Research, Inc.

The last two companies mentioned are in Boston and Cambridge, Massachusetts, respectively. The others are in New York City.

THE EXPATRIATE IN JAPAN

Suppose that you run an American company that has an important minority interest in a substantial joint venture in Japan. In that case, you should have an American resident at the Japanese company. He should not be the top man there, but he should hold an important position near the top, because you will want to use him as a liaison to get some new procedures and principles across to Japan. And, believe me, these procedures will not be adopted just by your mailing memos on them to the joint venture headquarters.

The resident American expatriate in Japan has a very important and very difficult job. He wears several hats: To the Japanese partners, he often represents you. To the joint venture, he often represents the American company, introducing into the Japanese medium some strange foreign procedures and principles. Your resident American has to proceed with patience, and he has to be familiar enough with Japan and sufficiently open-minded and intelligent to know which procedures will conflict too much with Japanese ways and should not be introduced.

When introducing your procedures in Japan, this American should persuade, not order. He should be quiet and discreet and show only a low profile for the U.S. involvement. When he wants to change the opinions of Japanese colleagues, he should try to do this without winning an argument with them, to save them from losing face. In a quiet way, perhaps without your ever knowing it, your man will get after many problems that would have become lost in the heap and remained unsolved had he not been on the scene.

To your U.S. company, your American resident represents the Japanese joint venture. It is he who has to explain why they don't buy the microswitches from you, but rather from a Japanese supplier. It is he who has to persuade your U.S. personnel to shorten the delivery time to Japan when your own supplies are tight.

And finally, when your American expatriate visits the United States, you will find him fighting you on behalf of some strange idea of the Japanese partners. Well, get out of your chair and shake his hand and thank him for fighting you, because he has probably found out that the strange idea fits the conditions in Japan perfectly. This resident American will constantly translate from Japanese thinking to American thinking and vice versa.

How do you find such a man?

Within your American company is, of course, the best place to look; and if you don't find him there, then there are Americans who have married Japanese girls or otherwise fallen in love with Japan. You can advertise for them in Japan, and sometimes even in the United States. Most authorities on the subject recommend that you not send a Nisei (a U.S.-born Japanese) to Japan, but I don't agree. I would prefer to look at the individual person and his capabilities, not at the slant of his eyes.

If the man is from outside your company, then he must be thoroughly trained before you send him. Although this seems obvious, companies

Figure 12 Form used to indicate applicant's foreign language ability.

Please list the languages you know on line (1); on lines (2) through (7) describe your ability in each language by using one of the following expressions:

Perfect
Excellent
Very good
Good
Moderate
Poor
None

1. LANGUAGE						
2. Reading						
3. Understanding the spoken language						
4. Speaking						
5. Writing						
6. Dictating to a good secretary (who can edit your dictation into a good rendition)						
7. Dictating to any stenographer						

On the reverse, please tell in a few words what other special knowledge you have about foreign languages and what experience you have gained from living in foreign countries. (This could also help in determining how your language knowledge could best be improved.)

often make a great mistake in not training this key man as well as they should.

Knowledge of Foreign Languages and Attitudes

Your executives abroad should naturally have adequate knowledge of foreign languages. But even though it is a less obvious requirement, it is at least as important for these men to have gained the knowledge of different moral codes, mores, legal systems, and foreign attitudes.

When interviewing someone for a position in a foreign country, I would be interested in finding out, for instance, whether he and his wife like the people there and why, whether they would enjoy living there and why, whether they would rather spend their weekends with Americans, third-country expatriates, or local nationals and why, whether they have read any author or seen any movie from the country, whether they have lived in any other foreign country with a similarly different environment, who their friends were there, whether they enjoyed living there and why, what they learned about the history, culture, and attitudes of that country, and so on.

It is totally insufficient to know whether or not a person speaks a foreign language. Does he read it? Write it? Dictate it? How well? Can he correct business correspondence or contracts written in it? Does he understand the different shades of meaning of the spoken language?

A form such as the one in Figure 12 is helpful in determining the language ability of an applicant, but it should be supplemented by spot checks on his own self-evaluation.

The first language an American must learn abroad is English, an English utilizing short, simple words distinctly pronounced in simple sentences that can be understood by those foreigners who have not had much exposure to the language.

Someone arriving in Japan begins by learning to understand and speak the English spoken in Japan, which is quite different from any other English. So is the English spoken in India. (You will find comments on the particular English that is used in the East Bloc in the chapter concerning that area.)

In the next chapter, we shall discuss further the English language and its pitfalls, foreign languages, and—very importantly—the nonspoken language of behavior, gestures, and other signals.

9

How to Cross the
Barriers to International
Understanding

I have covered this subject in the greatest detail because it concerns the aspects of international business that are generally understood least and handled worst. I suggest that the preceding chapter be read before this one, for they belong together.

Knowledge of Languages, Attitudes, and Culture: Some Further Remarks

In the preceding chapter, we discussed the knowledge of languages and the understanding of foreign attitudes that are so necessary for the international staff. By finding a staff that has this ability and knowledge, you can, in theory, cross the language and attitude barriers. But in practice, this achievement is much more difficult to accomplish.

In the first place, you will never find in your personnel all the desirable knowledge of languages and understanding of foreign attitudes you would wish. In theory, you would prefer this knowledge to be distributed among all the personnel and executives involved. In practice, you always have to work with much less than ideal resources.

Secondly, your top executives may not understand what they lack in understanding of foreigners. Let's look at an actual example.

A medium-sized French company I was very familiar with wanted to enter the U.S. market. They sent over to the United States a capable French executive who "spoke English." After a couple of years, their U.S. subsidiary had piled up a huge loss. Even after closing their subsidiary and licking their wounds, the French headquarters executives obviously still did not realize what had happened, because they turned right around and sent another French top executive who "spoke German" to run their German subsidiary. Again, fiasco!

Exactly the same thing happens to many American companies going into Europe.

What went wrong with the French subsidiary in the United States? The top executives in France never stopped to ask themselves, "Even though this man speaks English, can he actually communicate with American distributors and customers? Does he know what makes them tick, and if so, can he influence and motivate them?"

Knowing a language fluently allows you to be able to take the first step over the cultural barrier. But language is only one of the requirements needed to cross over. Unfortunately, an executive may not actually be aware that he hasn't accomplished the crossing until his business has already begun to go sour.

As it happened, there was excellent communication between the French resident manager in the above example and the French headquarters; but there was a barrier to understanding between the French resident manager and his American employees, and also between the manager and the American distributors and customers, a fact he was not even aware of.

The French manager knew good school English, which enabled him to order meals, chat at cocktail parties, and travel around easily; but much more than that is required to understand Americans, let alone to sell to them.

You might say that the solution should have been simple: The French company should have replaced their French resident manager with an experienced, capable American executive. But that would not have been the whole solution. It would have improved the situation, decreased the losses, and vastly improved the understanding between the manager and his customers. But what would have happened to the understanding between the manager of the U.S. subsidiary and the executives at the French headquarters? In all likelihood, it would have gone to pot.

Little more would have been accomplished than to move the cultural barrier from one location to another. Unless the American manager had excellent understanding of French executives—how to influence them, how to change their opinions, and how to make them understand the U.S. subsidiary's problems—the transatlantic communications would have been bound for very serious trouble.

Let's assume that the top executives at the French headquarters could not have been replaced (usually they cannot) with executives who possessed true international understanding. How could they have resolved this situation short of closing the U.S. subsidiary, as was actually done (and as is also being done with many foreign-owned subsidiaries in the United States under similar circumstances)?

Cultural Translation

The best way to solve a problem such as the one above is to hire the hard-to-find American manager who has the ability both to run the U.S. business and to communicate well with the French headquarters. But such a man is so rare that we might be forced to look for a second-best solution.

This would be to have a capable American executive running the U.S. subsidiary and a young, capable, flexible, open-minded international Frenchman on the staff of the U.S. company. This Frenchman should be able to communicate both with the French headquarters and with the Americans.

This man, in addition to fulfilling his other duties, would be what I call a *cultural translator,* a person who translates not only between languages but also between different ways of thinking, between different cultures.

The cultural translator can never fully educate the top executives at the French headquarters so that they understand all the aspects of their American business, but if he is capable, he can help them make the right decisions and keep them from making bad mistakes—and a smart one can achieve this without the headquarters executives knowing to what extent he has influenced them.

The only danger to the company arises when the French top executives, after the resulting U.S. success, start thinking that they themselves are now international experts and that they can now run, for instance, a German subsidiary and make the decisions without a German–French cultural translator. Sad times will invariably follow if they try.

Cultural translation goes far beyond just speaking the language, and a good American–French cultural translator is not necessarily a good German–French cultural translator, even if he also "speaks German."

As a matter of fact, a good cultural translator from American to French is not necessarily a good cultural translator from French to American. Quite different personal qualifications may well be required in the two opposing directions.

The above French–American example in reverse may concern an American-owned subsidiary in France run by a capable French executive. But in this case, and provided that the French subsidiary is big enough to warrant the large expense, the first choice for a cultural translator from French to American would be a young international American who resides in France and would work under the French head man— quite a different person from the cultural translator working in the French subsidiary in the United States.

Some people do have the ability to be cultural translators in both directions between two cultures. (The American expatriate in Japan described in the preceding chapter fills the role of a two-way cultural translator.) But few have the unique ability to play this role in all directions among several different cultures. I would call such a person a *multicultural translator*. If this person also has had business experience in several different countries, and if he is an able business leader, then he has the rare international-people-management ability described in the chapter on future trends. This quality is very little understood. The following is an actual example in which international-people-management ability was lacking.

A French company that operates in much of Europe has two top managers with many excellent qualities and many years of what they think is international business experience (actually, it is little more than export experience). Both men speak a couple of foreign languages, one of the men with fluency, the other one with difficulty. Despite their years in what they called international business, these two men do not really understand that people of different nationalities respond to quite different approaches in business and that they have different attitudes. These two otherwise capable executives do not realize that they offend Dutch and Danish customers, for example, with their normal French mannerisms and attitudes.

What is even worse, when they organize their company's international activities, they do not see the need for hiring people, perhaps at high salaries, who have this true international business ability that they themselves lack.

They ignore the fact that the company's telephone operator must speak English and German in addition to French. When hiring secretaries, they accept a knowledge of school English as a true knowledge of English. They know that their letters contain errors of grammar and spelling, but—much worse—they have no idea that their letters convey the wrong shades of meaning, and that they often offend the party receiving them.

When these two managers need an additional sales engineer for work in Germany, they find out if any of their French sales engineers speaks German; then they transfer him, ignoring whether he has any understanding at all of German culture, German customers, or desires uniquely German.

Quotations and service instructions from this French company to customers in Denmark and Norway are written in French instead of English (the second best alternative to Danish and Norwegian).

If the business results are good in spite of these mistakes, how much better the results would have been if the two French top managers had known the fundamentals of international business and hired international sales engineers who really could communicate thoroughly with the non-French customers.

There is an additional, typical fault in the same French company: French customers are given much better treatment, thought, and care and much more executive time than non-French customers. This is a fault that is particularly prevalent in the largest Western industrial countries: the United States, Germany, France, and the United Kingdom. It does not exist at all in the smaller countries such as Finland, Denmark, and Austria.

The French company in the above example happens to be a subsidiary of an American corporation. The top officers of the American corporation communicate well with one of the two French managers, the one who is fluent in English, but not at all well with the one who speaks little English, yet who is extremely capable within his specialty. As a consequence, the American top officers have become personal friends with only one of the two top managers. Unavoidably they give their ear much more to him than to the other manager, whom they don't understand as well. They have confidence only in the man who speaks fluent English.

As it happens, the success of the French firm is due principally to the efforts of the man whose English is poor, because his performance in his special field is outstanding. And yet he remains in an inferior position with respect to the other man, who doesn't happen to excel in any particular field but who can speak English better. Ironically, the man who is largely responsible for the company's success is paid less than the one who simply knows English well.

There are far too many such injustices done by international corporations to executives who are outstanding in one area of the business but who do not communicate well across a language barrier.

It is up to the top executives of the parent company to try to cross this barrier, to get full information on the performance of those with whom they cannot communicate directly, and to reward business results more than the ability to carry on conversations at cocktail parties.

In German there is a word for the ability that a businessman must try to acquire in any cultural environment: *Fingerspitzengefühl*, literally "sensitivity in the tips of your fingers." The word actually denotes that sixth sense which tells one good Brooklyn businessman how to get the best out of a bargain with another Brooklyn businessman, that sense which he may lack when he is confronted instead with Japanese, Norwegian, or, to a lesser extent, Texas businessmen.*

> *Some people have a natural ability to cross cultural barriers easily. Others must work hard at it. Most people never learn it, even though they may think they have.*

Keep in mind that it is not just a matter of your understanding the foreigners and what they say and don't say. No business will result from that alone. To be successful, you must influence them. This requires the opposite action as well, namely that they understand you—again, not only what you say, but also what you don't say.

To influence businessmen of another culture, you must have the rare ability to project yourself as one of their tribe. In competitive international industrial sales situations, it is often this projection, more than concrete product advantages, price, or quality, that in the end determines who gets the business.

We can summarize by repeating:

> *Learning another language is only the first step in getting along in a foreign country. The next step—learning the culture, habits, and attitudes of the country's people—is even more important.*

There is only one way to take both steps: Work hard at it and take a personal interest in it. Once you have learned how, you will be amply rewarded by the pleasure of truly communicating.

* The November 22, 1971, issue of *Time* magazine reported that all Japanese-owned manufacturing plants in the United States were experiencing difficulties because of the "culture shokku."

Language Study

"And how do you best learn a language?" I am often asked.

"By simple, hard work," I reply every time.

To speak and understand a language superficially, simple record courses are the cheapest and best solution.* The Berlitz method is generally more expensive but also effective. Total immersion is quick, expensive, and effective. But all these methods give only a superficial knowledge, and the language is quickly forgotten if not practiced constantly.

To learn a language thoroughly, to be able to write it *and* dictate it to any typist, and to be able to remember it without any practice over a long span of time, none of the above will suffice. For this purpose, it is necessary to study the grammar thoroughly and to practice extensively writing the language for years.

One manufacturer of record courses, Linguaphone Institute of Languages, combines efficiently the two approaches, listening and learning the grammar.

To people going abroad for an extended stay, I usually recommend studying the foreign language *before* going to the foreign country. That first study can be through records. Once they are in the foreign country, I recommend continuing regular language study, this time with emphasis on grammar and writing.

About Translations

Good translations are time-consuming and costly. For this reason, most companies get along with quick, rough translations in everyday transactions. But everyone working with these quick translations must remember that they are only rough, and it is necessary to demand a thorough translation of any important part that could be misunderstood or any part that seems to be wrong.

A good translator is much more than a person who knows two languages. A statement made in one language often means something quite different from its exact translation in another language. Here is an example:

A German service engineer kept adding this note to reports on occa-

---

* One practical detail about the use of language records: Start by transferring the recordings to one track on stereo tape, then use the other track for your own imitating. Listen to yourself on one speaker and to the teacher on the other speaker. Repeat the imitation over and over again until it is similar to the teacher's original. Use a tape recorder with the "sound-on-sound" feature that allows you to erase one track, leaving the other track, the teacher's, unerased.

sional defective parts from a trusted American supplier: "How could this happen?" In German, this note would be taken as a friendly reminder to find out how the particular defect could be avoided in the future. But the American manufacturing engineer who received these notes repeatedly took them to mean, more or less, "How can you make such stupid mistakes?"

A cultural translator would have known that the German sentence "How could this happen?" should have been translated to "Please investigate!"

> *A mediocre translator constantly causes ill feelings between parties of different nationalities.*

The wrong translation is easily amended. Much more dangerous is the imperfect translation, the one giving the wrong *shade* of meaning and causing adverse emotional reaction through an implied insult in the translation, one that was not present in the original language.

Good translations of business papers between certain countries with similar cultures, such as Denmark and Sweden or Spain and Portugal, can easily be made, but such translations are not so easy to make between dissimilar countries such as Denmark and Portugal. Differences in humor are one reason. Let's see how this difficulty affects advertising and public relations.

INTERNATIONAL ADVERTISING AND PUBLIC RELATIONS

In some eight cases out of ten, you cannot effectively translate advertising or public relations articles created in the home country into all languages, at least not between American English and a European language or Japanese, or between a European language and Japanese.

To get effective advertising and P.R., you must usually re-create it for each country, at least for those countries that are quite different from each other. Sometimes your advertising department can use the same photos or art or basic idea and only rewrite the text; but often even the same photos cannot be utilized.

Contrary to what most advertising and P.R. men assume, it is impossible for a professional advertising or P.R. man in one country to even begin to judge advertising or P.R. intended for another, dissimilar country, unless he has crossed the cultural barrier. If he hasn't, all he can do is judge whether the particular advertising or P.R. would have been effective in his own country. And that is immaterial.

> *Advertising and P.R. that are appealing in one country may be dull or even repulsive in another.*

Despite what has been said above, however, and despite what is said elsewhere in this book about presenting a Japanese corporate face in Japan, a German face in Germany, and so on, a global company should strive toward a uniform global *style* of advertising. What I mean by "style" here is the combination of such elements as page layout, typography, and use of art or photography. (Nevertheless, in small countries the low circulation of some media forces you to forgo some of the more costly elements such as full color and bleed.)

If such a characteristic, uniform style of advertising is used, international customers will tend to recognize the advertising at first glance as belonging to that particular global company, even before reading the company name, let alone any part of the text. This is highly advantageous.

It is very difficult, however, to get independent advertising agents in different countries to accept directives about style. Advertising art directors are often volatile, temperamental people, and they can easily react to a little remark as if you had asked Rembrandt to change the shape of a painting.

For this reason, international advertising requires diplomacy and sensitivity to different tastes in different countries. It requires independent creativity in almost every country, except in a few somewhat similar countries, such as Norway and Sweden, where translation is often enough.

Except for the countries with similar tastes, it is necessary to have a creative local advertising agent in each country. Don't use a British or an American advertising agent for Holland or Germany. You will probably waste a lot of money and not be happy with the results. (By this I am not saying that you cannot use the Dutch or German subsidiary of an American-owned group of advertising agencies, because they are generally manned by local people.)

One of the world's major advertising agencies spent its own money advertising its services in *Fortune* magazine with the message that it is only an old, dull theory that Italians and Germans have different tastes. The agency stated that, to the contrary, the same story line can sell the same product on a multicountry basis. I agree, but only in two cases out of ten. ("Put a tiger in your tank" was one exceptional campaign that translated well.)

If you are using a large Madison Avenue agency in the United States, you may be tempted to recommend that your overseas subsidiaries use that agency's local subsidiaries; but you should at the same time give your local overseas managers complete freedom to select another local firm instead, if they believe it is superior.

If a thoroughly cosmopolitan person compares the advertising of different countries, he invariably reaches the conclusion that U.S. advertising is tops in the world. But that does not necessarily mean that an American-owned advertising agency in Germany can do better there than a German-owned one. It does mean, however, that German, British, French, Japanese, and other advertising agencies, no matter who owns them, are learning a great deal from American advertising and P.R. methods. They are also transforming what they have learned to the tastes of their own countries and adding their own ingenuity and creativity.

American advertising leadership has greatly assisted the many American advertising firms that have established overseas subsidiaries, joint ventures, and affiliates. They serve not only multinational clients with headquarters in the United States but also locally owned foreign firms, and they do this on a very competitive basis.

Other comments on advertising may be found in the chapter on legal matters.

When to Use an Interpreter

Don't use an interpreter more often than necessary. Try to learn at least some words of the foreign language and make an effort to use them in unimportant matters in social communication. If you can give a brief speech in the local language, or at least say a few words, it will be much appreciated. It shows that you are at least trying.

In most day-to-day communication with foreign executives, it is preferable not to use an interpreter if you understand each other fairly well directly. The interpreter tends to make the conversations too formal and too laborious; the immediacy and spontaneity are lost. You also lose all those important bits of information that spontaneous cues from the foreign executive would likely have given you. Of course, if you do not understand each other fairly well, it is better to use an interpreter than to cause all kinds of misunderstanding by trying to muddle through without one.

In cases when it is especially important to ensure that there is no misunderstanding, it is a good practice to ask the other party to repeat to you his understanding of what you have said, and conversely, for you to repeat to him what you think he has said. You can sometimes do this even when you use an interpreter.

In formal business negotiations, when it is important to know the subtleties behind what each party is saying, and when the conversation may become a binding contract or lead to one, then use an interpreter, and spend the necessary money to get the best one available. Avoid bad interpreters! There is a big difference between a good one and an excellent one. And the interpreter can never be excellent if he does not know the subject matter to be discussed. Let him read up on it in advance and brief him well. Invite him to give you advice on the negotiation and help you achieve your objectives. It gives you a tremendous advantage if the interpreter is not just neutral but an additional member of your negotiating team.

When you use an interpreter and you also understand the other language, you will have another tremendous advantage, because you will be able to consider each statement for twice as long.

In formal negotiations in Japan (for example, in discussions with prospective partners of a joint venture), some Japanese advisors recom-

Avoid bad interpreters!

mend that the interpreter write down in both languages the essence of the main conclusions reached and have these signed by both parties, even though it is clearly stated and understood that these conclusions are tentative and not binding on either party. The Japanese advisors point out that by writing down the tentative conclusions, you save a great amount of time because you make it unnecessary to negotiate the same points over and over again. The Japanese respect the written word much more than the spoken one.

Don't be surprised if the interpreter occasionally uses a dictionary, if he sometimes translates a brief sentence into many words or a long one into a few, or even if he makes a few minor mistakes. That interpreter might still be better than the one who uses no dictionary and seems to make no mistakes, but fails to help the negotiations progress.

Don't be surprised either if your interpreter translates something in your language into seemingly entirely different wording, or into pure silence. This may show that you have got an excellent interpreter, because much of our daily verbiage means something entirely different from the dictionary meaning of the words.

Take, for example, the Texan who, as he comes into the office in the morning, passes slowly by the desk of a colleague, drawling, "How're ya doin'?" Translated to New York office language, this would be "Good morning, Jack." And translated to British English, it would be "Nasty weather today, eh, wot?"

Of course, none of these three expressions mean anything close to what the words say. They are only social sounds, independent of words. A psychologist might say that they mean something like "I'm in a pretty good humor today. If you want to talk to me, you can start now."

All languages contain many "nothing" expressions and words, such as *n'est-çe pas?* in French, *va* in Swedish, and *ja* in German when placed at the end of a sentence. The last two are in the spoken language but are usually never written.

A good interpreter does much more than interpret. If he works for an American in a negotiation with Germans, for example, he will see to it that the American addresses the Germans on a formal basis with title or family name; but if he works for a German in a negotiation with Americans, he will make sure the German addresses them informally, on a first-name basis. He may also urge the American to avoid resting his feet on the corner of the desk and coax the German to take off his coat and relax.

In important negotiations, *you* should hire the interpreter, rather than let the other party do it.

The Silent Language

Edward T. Hall, author of *The Silent Language*,* explained how American businessmen abroad often misinterpret foreign behavior, especially behavior connected with time, space, objects, money, friendships, and commitments. He called all nonverbal signals the silent language.

Misinterpretations of the silent language can get international businessmen into hot water. All of us constantly issue nonverbal signals. The trouble is that people of different cultures issue different signals, and signals that appear the same mean different things in other cultures.

For instance, I don't exactly enjoy it every time a mustachioed personal friend of mine in Moscow greets me by embracing me and bussing me on both cheeks, but to him this behavior means exactly the same as when a Swiss friend shakes my hand. For this reason, I have no alternative but to do in Rome as the Romans do. (My wife claims I look hilarious.)

In some cultures, the international businessman must positively shed all his own mores and accept new ones with an open mind. For example, when a Westerner is visiting a Moslem home where they observe purdah, the practice of secluding women from observation, the Westerner will find few clues to how he should behave. But even in less dissimilar surroundings than this, there are many differences to observe from country to country.

Say that you are an American businessman and that you have been invited for the first time to the home of an important Swedish business connection in Stockholm. "Come for dinner at seven," they said.

If you arrive at 7:25, you have committed an insulting blunder. Furthermore, if you brought no flowers for the hostess, it is an additional serious faux pas, which can be absolved only by sending her a large bouquet on the following day (and not two days later!).

"Dinner at seven" in Sweden means (or at least used to mean) that you should arrive between 6:55 and 7:05. At that time, the hostess will have the herring cold, the soup warm, and the whole meal calculated with precision so you will sit down at the table at 7:10. The guest arriving at 7:25 will cause the Châteaubriand to be overdone, the aquavit to be too warm, and other culinary disasters that the American guest wouldn't even notice. Probably he would never be told unless he were a very close personal friend.

If the dinner were instead at the home of a Colombian businessman in Bogotá, who had invited him to "dinner at seven," and the American arrived at 7:25, he would likely find that his host was just putting

* Garden City, N.Y.: Doubleday & Co., 1959.

on his shoes and the hostess was nowhere to be seen because she was still taking a bath. The next guest would probably arrive three quarters of an hour later, and most of the guests one to two hours later. The dinner would be served about 10:30, and the guests would leave right after dinner. (It is insulting to leave so abruptly after dinner in Northern Europe.)

An Indian customer once said to me, "We will order it right away." I inquired politely about what date we would receive the order, and I was not surprised to hear him reply, "In about three months," which was what "right away" meant to him.

Problems with English

In the preceding chapter, I mentioned that English is the first language an American going abroad must learn—an English containing only short, simple words that foreigners understand, one that contains no slang expressions whatsoever, and one with entirely new words or meanings, such as in the examples below.

Billion: In most countries this means 1,000 times more than it does in the United States. Instead of "billion," say "milliard" or "a thousand million" to avoid misunderstanding.

Native: In South Africa this word means "black." In many other countries, it means "savage."

Training: In many countries, this word connotes the kind of training given dogs or circus animals. "Instruction" will not have this bad connotation, even though it sounds a little wrong to an American.

America: In Spain and Portugal, this often means Latin America. "United States" is a much better term both there and in Latin America. (But it is of course best to refer to your own country as little as possible anyway, and concentrate on the place you are visiting.)

Feet, gallons, pounds, degrees Fahrenheit, etc.: In most countries, you had better state the measurements in meters, liters, kilos, degrees Centigrade (Centigrade is called Celsius in most countries), and so on.

Don't think for a moment that there are no barriers to understanding between England and the United States. British attitudes are very different from those in the United States, and even the language in England holds many pitfalls for Americans.

During World War II, some American soldiers were temporarily in charge of long-distance telephone communications for a British division. The number of lines for long-distance calls was limited, so the American operators were instructed to plug into each line every two minutes and ask, "Are you through?" The English, thinking this meant, "Have you got your connection through to the other party?" would answer, "Yes!"—whereupon they would be promptly disconnected and the line given to somebody else. Months passed before the constantly repeated misunderstanding was cleared up.

More on Differences in Attitudes

Here is an example of two experienced international businessmen reaching diametrically opposite conclusions.

At an American Management Associations seminar, a drilling superintendent of an international American oil company insisted that he had to have one American foreman on each drill rig, no matter whether he drilled in South America, North Africa, Southern Europe, or the Middle East. He said that many of the foreigners he had worked with in different countries knew the theories of oil drilling better than most American foremen, but that their attitude of *laissez-faire* or *no importa* could ruin several tens of thousands of dollars worth of equipment in one minute. This superintendent was "just not going to take any responsibility unless given American foremen."

He was probably right regarding *his* job; but hearing the above comments of the drilling superintendent at the seminar, the American manufacturing manager for a large agricultural equipment producer in West Germany exclaimed:

"Your attitude would be highly destructive in our company. As a matter of fact, after hearing you, I wouldn't let you in the door of our German plant. Only last year, we had a manufacturing engineer come over from Ohio. In only two weeks, he got our whole plant on edge, and half a dozen good German foremen were ready to resign.

"I went in and asked the American engineer what in the world he had told the foremen. He answered that he had only told them to do it exactly as we do it in Ohio. That was the worst thing he could possibly have done, and before he learned to let them do things their way, we had to send him back to the States. In a German plant, we must either operate in the German manner or not at all."

The manufacturing manager was, of course, quite right in his approach to *his* job.

As I mentioned in the chapter on subsidiaries, the main goal is to operate in the local manner, yet slip in some improvements in procedures and above all in management policies. The usual key is to adjust oneself to the surroundings and not try to change too much too quickly—never faster than can be absorbed by the local management.

On the other hand, in some matters, such as openness, honesty, and willingness to work hard, American attitudes compare so favorably with those of many other countries that they should not be adjusted but rather emphasized by Americans who travel abroad.

> *Disarm your foreign associates with your frank disclosures of both your strengths and your weaknesses.*
>
> *Gain the respect of your foreign affiliates and colleagues through your willingness to work hard toward the goals of the venture.*
>
> *Remind your people traveling abroad that the foreigners are going to be watching them, or better, send only people you don't have to remind.*

The differences in attitudes between Japan and the United States are constantly apparent to us all. But even experienced international business executives are often fooled by the superficial similarities between North European countries and the United States.

Consciously or subconsciously, many Americans remember that they have been to school with second-generation boys and girls of English, German, or French origin who seemed pretty much like other American boys and girls. So these Americans think that perhaps people over in Europe are pretty much the same as here, just as their schoolmates were.

In actual fact, second-generation Americans are totally Americans, whereas the attitudes of Englishmen, Germans, and Frenchmen differ from each other and from those of Americans. To discover the depth of the differences, you have to live for an extended period of time in each of these cultures, not just spend a few weeks there on quick business trips.

You might object, "But people are the same all over." Yes, that is true; but the cultures vary widely.

Many American companies with several European plants find that the differences in attitudes among Europeans cause them lots of problems.

They try many ways to minimize these problems, including working committees of middle managers from different countries and temporary exchanges of middle managers (very difficult).

Stereotypic categorizations are often misplaced, yet here I will mention a few. British and French executives sometimes have to restrain themselves from becoming exasperated by the need of their German colleagues to organize in advance even the smallest details, which the others would approach pragmatically as they go along. Also, Germans, Englishmen, and Scandinavians do not appreciate French and Spanish sharp-wittedness. The Spaniards do not understand British modesty or the careful thoroughness, self-control, and strong sense of responsibility of the Swiss.

Several important differences between Europeans and Americans are covered elsewhere in this book. Here I can add that some Americans are surprised to find in much of Europe:

Rather little appreciation for the value of time.

Sometimes more appreciation for large sales volume than for large profits—perhaps not always admitted, but often there.

Satisfaction with "normal" profits, rather than a preference for outstanding profits.

Much appreciation for manufacturing per se. Just trading in a product is not often considered as hallowed a job as producing it.

Little willingness to take risks. (In Northern Europe this has been caused largely by the tax systems.)

Appreciation for pseudoscientific explanations in technical discussions, no matter how useless they are (particularly in Central Europe).

The capable international businessman will make the best for his company out of whatever attitudes he finds. He knows that it is an uphill battle to change ingrained attitudes, so he will instead work along with the strengths of different nationalities and work around their weaknesses.

The comments that follow are always valid but are doubly important in certain less industrialized countries, where people may possess latent inferiority complexes in their relationships with Americans and West Europeans.

The good international businessman has an inborn sense of tact stemming from the conviction that he has his faults, just as others have theirs. He is deeply convinced that no people are either better or worse than any other people, just different.

The man who thinks that his own nationality is superior to any other, whether he is an American, a German, a Frenchman, or a Japanese, will not be able to hide it. He will cause deep resentments in his relationships with foreigners.

The good international businessman long ago discovered that it is no use getting upset and irritated by unusual foreign conditions and barriers obstructing good business. Those are the rules of the game, and there is no more use wanting to change them than there is wanting to lower the tennis net if your ball keeps hitting it. Change yourself instead!

The good international businessman finds the differences between cultures and countries a constant challenge and a source of deep enjoyment, rather than a barrier. He travels from country to country unencumbered by convention and prejudice, but instead with great curiosity and openmindedness.

How to Overcome the Communication Barriers Through Better Transmission

In domestic business and in intra-European business, good communication is taken for granted. Generally, not enough consideration is provided for communication in transoceanic business.

The main reason for the lack of proper transoceanic communication is differences in attitude and language. The next biggest reason is simply money: People don't jump on a plane to go over to iron out their differences often enough when the air fare is $600, and people don't discuss enough over the telephone when a 15-minute call costs $30 or $40.

A Chicago headquarters that communicates exceptionally well with its branches in New York, Louisville, and Dallas often runs into real trouble when trying to communicate with subsidiaries in Düsseldorf, São Paulo, and Sydney, without quite knowing why.

Part of the reason stems from trouble with transmission of communications. To see this matter more clearly, we shall divide the thoughts to be communicated into three different categories:

Type 1. One-way "shots" of information: Simple orders or statements of undisputed facts, such as "Ship 15 parts number 15053 soonest."

Type 2. One two-way pair of "shots" of information: Simple questions and answers, such as: "Have you included overhead in your July 3 cost estimate?" — "No. For overhead, please add 30%. For profit, please add an additional 25% on cost and overhead."

Type 3. Back-and-forth communication: Discussion of why you should purchase rather than manufacture gizmos and what style dresses you should sell next year.

Type 1 and type 2 messages are communicated well by telex* or by letter. They cause few difficulties. Type 3 messages are best communicated in a face-to-face discussion, in a give and take of ideas bounced back and forth. Failure to acknowledge this need causes most of the breakdowns and difficulties in communication.

The simplest type 3 messages can sometimes be communicated by a combination of letters, reports, telexes, and telephone calls, especially if the two parties know each other well and think alike. Alternatively, it may be possible to break them down into a series of type 2 items. However, many type 3 messages cannot be communicated through written or telephoned messages.

Let's look again at the example of type 2 communication. The person who answered this question was a good communicator, because he thought of and answered the two additional questions that were not asked originally. This is one of the first requirements for people in international business.

Had the receiver been a mediocre communicator, the exchange of telexes could have been three times longer. Even for type 1 and type 2 items, it is important to have capable people who think beyond the immediate horizon, people who consistently put themselves in the other party's shoes.

Today the telex usually provides the best means of transoceanic communication for type 1 and type 2 items. Compared to the time required

---

* I am using the term "telex" broadly to indicate most types of teletype transmission. Facsimile systems may well take over part of this work in the future, when their cost decreases and their speed increases.

to write letters, the telex is a whiz, saving executives and secretaries precious hours. Telex messages are usually much more complete and cost less than cables (unless they are extremely short). Although telex costs the same or more per minute as telephone, it is much cheaper to use because you communicate much more information per minute by telex than by telephone.

For type 3 items, frequent travel is by far the best means of exchanging ideas, the most effective means of communication. *Who* is traveling is important. A message-carrier can bring type 1 and type 2 messages, but never type 3 messages. To achieve the best communication on type 3 items, it is necessary that the two people who communicate with each other both know the basic subject matter thoroughly. This requirement is often ignored, with disastrous consequences.

Suppose the U.S. headquarters of an automobile manufacturer wants to make two complex changes within their European plants, one involving engine machining and the other involving body welding.

If they send a capable body welding specialist on a round trip to their European plants with orders to get the two changes implemented, chances are that he will get them to adopt the body welding changes but not the engine machining modifications. He probably cannot counter their arguments against the new engine machining procedures. He does not know why all the other alternatives suggested in Europe are worse than the one recommended in the United States.

For the engine machining modification, this man functions only as a message-carrier; but since the message is of type 3, no mere message-carrier can achieve good communication between two parties who do know the subject. In fact, a message-carrier can often impede such communication.

If you are given a task as a message-carrier, you have two alternatives of action. If the subject matter is not too voluminous, you can learn it and thus become more than a message-carrier.

If the subject matter is voluminous, then you had better refuse the task as a message-carrier and try instead to function as a catalyst and get the two parties who do understand the subject into direct communication with each other.

Here is one more example of difficulties in transoceanic communications: Suppose lengthy service instructions for a piece of American machinery are printed, and the machinery is then distributed for use throughout the United States and in several other countries.

Shortly thereafter, there is severe trouble with the machinery in Germany. This particular problem has developed not because of a misunderstanding of the instructions (which is sometimes the case), but because somebody in Germany had the idea to use the equipment in a manner a little different from that described in the written instructions.

Suppose somebody in Ohio had already gotten the same idea—had also tried to use the equipment in the different way. At the first sign of trouble, the man in Ohio would have telephoned the Chicago headquarters and would immediately have been put straight.

But the man in Germany would not dream of telephoning Chicago when his problem arises. Instead, attempting to improve things, he tries some further improvisation that only gets him into more trouble. By this time, no telephone or telex can get him out of it; only a visit by a knowledgeable serviceman can put things aright.

The main shortcoming of most technical service literature, in terms of good communication, is that it can state how to use something but not why all the other possible alternative ways of using it will not work.

One important type of communication that goes beyond type 3 is the transfer from Country X to Country Y of a whole block of complex knowledge in a certain field. The best way to transfer such a large mass of information is usually to send employees from Country Y to Country X, people who already have the necessary background to learn the material. They must learn it directly from the people who compiled the information. The training can take place either in a formal training program or through working with employees who are thoroughly versed in the material.

An attempt to transfer all this information by sending over a thick ring binder in which the principles and details have been stated will not communicate the new know-how if it is sent to people inexperienced in that particular field. Such a method can help only people who already have the necessary related experience.

An example of the transfer of a block of knowledge is this very book. Nobody will become an expert in international management just by reading it, but the person who already has background and experience in the field might clarify some ideas of his own and add others, particularly in those areas where the book tickles his imagination through the recognition of problems that he has already battled himself.

Between countries, there is often strong resistance to new know-how from outside, resistance that can be overcome only in face-to-face discussions. This resistance is due partly to misplaced nationalism and partly to the NIH (Not Invented Here) factor.

Many otherwise experienced executives make the mistake of assuming that know-how can be transferred from one country to another simply by sending paper: reports, articles, instructions, specifications, and drawings. This is definitely not possible.

> *Know-how is not primarily stored in articles, books, draw-*
> *ings, reports, or specifications. Know-how is stored in people.*
> *If you want to transfer it from one country to another,*
> *you should send the people and let them talk to those who*
> *have the background necessary to absorb the new know-how.*

To put it simply, mail does not transfer know-how from country to country as much as airlines do.

Three Organizational Impediments to Good Communication

If transoceanic communications on a certain subject cause particularly strong conflicts between the two communicating parties, examine the reasons. Perhaps the corporate organizational structure is wrong, or somebody has misunderstood his place in it.

Possibly the conflicts result from *unclear assignments of authority.* For example, there may be too much second-guessing by the staff at headquarters, or even by headquarters top managers, who should leave the particular type of decision under consideration entirely to the local subsidiary.

Conversely, strong subsidiary managers must be made to understand now and then that certain decisions will be made at headquarters and that the subsidiaries are part of the worldwide group, not a collection of companies that are run by their managers as their personal property, with disregard for maximization of group benefits.

Many problems of communication are caused by *insecure bosses* who insist that all communications should flow through them. Often they don't understand the subjects as well as their subordinates at the front line.

Take the case of the department manager who insists that he himself be sent to Sydney, rather than the engineer who can best solve the problem at hand there. This department manager is a bad communicator—and a bad manager.

A frequent problem that seems to be a communication problem, but is not, is caused by the *insubordinate manager* who does not want to do what he is told to do. He will often invent communication barriers with ingenuity:

"The message arrived too late."
"I did not understand the message."
"It seemed better to do it the other way."

"We could not borrow the necessary funds."
"The order had been shipped before your cancellation telex arrived."

Many similarly transparent replies are given as excuses.

Experienced international executives welcome differing opinions, but they also realize that someone has to make the final decision, and once this is done, no company can permit disunity, obvious or hidden.

Experienced message-senders also know that if the message is contrary to the opinion of the receiver, or if it imposes on his territory, then it must be followed by a sentence such as "Please report when accomplished," or "Telex in case of delay or obstacle."

Even so, it is best to follow up such a matter at the proper time. A distance of 4,000 miles is no excuse for lack of supervision or for permitting insubordination.

Tell the Truth

Total truth is one of the best and simplest aids to good communication.

This simple fact is far too often forgotten. Whenever there is a risk of delays in deliveries, or whenever a mistake has been made, tell the man across the ocean about it right away and in full detail, so that he can start immediately to minimize the consequences.

The slight initial disadvantage that comes from telling the full truth early is far outweighed by the additional credibility given to everything else you are communicating to the other party. His confidence is, after all, essential. You can issue a stream of memos and reports, but if the other party does not believe them, you have communicated nothing.

Most business people who meet personally now and then, or who discuss things frequently by telephone, tend automatically to establish between themselves an atmosphere of mutual trust. But if the two parties are on opposite sides of an ocean, if they see each other seldom and telephone each other rarely, there is no such automatic establishment of mutual trust. That trust has to be created, nursed along with care, protected, and nourished through a habit of always telling the whole truth, the bad with the good.

Once distrust sets in, it is hard to dispel. Between two sister companies, and between subsidiary and parent company, there easily arises an atmosphere of "we" and "they," rather than the proper corporate family relationship. Such a situation can be costly.

It is not only in the form and content of the *outgoing* messages that you must guard against distrust. It is just as important to teach all personnel again and again to interpret the *incoming* messages in the most favorable light, to remember that the other party does not know the language well, that his words just *seem* insulting, that circumstances beyond our knowledge probably caused him to write the strange request in the telex or letter.

Teach your employees to take the positive, constructive approach to incoming telexes and mail from overseas, rather than the negative, destructive approach. Don't let your people get mad at "them." How will that solve anything?

If all these efforts fail and distrust sets in, then let the two parties travel to meet face to face to iron out their conflicts. Don't let them fight each other for months across the ocean about a matter that they can clear up in a few days of personal communication.

10

Painless Financing, Pricing, and International Economics

FOR the ABCs of the financing of foreign operations, please refer to one of the excellent books available. (Some of them are mentioned in the list of recommended information sources at the end of this book.) I will not repeat here what has been stated better by others, but rather give you some personal observations, most of which I have not seen in print elsewhere.

The chapters in this book on statistics for monitoring operations and on planning partly concern financial measurement and control.

Painless Financing

The easiest way to avoid major financial problems is to be associated only with profitable companies in industries that are not capital intensive. In my personal experience, capital has always been the easiest item to get. In industrialized countries, the company with a profitable idea certainly has no trouble getting capital for it. There is more of a dearth of good ideas than of capital to finance them.

Moreover, my strongest piece of advice about financing is an obvious one: Do everything else well, so that you make good profits. Then financing is quite painless.

KEEP THE EQUITY RATHER SMALL

Suppose you are founding a new European subsidiary. You expect it to lose money at the start and be quite profitable thereafter. In this case, you might do well by putting into it only the minimum equity capital required by local laws. In most countries, the point of time for which the minimum equity capital must be calculated is the date of expected break-even, because the total losses may not exceed a certain proportion of your equity. This proportion varies from country to country, and in some countries there is no such rule at all.

The remaining funds, beyond the equity, can be borrowed locally in Europe from bankers, insurance companies, suppliers, or other subsidiaries. Marketing subsidiaries that import from the parent company often borrow from the parent simply through a long open trade account during their first years of operation. Should the new company need more funds than expected, additional loans can usually be secured to tide it over.

Many new subsidiaries keep their initial capital needs low by renting rather than building or buying their quarters. (Japan is the exceptional country where this is not recommended, for reasons given in the chapter on staffing.)

One way of keeping the initial capital need small is to limit strictly the amount of growth permitted the new company before it reaches break-even. Once the new venture has become profitable, it can of course be permitted to grow again to the extent that it can finance its growth out of profits and further local borrowings, and to the extent that its further growth promises further profitability.

The above remarks concern Europe. If instead you are founding a subsidiary in a less industrialized country, the matter becomes more complex. Minimum equity is not necessarily the best solution there, because there is little medium- and long-term capital available in most of the less industrialized countries. More complex financing procedures and sources are used, such as swap, Cooley funds, and Edge Act corporation loans. Unfortunately, a book is not a suitable place to describe the various sources of international funds available, because the situation changes too much for such a description to stay adequate.

Japanese joint ventures should generally be relatively well financed with ample equity, partly because the Japanese company may go through some periods when it becomes difficult to borrow in Japan. Joint ventures in Japan do nearly all their borrowing from banks against 60- to 90-day promissory notes. Medium- and long-term credits in Japan are usually not made available to joint ventures with foreign partners. The corporate bond market in Japan is also closed to such joint ventures, but this state seems to be changing.

Let's return to a subsidiary in Europe to examine two of the advantages of having the smallest possible equity.

The initial losses of a new subsidiary are usually caused by start-up expenses, including the hiring and training of new personnel. For accounting purposes, these expenses are of course written off immediately as losses; but they really are an investment in the going-concern value of the new company. Accountants treat this investment in human resources quite differently from investments in concrete things. Suppose that it is financed out of borrowed money that is later repaid out of pretax profits (pretax because of loss carry-forward); then the new company has a good chance of ending up with a high percentage return on its equity, because the equity is small in relation to what has actually been "invested" at one time in the going concern. Secondly, interest on debt is of course paid from pretax profits, whereas the return on equity is taxed.

The policy of keeping the equity small causes much static from overseas subsidiary managers, particularly if they have no formal business training. In many European countries it is much more prestigious to be managing director of a company with $10 million share capital than of one with only $50,000. No matter how long you talk to these managers about it being a bigger achievement to have $500,000 net profits from a $50,000-share-capital company than from a $10-million-share-capital company, they will not listen to you. For this and other reasons, it is up to the parent company alone to determine how much equity capital makes the most sense for each subsidiary.

It is also the parent company that must see that total investments, including inventory and accounts receivable, are kept within reasonable limits.

Hardly any new subsidiary can borrow much money in the beginning without parent company guarantees, because it cannot show the bankers a "track record." In some countries, such parent company guarantees are taxed. In others they are prohibited. But one of your friendly bankers will usually have some good confidential advice on how to overcome the problem.

FINANCIAL ADVICE

Many domestic and foreign laws and regulations affecting international finance are initiated by politicians who are ignorant about international finance. These regulations would do a lot of damage to the countries they are supposed to help if capable bankers and international businessmen did not find legal ways of getting around many of them shortly after they are written.

To benefit from the valuable knowledge of more than one such team of international bankers, multinational companies usually maintain accounts with at least a couple of the large international banks. Since the fairly recent establishment of large European international banking alliances, one or more such European groups are usually added to the financial teams consulted frequently by the multinational companies. In the future, more Japanese banks will probably join some of these groups.

One of the matters on which international companies want constant advice from international bankers is hedging against changes in currency exchange rates. Sometimes people who hedge drive the premium way above what it should be, so that one can actually earn money by doing reverse hedging.

Companies can take three different approaches to their role in parity changes: the passive one, the medium-active one, and the speculative one. Companies taking the passive approach hedge all foreign investments as a matter of policy. They assume the cost to be about the same over a period of time as if they had lost on an uncovered position. To them, the advantage is to spread the cost rather than to protect the loss.

In the past, I have advocated instead a medium-active approach and have come out ahead. Using plain common sense, you can save money by thinking ahead and planning for your needs in different currencies, taking calculated risks along the way.

A company that follows the third approach and positively speculates in foreign currency changes must have a real monetary expert on its staff. Only large companies can justify this expense. Furthermore, even the best of the experts in this field are often wrong, because the governmental actions depend to such a large extent on unpredictable politics. For these reasons, most companies do not take this speculative approach, but stick to protecting some commercial risks rather than playing foreign-exchange roulette.

Some companies even hedge fixed assets to protect themselves against the apparent loss when the currency for which the assets have been bought is devalued. I consider this principle wrong (except in cases of pure speculation) for two reasons: (1) The fixed assets are in reality not worth anything less after the devaluation, and (2) price rises invariably follow devaluations. A devaluation shows only that the currency has changed value, not that the assets have changed real value.

In a country with heavy inflation and periodic large devaluations, it is, of course, particularly important to keep as low as possible the amount of those assets exposed to devaluation.

Another subject on which companies want the international bankers' advice is where to borrow money. It used to be possible to find greater bargains by borrowing money in the country with the lowest interest rates or the highest devaluation chances; but the over-all advantages have evened out somewhat. They will probably continue to even out more, as a larger and larger portion of the total amount is borrowed by financial managers in multinational corporations rather than by people with a narrow national outlook. The multinationals will invariably spot the remaining bargains and bid up the prices to the world level, whether

You can save money by thinking ahead and planning for your needs in different currencies.

this be 7 percent in a country with stable currency or 29 percent in a country with expected 20-percent devaluation per year.

Outside financial and tax advisors are indispensable to most companies when they are going to decide between many different borrowing possibilities, such as revolving lines of credit, medium-term loans with fixed and floating interest, long-term loans, and straight or convertible debentures in several alternative countries and currencies.

Because of the likelihood of recurring credit squeezes from time to time in Europe over the next few years, it may be well in several countries to pay a commitment fee of $\frac{1}{4}$–$\frac{1}{2}$ percent per annum for the unused part of at least one revolving credit line. It may also be good to cover some medium-term financial needs with term borrowing rather than with revolving credit lines, despite the widespread popularity in some European countries of the revolving credit lines.

Two types of governmental aids available in some parts of Europe should not be overlooked. These are capital incentives to locate manufacturing in certain places and export financing or guarantees available in some countries, such as from Ducroire in Belgium, the ECGD in England, and the BFCE in France.* Some of these export aids are also available for exports to related companies. Thus, they can be utilized for internal corporate financing when used in intercompany trade.

It is useless to discuss in a book the regulations of the Office of Foreign Direct Investments of the Department of Commerce, because they vary from year to year, they are available from the government, and any large accounting firm will gladly give good advice on how to comply with the OFDI without needlessly hampering your foreign operations.

The large multinational companies have become very sophisticated in decreasing their cash needs through central management of all their small pools of cash around the world and investment of any unneeded cash at the best interest rates available. A few multinational companies, including Dow Chemical, Cummins Engine, and Siemens, have taken the ultimate step in their worldwide money management and gone into international banking. Probably more multinational companies will do the same.

SELLING BOND ISSUES TO CUSTOMERS OF SWISS BANKS

To obtain large amounts of long-term funds, well-known companies can issue bonds in the Netherlands Antilles, Luxembourg, or the state of Delaware and place them through a consortium that eventually sells

* The initials stand for Export Credit Guarantee Department and Banque Française de Commerce Extérieure, respectively.

most of them to Swiss banks. The ultimate investors are largely customers of the Swiss banks, mainly individuals from politically and economically unstable countries or high-tax countries. These individuals are usually stable, long-term investors. They generally prefer bonds of well-known corporations, so a lesser known company cannot raise money in this manner.

Some criminals have succeeded from time to time in using Swiss banks for depositing their loot; but Swiss bankers do not want such customers at all. They make a serious, though discreet, attempt at ensuring that their depositors are serious investors who have come into their money honestly, or at least without breaking any Swiss laws.

The investment pool in Switzerland, the largest one in the world outside the United States, is put to excellent industrial and commercial use by the capable Swiss bankers. It is estimated that this pool totals over $70,000 million. (This figure includes all currency denominations involved in the pool.) The Swiss bankers can at any time give good information regarding the yield at which a bond issue can be sold.

Because the names of the three main Swiss banks undergo some confusing changes when they are translated, I will list them in English, German, and French. The street addresses in Zurich are given under the English names:

English	German	French
Swiss Credit Bank 8 Paradeplatz	Schweizerische Kreditanstalt	Crédit Suisse
Swiss Bank Corp. 6 Paradeplatz	Schweizerischer Bankverein	Société de Banque Suisse
Union Bank of Switzerland 45 Bahnhofstrasse	Schweizerische Bankgesellschaft	Union de Banques Suisses

The names of the next two banks (which are also members of the Swiss cartel of big banks) are:

Peoples Bank of Switzerland	Schweizerische Volksbank	Banque Populaire Suisse
Leu & Co. Bank Ltd.	Bank Leu & Co. A.G.	Leu & Cie

The private Swiss banks are named after their owners. They include Pictet, Gottardo, Vontobel, and Bär.

Some of the Swiss banks specializing in barter and switch deals are mentioned in the chapter on East Bloc business.

WORKING WITH YOUR BANKERS

For your foreign financing needs, whether you depend mainly on a Swiss bank, a large international bank, or a European investment banking group, you will be well advised not to depend on only one banking group. Rather you should let it be known that you do compare interest rates and that you will not easily accept the reply that "no funds are available for lending at present" when you happen to need more funds than estimated in a country where money is tight for the moment.

To gain the bankers' confidence, you should make it a point to inform them thoroughly from time to time about what your companies are doing and planning to do, at least so far as it affects the companies' financial needs and strengths. You should tell the bankers both good and bad news about your domain. Don't let them hear the good news from you and the bad news from your suppliers and customers.

European investment bankers make it an important point of professional pride to keep well informed about the companies they assist, whether or not the company managements help them. It is only human for them to be more helpful to those customers who make their work easier.

You want to show as far as possible a French corporate face in France, an English face in the United Kingdom, a German face in Germany, and a Japanese face in Japan. This extends to your commercial banking connections for business *within* each of those countries. Experienced companies choose a bank of local nationality and origin in such countries, even though they may use a multinational bank for their international banking needs and an investment bank for their main borrowing needs.

The multinational banks don't care for this division of the business. They sometimes claim that you will get better service by giving them all of your business. I doubt it, and I don't recommend it.

BLOCKED CURRENCIES

International companies sometimes find themselves with perfectly good liquid assets in blocked currencies. Usually this occurs in countries that have an unrealistic rate of exchange backed by equally unrealistic currency controls.

It is hard to generalize about what to do in such a situation, especially if it occurs in a country where you have a business establishment and it can be difficult to get the money out. But suppose it occurs in some

minor country where you don't have any operation of your own and
don't want any; then the procedure of converting the funds is simpler.

This procedure is usually illegal inside the blocking country; but
outside that country there is nothing illegal in changing the money on
the free market in Hong Kong (mainly Asian currencies), Switzerland,
or New York. To international thinking, it is, on the contrary, wrong
for a country to try to restrict the free movement of honestly earned
assets. It is also in the long run useless.

In New York, the normal procedure for freeing blocked currencies
is to find a reputable foreign currency dealer through recommendations,
to ask him for an exchange rate quotation, and to order the blocked
currency paid into an account indicated by him in the blocking country;
then sit back and wait for a couple of months until you receive the
money in a bank account you have indicated in dollars, marks, yen,
or whatever you had ordered. During the waiting period, you will usually
not have any guarantee, other than the dealer's reputation, that you
will ever see the money again.

Don't ever ask the dealer how he does it!

International Pricing

PRICING TO CUSTOMERS

The basic rule of thumb followed by most multinational companies is
very simple:

> *Your prices in each country should be what the market
> will bear in that country and independent of your prices
> in other countries.*

You might ask, "Why state such a self-evident rule?" But you would
be amazed at how many arguments are raised against it in practice.
I will answer a few of the objections to the rule here.

Objection: This policy will cause a company to have different prices
for the same product in different countries.

Answer: Sure, it will. If the product can bear different prices in different countries, it should.

Objection: What about international industrial customers who buy
the same product from you in different countries? Won't they object?

Answer: Yes, they will. But if they are at all sophisticated in their own pricing, they will also be charging different prices for their products in different countries, so they will understand your reasoning—even though they may not admit it at first. Usually the advantages to them of getting service, spare parts, and assistance from the local supplier of your products in each country outweigh what they may save by buying your products in the country where you have your lowest prices and shipping the products to the countries where you have your highest prices. For consumer goods, the language or packaging problems may cancel any price differential to an international customer. Finally, the countries where you have high prices are likely to be countries with high customs duties or other high costs of doing business.

Objection: Shouldn't the price elasticity and the price for maximization of profit be calculated for each country?

Answer: That is saying the same thing I expressed a little more simply. Price elasticities are often difficult to find, but many products have a price (or a price range) below which the sales volume would increase only moderately and above which the sales volume would fall off substantially. That price is what I called "the price the market will bear."

INTERCOMPANY PRICING

This is such a complex subject that for most companies it requires substantial outside advice from tax lawyers, customs duty advisors, and accounting firms. But usually the advisors leave you a margin between the minimum price you can charge without upsetting the authorities in one series of countries and the maximum price you can charge without unduly alarming the authorities in another series of countries. The customs and tax authorities of the importing countries are usually on opposing sides of the fence.

Of those prices you are left with that fall between the minimum and maximum, you end up charging the price that maximizes global net after-tax profits.

Of course, in some cases the minimum and maximum prices are the same, so you have no choice. In other cases, the minimum price allowed by some authorities may be higher than the maximum price allowed by other authorities, leaving you with *no* price that is allowable by both. Then you have to go back and try to enlist the help of the authorities in settling the matter.

Painless International Economics

Don't lose as much time as I have trying to understand much of the mumbo-jumbo about international economics that you hear in many political speeches or read in many seemingly responsible newspapers. Instead, learn just the fundamentals of international economics and use your own common sense for the rest. After that, if you still have trouble understanding some article or speech, you can bet that it is probably wrong anyway.

It is incredible how much pure nonsense about international economics is written in newspapers by reporters, pseudoeconomists, and prominent businessmen. Furthermore, economic facts and figures are turned around by politicians for their own benefit, either willfully or through ignorance.

Since most people have not taken the time to learn the fundamentals of international economics, it seems that anyone who wants to be elected mayor or even PTA chairman assumes that he is free to demonstrate his understanding of the world we live in by speaking on the subject, using a few specialized terms so that he can sound like he knows what he is talking about.

This bad habit is by no means limited to the United States. It is practiced shamelessly throughout the world by people who would never dream of making similarly ignorant statements in other fields, such as medicine or geology.

If, for example, a country's currency is beginning to weaken, people will make long speeches about the reasons for this, often completely missing the main one—which is the same as the reason for your starting to doubt the value of someone's IOUs: If a country with small reserves spends more abroad than it earns year after year, and if you see no sign of a change ahead, then the value of its currency comes under suspicion from other countries. Internal inflation contributes directly to this overspending abroad, and if the country's government itself spends more than it takes in, this contributes in turn to internal inflation.

The West German government has been prohibited by law from deficit budgeting over a long period. This law and the German willingness to work hard, save, and invest are two of the various factors that have contributed to the better maintenance of the value of German currency than of the value of most other currencies.

As another example of wrong public statements, consider what has been written during the last fifteen years about the Eurodollar and where it comes from. I tried long and hard to understand all the conflicting statements with their scientific jargon coming from seemingly reputable sources, but I never succeeded in grasping it until I read a simple little article by Milton Friedman: "The Euro-Dollar Market: Some First Principles."*

He explained in clear, simple language that any businessman could understand at once that the Eurodollar market is simply the market of deposits and loans with European banks, denominated in dollars.

In other words, Eurodollars are just the bookkeepers' denomination of what is lent and borrowed. The Eurodollar maintains by definition the same value as the U.S. dollar, but it distinguishes itself favorably from the real U.S. dollar by being totally outside U.S. controls, U.S. taxes, and other U.S. interference when used between non-U.S. corporations, banks, or individuals.

Take this simple explanation by Milton Friedman and combine it with your own knowledge about the effects of supply and demand, and a whole new world of enlightenment opens up toward understanding the increases and decreases of Eurodollar interest rates.

If confidence in the real U.S. dollar should decrease again in relation to confidence in the German mark, we would get an increasing market in Euromarks. The name "Euromarks" is itself pure nonsense, because the currency referred to need be neither European nor marks. But at least people are beginning to know what the term refers to, whether they borrow Euromarks in Zurich, Singapore, or São Paulo.

A "Euromark" is a precisely defined unit of measuring value, equivalent to a German mark. Just as the measure "foot" is no longer the foot of a person, so also the measure "Euromark" is no longer a mark.

The Euromark is the measuring unit in a transaction where surplus funds, say Lebanese pounds, of someone, say an oil sheik, are lent to others, say a new Japanese factory in Singapore. Usually both lender and borrower are nonresidents of West Germany. Although none of the currencies lent, borrowed, and repaid need to be either marks or European, they do need to be transferable into marks, in order that they can be measured precisely in "Euromarks."

Although the center for Eurodollars is London, its market is worldwide. In Hong Kong and Singapore, exactly the same unit of measurement is called an "Asian dollar," which is an equally nonsensical name. The nominal supervision of the Eurodollar market is by the Bank for International Settlements; but the leading traders in it are the overseas branches of the First National City Bank of New York and the other big overseas U.S. banks.

Behind the creation of the Eurocurrency entrepôt there are such

* *Morgan Guaranty Survey,* October 1969, pp. 4–14. (Reprinted by University of Chicago Graduate School of Business, Selected Paper No. 34.)

basic factors as increased European rates of savings, and insecurity for capital in many less industrialized countries outside Europe; but it is U.S. governmental actions that have spurred the amazing growth of the Eurocurrency market by obstructing New York's previous role as banker to the world. These governmental actions include the 1963 interest equalization tax and the various foreign direct investment restrictions that followed.

So little is known in international economics that there are still people in authority who dispute Milton Friedman's lucid explanation of Eurodollars. Their involved explanations make no sense to me, but Friedman's clear and simple one does.

At the end of 1972, the Eurodollar pool was around $60,000 million. To businessmen, it is enough to know that the pool is big, so that a demand for a couple of million more or less will not cause waves. Besides Eurodollars, there were, at the end of 1972, over $20,000 million worth of other Eurocurrencies around the world.

It is strange that in this day and age there is a total of over $80,000 million worth of a commodity that is growing at $15,000 million a year and is traded around the world by thousands of companies and prominent, knowledgeable bankers—a commodity that is blamed for upsetting some of the strongest governments in the world—and yet the experts are still disputing what the stuff is and where it comes from!

Nevertheless, their lack of knowledge has not stopped politicians from making long, fine speeches about the need to control Eurocurrencies. The politicians' only snag is that since they don't know what Eurocurrencies are, they haven't yet figured out a good way to control them. I hope it will take the politicians a long time, because in the meantime Eurocurrencies are a very useful commodity to businessmen.

SOME GOVERNMENTAL ATTITUDES TOWARD FOREIGN TRADE

Basically, most governments through their actions seem to regard imports as evil and exports as good. Governments put all kinds of barriers, some subtle, imaginative, and fancy, in the way of imports. Then occasionally various governments get together and point out to each other what bad boys all the others are, and they agree to dismantle or lower a few of these barriers. At the same time, the individual governments pay bureaucrats to sit and invent newer and fancier barriers to imports— preferably so designed that they will not attract the attention of other governments.

If they cannot get away with more import barriers, they invent export subsidies, because most governments consider exports to be wonderful and wholesome. These subsidies sometimes constitute a great expense to ordinary taxpayers, who would be shocked to learn what their hard-earned money was used for.

Even when a government—Japan's, for example—finds itself with far too large surpluses in its foreign trade, it takes its time dismantling the import barriers.

In the long run, many of the governmental actions for balance-of-payments purposes are self-defeating. If the exchange rate for a currency is unrealistic, it would be better to change it. We have seen over the last several years that currency exchange rates cannot be pegged too rigidly between countries, unless these countries also closely coordinate their fiscal and monetary policies, which few do.

It is advantageous to allow currency parities to move freely, within a small range, in relation to each other. This decreases the "slushing" of enormous amounts of money back and forth between countries.

If, for example, the Swedish crown were to be pegged rigidly and a few financial managers were to get the idea that it might be slightly overvalued and might become devalued, then they would see to it that all payments from Sweden were made promptly, perhaps even prepaid, and that payments to Sweden were delayed. International business magazines would report the initial trend, causing thousands of traders to do the same leading and lagging. As a consequence, Sweden would be drained of foreign currencies, and this drain might force a bigger devaluation than would otherwise have been needed.

If instead the Swedish crown is free to move down slightly after the action of the first few financial managers, then most of the remainder may decide that that small move makes the leading and lagging uninteresting. Thus, "slushing" is decreased.

Politicians sometimes have blamed "slushing" on wild-eyed speculators or the "Gnomes of Zurich," whereas it is only their own actions that have caused serious businessmen to take these steps to protect themselves.

11

Living Statistics
on Market Potential

IN the chapter on where and when to use the various types of foreign operational setups, we concluded that the foremost determining factor was the size of the potential market in each country. Many serious mistakes are made in establishing subsidiaries in countries with too small a market and, conversely, in having independent distributors in countries large enough for very profitable subsidiaries.

For this reason, it is important to work out good, clear, living statistics on the potential market for your products in each country. I call them living statistics because they should be statistics you can use, rather than mind-numbing pages of endless, dead figures.

Since it is impossible to describe how to work out statistics for each product, I will give only a few general hints.

Which Statistics to Use

If there are no statistics available showing the need for your specific product in each country, then you must find available statistics divided by country that correlate to the need for your product. But when you do this, watch for the traps. First of all, completely forget the map, because little Luxembourg has a bigger market for most products than big Mauritania, Mali, and Chad put together.

Second, I have often heard experienced businessmen compare countries by the number of people they have. I cannot think of any product for which the market is proportional to the population figures.

Actually, the number of telephones used in each country* is a much better guide for many products than population figures. Telephone statistics have the advantages of being fairly up-to-date, defined uniformly from country to country, and available not only by country, but also by city and district, so that you get a quantitative idea about where in each country to find your main market.

Another guide for market size that correlates to the potential market for many products is the gross domestic product or gross national product. The figures published annually by the United Nations on GDP are particularly reliable because the UN has a large staff of statisticians who make sure that the figures are either based on uniform definitions from country to country or adjusted in such a manner that they can be compared.

Now, how do you make those figures come alive so that you can use them? Here are a couple of hints.

First, the GNP for last year or the year before last is really not as significant as that for some years in the future. By studying past growth rates and future prospects,† you can determine fairly well the likely GNP figures in the near future.

Second, these figures mean little when expressed in so many billions of dollars, yen, or rubles. Suppose you have a good grasp of the size of the U.S. potential market, and you want to try to visualize how big other markets are in relation to that of the United States. If you divide all the GNP figures in dollars by one divisor, so chosen that the result for the United States is 100, the resulting figures for all the other countries indicate their GNP as a percentage of that of the United States.

If your potential market is proportional to something other than GNP, you may be able to find the appropriate figures, or at least something that correlates to them, among the United Nations statistics. The following are some categories for which statistics are available by country in UN statistical yearbooks:

Industrial production	Textiles
Value added by metal-	Steel
working industries	Lumber

* These figures can be found in *The World's Telephones*, published annually by the American Telephone & Telegraph Company, 195 Broadway, New York, New York 10007.

† See the recommended information sources at the end of this book.

Motor vehicles (production)   Cement
Motor vehicles (in use)   Paper
Tractors (in use)   Chemicals (by product)
Harvesters (in use)   Energy
Radio and TV receivers   Shipping fleet
   (production)   Civil aviation
Mining (by product)   Tourist travel
Construction   Housing
Agricultural production   Education
   (by product)

Of course, the market projections will be entirely different for each item. A projection of the future markets for mercury mining, for example, will show Spain, Italy, and the U.S.S.R. as by far the most important countries, followed by only half a dozen other countries of any significance in the world at all.

The United Nations is the only organization that assembles a great amount of varied statistics based on the same definitions from country to country. If you were to try to use instead the different countries' national statistics, you would find that what is called, say, steel sheet in one country is quite different from what is defined as steel sheet in another; so if you try to compare national production figures for steel sheet, you are likely to be completely misled. The same goes for most other products.

Many of the statistics prepared and used in industry give the impression that the person who put them together must have thought that he would be paid by the volume of figures he presented. Good statistics are distinguished by how few figures are presented in the final result, how simple the result is, and how applicable the result is to the problem at hand.

It is, of course, necessary to consider carefully applicability of any statistics. Let's take, as an example, a product I am not familiar with. Assume that you make heavy stamping equipment used by automotive manufacturers and you want to know your potential market size for each country in relation to that of the United States.

You can find the figures for automobile production by country. But those are inadequate because you must subtract vehicles that are merely assembled from imported parts.

So instead, you locate statistics showing the net number of vehicles totally produced in each country. But that is no good either, because in a normal market your sales may be, say, 20 percent for replacement of worn-out machines and 80 percent for new manufacturing lines added.

So you can determine 20 percent of your market in each country from the figures you got above for the *current* net number of vehicles totally produced in each country.

You may find that the other 80 percent of your market in the past has been roughly proportional to the *growth* in net number of vehicles totally produced in each country. You can then calculate the statistics for past growth and make estimates for future growth, make allowances for percentages of production capacity presently utilized, and thus develop figures for adjusted estimated future *growth* in net number of vehicles to be produced in each country. From these statistics, you can possibly determine the remaining 80 percent of the potential market in your field for each country.

Adding this figure to the previous 20 percent, you get figures that can be tabulated as the result. For your specific company, you may then want to reduce some of the figures because of competitors or national preferences, or because some of the plants are too small to use your products.

In the same manner, you must always make a habit of asking whether the latest figures you were given really correlate as well as possible to what you are after. You have to adjust the figures, readjust them, and readjust them again. The few significant figures that remain after all the refining are what I call living statistics. All the rest are only dead, useless figures.

Compiling Your Own Statistics

If there are no statistics available that correlate to your market sizes, then the only alternative is to develop your own figures by going out into the market and collecting them. This is obviously very time-consuming and expensive. The resulting figures are usually inadequate unless collected by capable people who are trained to do this job. For consumer products, this collection of statistics can usually be done best by outside consultants; but for industrial capital equipment, it is sometimes better to use your own personnel, for two reasons: (1) Collecting statistics may require more transfer of know-how about your industry to the consultant than you care to allow time for or desire to tell him; and (2) while your own team is gathering statistics, you can often pick up much additional useful information about competitors, outstanding distributors, and the like. Your own people know which of this information is valuable. The outside consultant sometimes does not.

On the other hand, the outside consultant often has an advantage through keeping secret the identity of his client. This may enable him to get more information. In some cases you may want to use a consultant to avoid letting your competitors get wind of the fact that it is you who are investigating a new, promising market.

Some consultants will gather both statistics and market information for a whole industry and sell it to all companies in the industry that they can. This way you may not get any better information than your competitors, but you will get it for a fraction of the cost of statistics ordered just for your own company. And you can always try to utilize it more ingeniously than your competitors.

12

Usable Statistics
for Monitoring Operations

IF your company is typical, you get a great mass of figures from overseas on the operational results. The trick is to get someone to organize these figures in such a way that they give you intelligent information on the essentials, but none of the useless details. This chapter contains some examples of how to organize these data for overseas operations that are mainly distributing companies, rather than manufacturing operations.

What really interests you is whether your net profit from each major foreign operation is reasonable in relation to the potential market size and your domestic profits. This can best be illustrated in a profit performance chart, as we shall see shortly.

To throw further light on the above figures, you would also want to know several additional figures for each operation, such as gross sales in relation to market size, sales per employee, sales per salesman, and net return on capital invested after adjustment for political risks and other factors. These figures can best be illustrated in a performance table for each foreign operation; performance tables will be discussed later in this chapter.

Developing the Profit Performance Chart

If the United States is your major market and the one you know best, you may want to show the net profit for each major foreign market

as a percentage of the net domestic profit, rather than in absolute dollar
figures. Figure 13 is an example of some typical relationships. The advantage in doing this is that you can then see graphically how well
you are doing in each market in relation to its size.

For joint ventures it is preferable to show both total net profits of
the venture and net profits to you as a partner. Even more significant
than such a chart for each year may be one for the average of the
past five years and for the projected average of the next five years,
because such a chart eliminates the considerable yearly fluctuations in
profit due to various external factors in different markets.

Suppose that some subsidiaries handle both one major and several
minor countries. In that case you want to divide their revenue by major
markets and allocate expenses and overhead as well as possible among
the markets, so that you can find out the net profits for each major
market independently of corporate shells that might include more than
one market or less than one market.

Your direct exports from the parent company should also be analyzed
separately in a similar manner.

If sales volume is also shown in a chart, then it is often preferable
to divide total sales into major product categories, so that it becomes
clear which product categories are performing badly in each market.

If sales volume is compared for different countries, some of which
are handled by distributors and others by subsidiaries, then you must
use the estimated gross sales of the distributors, not your own sales to
the distributors, because they are not comparable to subsidiary sales in
other countries. In other words, for management use, you must compare
the sales at the same level in each country: retail, wholesale, or import.

This is contrary to what is done for accounting purposes. There,
figures that cannot be compared at all are lumped together, figures
such as net income from licensees, export sales volume to distributors,
and gross sales volume from consolidated subsidiaries. These accounting
figures originating from different levels are quite unrelated to each other
in terms of usable information for management.

If your company is at all diversified, you probably also want some
of the sales figures by product line and, if possible, estimated net profit
by product line. If it is not possible to estimate net profit by product
line, then you want at least gross profit contribution by product line.

PERFORMANCE TABLES FOR EACH MARKET

For each major distributing operation shown in the preceding chart,
I like to see an analysis sheet. Table 1 is an example of what a performance table may contain for one company. (If an operation involves

Figure 13   Profit performance chart showing potential market size and net income as percentages of those of the United States.

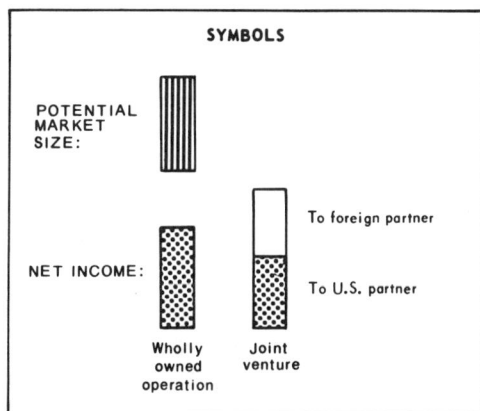

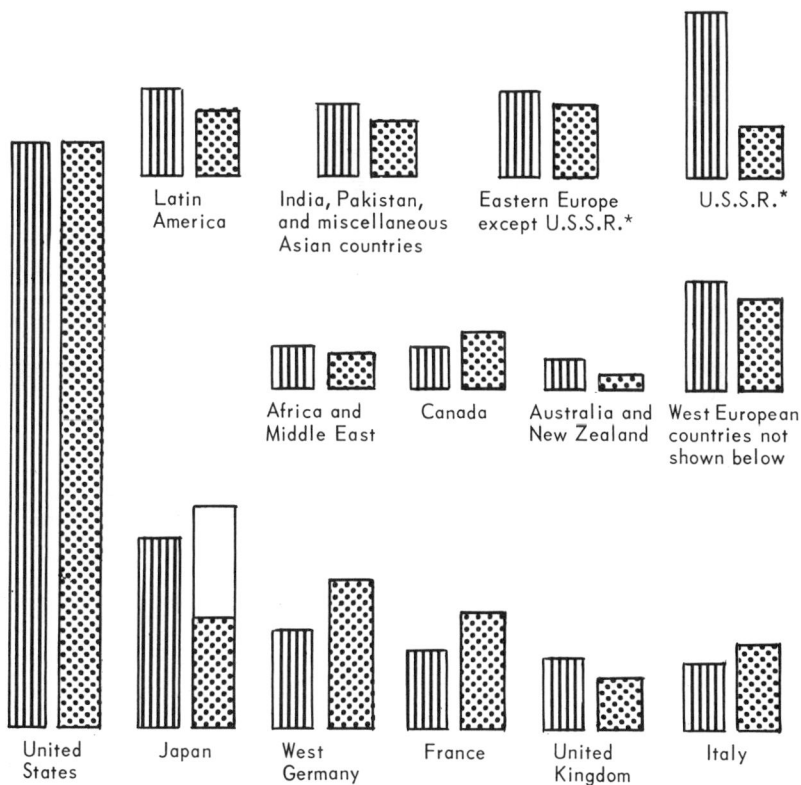

Table 1   Sample performance table for a distributing operation.

PERFORMANCE OF ___(subsidiary or operation)___
FOR THE YEAR(S)_____

PART A. ENTIRE OPERATION

Potential market size	$_____	= _____% of U.S. market
Net profit	$_____	= _____% of U.S. net profit
Unusual expenses incurred for long-range benefits	$_____	
Gross sales	$_____	= _____% of U.S. sales
Return on sales	_____%	vs. _____% for the U.S.
Total invested capital	$_____	
Return on invested capital	_____%	vs. _____% for the U.S.
Equity	$_____	
Return on equity	_____%	vs. _____% for the U.S.
Estimated political and economic risk factor	_____%	
Sales per employee	$_____/person	
Sales per salesman	$_____/man	
Sales divided by total invested capital	_____	vs. _____ for the U.S.
Sales divided by inventory	_____	
Average collection period	_____ days	vs. _____ days for the U.S.

PART B. DEPARTMENTAL ANALYSIS

	Product Department A	Product Department B	Product Department C
Departmental sales	$_____	$_____	$_____
Percentage of total	_____%	_____%	_____%
Gross profit contribution	$_____	$_____	$_____
Estimated net profit	$_____	$_____	$_____
Sales per departmental employee	$_____	$_____	$_____
Sales per salesman	$_____	$_____	$_____

major manufacturing, the performance table will have to be changed considerably.)

In order to get figures for management purposes, it will usually be necessary to make adjustments from the accounting figures to cover special intercompany pricing, intercompany transfers, and intercompany assistance.

Devaluations, revaluations, and inflation can play havoc with most of these figures. A good accountant, however, can make adjustments for the changes in exchange rates so that the final results will not be misleading to managers. For that purpose, he will often use exchange rates that are different from those used for normal accounting purposes. The effects of unusual inflation in a country should also be eliminated from these figures by the accountant.

The net profit shown in the performance table can be either before or after income taxes, as long as it is shown at the same stage for all markets. I prefer to show net income after global income taxes, because that is what matters most. I also prefer to show it whether or not it is remitted; but if there is risk that it might be impossible to remit part of the net profit, then this fact, and the amount subject to risk, should be annotated.

"Unusual expenses incurred for long-range benefits" should include investments (beyond the normal ones) in human resources, research and development, local public and governmental relations, and so forth. Amounts included here should of course always be explained. If some of these are of unusual long-range benefit to the company, they can, for comparison purposes only, be added to net profits before income tax, in order to give proper credit to the manager who is consistently working hard for the company's long-range growth and benefits, rather than squeezing out every short-range profit dollar he can find at the expense of the company's future.

The return on equity is shown partly to give credit to the manager who succeeds in raising a large part of his needed funds locally.

The estimated political and economic risk factor is a subjectively estimated percentage figure showing, in general, how much higher percent return on capital will be needed in the country in question, as compared to the United States, in order to allow for the political and economic risks of investing in that country. (Since all figures are converted to dollars, this particular percentage should not reflect relative current inflation, only political and economic risks.) Some examples may clarify this item.

The risk factor in a country like West Germany might be 0 percent, indicating that political and economic risks there are about the same as in the United States.

A risk factor of 100 percent would indicate near certain confiscation of the company in about a year, without reimbursement—and without domestic insurance against the loss.

A risk factor of 10 percent in Country X would indicate a 10-percent risk of losing the whole capital investment there within a year (principal as well as return). If a venture in Germany (where there is no political risk of loss) shows a potential return of 14 percent on total investment, it should in theory be as attractive as a venture in Country X that shows a potential return on investment of about 27 percent. The figure 27 percent is obtained by use of the following simple formula:

$$\begin{pmatrix} \text{Probability of} \\ \text{retaining the} \\ \text{principal and return} \\ \text{in Germany} \end{pmatrix} \times \begin{pmatrix} \text{principal} \\ \text{and return} \\ \text{in} \\ \text{Germany} \end{pmatrix} = \begin{pmatrix} \text{probability of} \\ \text{retaining the} \\ \text{principal and return} \\ \text{in Country X} \end{pmatrix} \times \begin{pmatrix} \text{principal} \\ \text{and return} \\ \text{in} \\ \text{Country X} \end{pmatrix}$$

In this case we have

$$(1.00)(1.14) = (.90)(x)$$
$$x = 1.27$$

where x = principal plus return in Country X.

In other words, a company must earn a return of 27 percent on principal in a country where there is a 10-percent risk of total loss to have an investment which is as attractive as a 14-percent return in a country where there is no risk of total loss. In actual fact, the complete considerations will be much more complex, but this risk factor gives at least an arithmetical starting point.

If the political risk can be insured, then it is necessary to include only the exposed risk and the insurance premium in the above factor. For example, suppose that you estimate the risk of complete confiscation without reimbursement to be 50 percent in Country Y, and suppose that you can insure 80 percent of the investment. The exposed risk is then in theory 50 percent of 20 percent, or 10 percent. To that must be added the cost of the governmental insurance, say 7 percent, for a subtotal of 17 percent.

But that isn't all, because there might also be a risk that you will lose the use of the assets without formal confiscation, as in the case of political-economic stagnation, so that you cannot get payment on the insurance. Furthermore, even in the case of confiscation, there might be a delay before you are paid. During that time, you don't get any benefit from your investment. Suppose that you judge the total of these two factors to raise the previous 17-percent risk to a total risk of 30 percent. Suppose furthermore that in a country like Germany you expect a 14-percent net return on investment and you ask yourself what return on investment in Country Y will be equally attractive. The same simple calculation tells you 63 percent $[(1.00)(1.14) = (.70)(x); \; x = 1.63]$. Tax and other considerations may make the calculation much more complex, but don't let that scare you and keep you from following it through arithmetically to see where you come out. If you assign arithmetical values to all considerations of this nature, the final result will be much more accurate than just flying by the seat of your pants.

The figure for sales divided by inventory in Table 1 gives only the apparent inventory turnover, not the true one. This must be analyzed separately.

In Part B, the last three figures for each department can assist in putting a brake on the empire-building department manager who wants to hire additional personnel although his department cannot support it.

Limitations of Performance Statistics

I would advocate distributing statistics such as the preceding table and bar chart to the managers of each operation and their department managers, provided the data are accompanied each time by a letter stating that no results can be judged only through statistics, and that many nonquantifiable matters also have to be given proper weight. As stated above, numerical values should be assigned to as many factors as possible. But the human judgment applied is much more important than the statistics alone, no matter how refined they are.

In addition, the letter of transmittal should remind the managers of the great importance of investments in human resources, in establishing and maintaining a positive company morale, and in research and development, as well as in public relations and advertising.

Turnover among middle managers and other employees is another factor to watch carefully. If several of the best people leave, serious management shortcomings are usually indicated. Take warning from these very early indications, don't wait until the problems become visible in the accounting figures.

Build-up of capable personnel and executives, clarity of organization, and delegation of responsibility and authority to achieve a smoothly functioning, efficient enterprise are important factors to be evaluated separately from the performance table. So are the relative strength of the competition in each market, the difficulties of importing into each market, patents, and other external factors.

The figures I have described are some of the data developed annually. Simpler key figures should be sent to headquarters monthly, and they should generally arrive by the fifteenth of the month following the month being reported. Incredible as it may seem, some companies get only annual data from foreign joint ventures; therefore they really know very little about what is going on.

13

Getting the Most
Out of Planning

WITHOUT planning, a company becomes a ship without a rudder, drifting with the winds of the moment. After some years, such a company could well find itself in a field overcrowded with more determined competitors. A company should plan in order to *make* its own future, rather than drift into it.

A company is often hostile to major change. It is instead bent on cost-cutting, production scheduling, and very minor changes that might increase efficiency slightly. Yet change in a major way it must, if it is going to grow and prosper. It must try to introduce new products and new processes near the beginning of their life cycles.

Long-range planning should be one of top management's means of constantly checking on what the company is doing, and what it really should be doing to achieve the greatest long-range success. It is a means of getting middle management to search for major ventures in big new fields, rather than only small completions to the existing lines. Planning is also one of the vehicles for cultivating more interdepartmental exchange of information and overcoming the NIH (Not Invented Here) factor.

Who Should Plan?

Experienced line managers often are too busy with day-to-day operational matters, with the latest crisis, with the ringing telephone and the stream of people coming into the office. Planning for the future does not need to be done immediately, so it is postponed, not done at all, or delegated completely to young, eager staff people. Having learned about planning only at college, they do not have the practical experience to steer them past all the impractical alternatives and into the channels that lead to fastest net after-tax profit growth and highest return on invested capital, two of the main goals of planning. Therefore we conclude:

> *Those who have the least time for it, the experienced line managers, should provide the main input into planning, despite all their other work.*

There are three reasons for this. *First,* their all-round experience is needed for planning, which is one of the most complex of the fundamental management functions.

Certainly, the routine technical phases of planning, the gathering of information, the secretarial duties, and even the main assembling and writing of the plan can be delegated to staff employees, but not the creative phases of planning.

Second, the executive who provides the main input for the planning can't help but be greatly stimulated in the process. Planning raises his sights beyond today and toward the all-important future. The mental discipline involved in thinking through various alternative future courses of action step by step to their end effect is beneficial to every executive. The mental work involved in formulating corporate objectives, setting future targets, planning all the steps to reach these targets, and preparing for minimization of future risks makes the manager better prepared to cope with what actually does lie ahead.

The executive will attain a feeling of new security once he has surveyed the whole area in which his company operates and studied the future through which he will move during the next few years.

Third, only if a plan is properly executed will it achieve its full value. The line managers have the responsibility for executing the plan.

If the plan is developed not by them but by young staff assistants, who present it written and ready to the experienced line managers, then the line managers will find many reasons why they should go different routes.

Under these circumstances, the line managers have no personal commitment to carry out the plan; they have not thought through those alternative routes that they are so willing to try. Why should they adhere to this paper created by some young staffers?

On the other hand, if later evidence and new circumstances do, in fact, give promise of better results from alternative routes than from those in the plan, then the line managers who have been active themselves in the development of the plan will be better able to evaluate and decide on the course of action as they go along. And chances are that they will make better decisions.

Who should be in charge of planning? The chief executive should, but he is usually too busy to dedicate the necessary time to it. In a large company, there must be a planning coordinator to guide all the planning activity. That man should preferably not be a staff assistant only versed in theory, but an experienced executive commanding the respect and cooperation of the line managers.

One British company solved the problem of having the right man for this job simply by rotating the job among its line managers. The disadvantage of not having a trained planning coordinator was outweighed by the fact that the company ended up with better and more well-rounded line managers.

UPSIDE-DOWN PLANNING

Normally, short-range planning originates at the bottom and is submitted to the top, whereas long-range planning originates at the top and is communicated downward. But for an occasional year, the reverse process can be tried. (Singer, for example, tried it in 1967.) It gives to the various managers a better understanding about what goes on at the other end of the organizational ladder.

Four Types of Plans

ONE-YEAR BUDGET PLAN

The one-year budget plan is usually developed as close to the firing line as possible, in each foreign subsidiary and in each domestic division. Normally, it should be updated quarterly, each time for the four quarters ahead.

When the budget plan is submitted to the corporate head office, it is checked to make sure that it meshes with the budget plans of other parts of the company, with the initial steps of the longer-range plans, and with top management expectations. Typically, the one-year budget plan includes:

Sales forecast (with reasons, reservations, and comments).

Budget.

Personnel plan.

Capital investment plan.

Financing plan.

New product needs and suggested steps toward satisfying them; old product phase-out.

Manufacturing plan.

Other major actions to be taken, their likely consequences, alternative actions, and the consequences of each.

Short-range opportunities to be sought out and threats to be prepared against.

TWO-YEAR FORECAST PLAN

The two-year forecast plan is usually prepared by each subsidiary and each domestic division once a year and for the year following the budget year. Typically, it contains the same type of material as the budget plan, but more alternative policies and actions are usually explored more deeply in the forecast plan. It normally leaves more room for changes along the way.

True planning work requires thorough consideration of alternatives. If it is well done, it will point out the direction in which the company should go.

The two-year forecast plan differs from the budget in that the plan indicates what should be made to happen, not merely what is likely to happen.

LONG-RANGE PLAN

Long-range planning should be the function of the parent company's top corporate officers. Although a formal, written long-range plan might be issued only once a year, long-range planning and the examination, up-dating, changing, and reexamination of the existing plan should be a continuing function during the year.

The execution of past plans should also be carefully analyzed. Those cases where a subsidiary or a division has found itself lagging behind established targets or launched out in directions different from those in the plan must be questioned and explained.

The length of the time span to be included in the long-range plan has been discussed endlessly; no one period of time will suit all companies. If the typical product life cycle of a certain industry is seven years, it obviously makes little sense to have long-range planning cover only five years. In another industry, technological changes might come so rapidly that nothing can be predicted beyond five years and, therefore, that space of time becomes the logical long-range planning period.

On the other hand, mining and certain heavy industries require ten- or fifteen-year plans because of the long write-off periods of new ventures and certain equipment. The long-range plan typically contains:

Restatement of corporate objectives and the main steps to be taken toward any unusual objectives.

General business strategy planning toward the normal corporate objectives of profit maximization.

Forecast of annual financial statements for the period included in the long-range plan.

Planning of: investments and financing; new product development and old product phase-out; manufacturing; acquisition and divestiture goals and steps toward achieving them; other major new projects; personnel resources and executive development.

This type of planning analyzes where the company is, where it should be going, and how and when it can get there. It analyzes the company's internal weaknesses and strengths and the company's external opportunities and threats. Thus, it is the most important of the various types of corporate plans. To develop a good long-range plan, you must first consider many alternative courses of action for the company and then distill out the one plan that is likely to give the best results.

BLUE-YONDER PROJECTIONS

This is not really planning but a mixture of guessing, dreaming, estimating, and projecting for the future that lies beyond the time period for which planning can be done with some confidence. In a company that can make a five-year plan, it can be a worthwhile exercise for the top managers to get together once a year to try to project where the company should be in ten and in fifteen years, as well as what should be done during the next five years toward achieving these longer-range targets. Naturally, what is put down in writing about these blue-yonder projections is very nebulous.

Four Common Faults in Planning

Keeping the long-range plan too secret. This is a major fault in many international companies because it keeps the plan—or essential portions of it—from being communicated clearly to all the line managers. These men should know at least most of these plans in order to make their work fall in line with them.

Excessive secrecy on the part of R&D. The main planners need to know what the research and development department of the company is coming up with. However, R&D often considers its work too secret. In these cases, R&D together with the marketing department can pass on to the planners information on at least what effects the new gizmo will likely produce.

For example, they might state that by a certain future date, the likelihood is 80 percent that a new woodworking machine tool in the $30,000 bracket will be released, and that there is over 50 percent likelihood that the U.S. sales will reach about fifty units annually within two years after release. Other countries might consume proportionately many units. Fair patent protection is hoped for, but some competition is nevertheless expected, so normal sales efforts will need to be expended.

Excessive secrecy regarding costs or cost accounting procedures. For reasons that are usually invalid, some companies in the same group often keep secret from each other certain costs, or the procedures used in cost accounting.

Of course, it is impossible for a planner to do a complete job if he does not have correct cost information, but this type of secrecy should be prevented anyway among managers in the same corporate family, unless there are exceptionally good reasons for it. Secrecy hinders other types of management activities as well as planning.

Too rigid adherence to the plan. The plan must never become a straitjacket. The same, of course, is true about the budget. These devices are only tools and must never be binding. Central management should never be allowed to usurp decision-making power from subsidiary and divisional managers, who must be able to make quick decisions when necessary for their own profit centers. Decentralization of decision-making power gives the corporation flexible strength and the ability to act fast with a minimum of red tape.

Thus, as we discussed elsewhere, a subsidiary manager should feel obliged to grasp a passing opportunity for his company without awaiting approval from above, *when the matter is urgent.* He should feel free to act independently, whether or not the particular action was provided for in the plan. (But he should report his action.)

On the other hand, this freedom does not absolve the same manager from consulting with headquarters *when time allows it,* and when the action has substantial consequences. In this manner, the manager can insure that the action does not conflict with over-all objectives or plans of action elsewhere, which he might not be aware of.

Risk Planning

It is often tempting for planners to choose the alternative with the least risk and the least investment. If they do, then they are most likely to avoid criticism. But this course of action is totally wrong. It should not be the objective of planners to avoid criticism. It is not even their first objective to minimize risk.

Of top priority is maximizing future profits. To do so, it is nearly always necessary to take measured risks.

There are always some disadvantages to any good solution. Planning has to find the alternative that has the most favorable sum of large

Planning has to find the alternative . . .

advantages and small disadvantages, not the alternative that has no disadvantages; that alternative is usually not bold enough.

The planner who tries to avoid criticism is a bad planner and a misguided businessman.

International Planning

Most of the general rules about planning given above apply just as much to domestic as to international planning, but the planning work itself is vastly different in an international company as compared to a domestic one.

Communication difficulties and differences in attitudes present special challenges to the international planner. He can assist greatly in getting all companies in the same corporate family to pull in the same direction.

The planner can also assist in avoiding product proliferation and duplication of costly facilities and efforts. For example, suppose a French subsidiary wants its products to be a little different from those of the German subsidiary, and neither of them cares for those of the British subsidiary. All three want their own product engineering departments and other related facilities.

A high degree of judgment, diplomacy, and persuasion is required to act on these types of requests from different countries. Only experienced international executives who can cross the cultural barriers should attempt to do this sensitive job.

The planning of personnel and know-how resources as well as of executive development in international operations is totally different from the same type of planning in a domestic company. The international planner must provide for future personnel, know-how, and executive needs within each country where the corporation operates. It is usually difficult to fill a lack of human resources in one country from an oversupply in another country.

14

Location of Manufacturing

IN Chapter 1, we noted that a product will not have to carry international trade costs if manufacturing is located within each major national and regional market, rather than being centralized in one spot for the whole world. We also noted that a product must sometimes be different for each major market because of local differences in taste or variations in governmental regulations.

In this chapter, we shall first briefly examine each major aspect that must be considered in order to optimize the manufacturing location; then we shall see how these often conflicting aspects are weighed against each other. In the chapter on Operation Europe, we shall apply some of the viewpoints presented here to manufacturing in Europe.

Tax Aspects

To many profitable companies, the foremost consideration for location of manufacturing will be the corporate tax aspects, because to many companies, corporate taxes are the highest single expense item.

When they consider various alternative locations for manufacturing, companies should make projected profit-and-loss statements for each location and move the taxes up from their traditional place on the statements, second from the end, to follow cost of goods sold. Thus, labor cost and tax costs are shown together. Both depend on the location, so making a clear comparison becomes easier.

If the right tax holiday area is selected for a manufacturing operation, the profits from that operation can be used for reinvestment in facilities, inventory, accounts receivable, and so on, without first being cut in half by taxes, at least during the term of the tax holiday.

If the tax holiday area also has customs-free access to a major market, it naturally becomes that much more attractive. It is no coincidence that the world's two most important tax holiday areas with moderate labor costs have such duty-free access to the two largest markets in the Western world: Puerto Rico for the U.S. market, and Italy's Mezzogiorno for the Common Market.

Italy's tax holiday area used to include only parts of southern Italy, but some northern mountain locations are now included.

With Portugal's new free-trade agreement with the Common Market, some development areas in Portugal may become quite attractive as manufacturing locations (provided Portugal achieves more than superficial political peace and stability).

And now that Ireland has entered the Common Market, it may also become more attractive as a location for manufacturing, especially if the political situation north of Eire clears up.

Even if you cannot locate your manufacturing in a tax holiday area, it is very important to find a location with reasonable corporate income tax rates. The difference between 38 percent and 68 percent becomes evident quickly. Not only the main corporate income tax rate, but also depreciation allowances, dividend taxes, capital taxes, certain sales taxes, and municipal and other local community or cantonal taxes must be carefully compared.

Within the EEC countries and their new free-trade associates, several other locations are available with corporate tax incentives and capital incentives. They should all be considered and compared if you are locating manufacturing in Europe.

Labor Aspects

COST, PRODUCTIVITY, AND RELIABILITY

Not all industries by far can utilize lower overseas labor costs. Many find that the labor cost per product unit is higher overseas, despite the lower labor cost per hour. Even in cases where the labor cost per unit is lower overseas, many other factors may make total costs higher than in the United States.

But those industries that have much routine hand labor on small, light parts are increasingly locating parts factories and assembly plants in places such as Taiwan, Singapore, Hong Kong, southern Italy, and even Yugoslavia (through cooperative production agreements) and northern Mexico.

The flight to areas of lower labor costs is by no means limited to U.S. industries. It is also increasingly practiced by others, such as Swedish, German, and lately even Japanese and Italian industries.

I must warn against overestimating small differences in labor costs, such as those existing between France, Germany, Belgium, and the Netherlands. To some extent, they may be outweighed by productivity differences. They also vary with time, or with devaluations and revaluations.

Not only the cost of labor but also the reliability of the labor force should be considered. The United Kingdom, for instance, has many wildcat strikes. Even if strikes don't hit your production directly, they may paralyze it for frequent and extended periods by hitting suppliers, truckers, or other indispensable services.

ECONOMIC CONSEQUENCES OF THE FLIGHT TO LOW-COST LABOR

U.S. and West European labor leaders have been cool toward the flight of industry to areas of cheap foreign labor. The long-range economic effects of this flight, however, are a little different than they seem at first glance.

The transfer of routine manual manufacturing operations to cheap-labor countries allows the industrialized countries to upgrade their own labor for more sophisticated work. This work yields higher hourly earnings and involves fewer of the more tedious, repetitive tasks. Thus, we conclude that

The flight of manufacturing to cheap-labor countries has an economic effect on the industrialized countries similar to that of automation.

That is, it causes a need for reeducating some workers to higher grades of work. Failing that, it produces some painful unemployment. One can only hope that such unemployment can be minimized through more reeducation.

The unsettling effect of the need for reeducation is one of the two short-term disadvantages of the flight to low-cost labor. The other disadvantage is a temporary negative effect on the trade balance of the industrialized countries—temporary because the long-term effect of upgrading the types of work done in the industrialized countries is a positive one for their trade balance. By upgrading their jobs to the most sophisticated levels, the industrialized countries will be able to sustain or improve their high standard of living, yet compete in the world market—something they will be totally unable to do if they continue to insist that routine manual labor be carried out locally when it can be avoided.

Both short-term disadvantages are outweighed by the long-term advantages.

It would be no more useful to try to stop the flight of manufacturing to countries of lower labor costs than to try to stop automation. The flight also has a slowing effect on inflation in the industrialized countries, just as automation does.

Fortunately, the new industries provide a welcome source of jobs, training, and hard-currency income to the cheap-labor countries. Thus, as with most international business, both seller and buyer benefit.

Customs Duty Aspects

As we saw before, you naturally try to locate your manufacturing within the tariff walls of your major markets; but there are several less obvious customs aspects to be aware of.

Assuming that your new factory needs to import components and materials, there are important differences (even among the original six of the nine EEC countries) in how much red tape is involved in meeting customs requirements, how much time it takes to cut through the red tape, and how costly it is ultimately to clear the goods through customs, even though the actual duty is the same. Among the first six EEC countries, Italy is the worst and the Benelux countries are the best in these respects.

One European country, the United Kingdom, has for many years had particularly difficult customs laws that required a lot of red tape, costly time, and often uplift in the value of products for duty purposes. Hopefully the United Kingdom will be forced to radically change this situation.

Among members of the Latin American Free Trade Association (LAFTA), such differences from country to country are, of course, much broader than among EEC members.

Appeal of the Country of Origin

The fact is seldom found in print, but to the ultimate customers, some locations of manufacturing have a large emotional advantage. Most likely, you should locate a perfume factory or a cosmetics factory in France and a watch factory in Switzerland, so the products can carry the influential labels, "Made in France" or "Made in Switzerland," respectively. Similarly, considering the emotional advantage alone, a heavy industrial equipment factory for the world market should best be in the United States. "Made in U.S.A." is a good label in this field. For much of the Common Market, though, an even better label might be "Made in West Germany."

Within the industrial equipment field, there is a strong preference in the United States for American equipment, in Germany for German equipment, and in France for French equipment; but many other countries have no significant preference for locally made products. In many less industrialized countries, private buyers have a definite preference for equipment made in industrialized countries. They expect the quality to be higher.

Some manufacturing locations have a large emotional advantage.

Political Risk

For a manufacturing subsidiary, the political risk is larger than for a distributing subsidiary, simply because the fixed investment is higher. In fact, the political risk is often the single largest deterrent to locating a factory in a less industrialized country.

We saw in the chapter on statistics for monitoring operations that if a country's political situation is unstable, the actual risk undertaken there must be quantified, and the required return on investment must

For a manufacturing subsidiary the political risk is larger than for a distributing subsidiary.

be correspondingly higher for that particular country. Otherwise, it is better to invest elsewhere, no matter who claims that "we have to protect our market in that country," or "we've got to lower our labor costs."

In the countries with lower labor costs, there are always substantial political risks. This is not a coincidence but a two-way cause-and-effect relationship. It is easy to see that low labor costs can give an unstable political situation, but the reverse is also true: An unstable political situation in a country causes companies to hesitate investing there; therefore unemployment continues to rise, causing labor costs to drop.

Executives inexperienced in international business are often surprised to see the high return (even in constant dollars) on capital in some Latin American countries. But nobody would invest there if they could expect only the modest return on capital that is common in the United States or Switzerland.

Political aspects are, of course, most important in less industrialized countries, but political aspects must also be given full consideration when locating in most of the industrialized countries.

Such considerations include, for South Africa, the long-range outlook for the apartheid system; for Australia, the increasing desire for local ownership; and for most of Southern Europe and the United Kingdom, the risk of strikes and political instability caused by a faster growth of expectations for improved standards of living than of productivity to support the improved standards.

This difference for the United Kingdom may well increase. The gross domestic product per capita of the United Kingdom has fallen behind those of all noncommunist countries in Northern and Central Europe, excepting Ireland and Austria, and it will be behind that of Italy in a few years, according to the OECD (Organization for Economic Cooperation and Development).

Availability of Components

That this consideration is important was mentioned in Chapter 2. Let's take an all too common example: An American manufacturer can no longer export his gizmo to Argentina because a local competitive Argentine gizmo factory has been set up, making imports difficult. To protect its Argentine sales, the American company decides to start making gizmos in Argentina and to export them from there to other LAFTA countries.

But very quickly, the American company discovers the difficulty—that instead of having had trouble importing one article to Argentina, it now has much more trouble trying to import 20 different components that are unavailable in Argentina but necessary for gizmo production. The experienced international executive plans company actions so far ahead that the company usually is spared such a predicament.

Other Governmental Interference

Apart from taxation and import hindrances, some governments interfere in other ways with the freedom of action of private industry. For example, they may prevent the expansion of a building or hinder surplus labor layoffs. The purpose of such governmental interference is generally to improve the standard of living in the country. It actually works exactly the opposite way by hampering private industry.

Such governmental interference is very serious in many less industrialized countries, such as India, but it also acts as a heavy wet blanket covering private initiative in several industrialized West European countries, which have had social democratic governments for a long time.

Weighing All the Aspects

Clearly, many of the aspects of location are conflicting. Say you want to manufacture in Singapore, but you fear the political risk. Or you can buy an existing plant in England at a very favorable price, but the disadvantages of the country outweigh the low initial costs. In the final analysis, it becomes necessary to quantify all the aspects, including those that are very difficult to quantify. Return-on-investment calculations may help, and it will be necessary to use many figures that were arrived at subjectively, such as the political risk factor explained in Chapter 12.

The planning of manufacturing locations often becomes a matter of deciding which component parts should be made in only one location, in order to gain the benefit of mass production, and which parts must be made in other countries as well, to gain buyer acceptance, to decrease customs duties, or to comply with varying safety codes.

15

About
International Shipping

WHEN a company that has operated only domestically goes international, it is imperative that it upgrade its personnel in the packing department. If a mistake is made, say, packing wrong parts, in a shipment from Illinois to Ohio or California, the customer will soon be on the phone, and the matter can be corrected within days without great harm or expense. But if the same mistake happens in a shipment to Brazil or India, it easily causes months of severe difficulties, often great expense, and even permanent loss of customers.

If a company ships by surface to many different international customers, the company's shipping and accounting personnel are forced to do much more complex paperwork than they did when they were shipping only within the United States. Capable, accurate, and responsible employees in shipping and documentation can save such an internationally active company a lot of grief and loss by avoiding mistakes. They can also save time and money by finding the best ways of shipping the goods.

In addition, not every carpenter knows how to make seaworthy boxing and crating.

Those who think that goods in international trade will move automatically will be badly disappointed. Only conscientious surveillance by company personnel on both sides will keep the goods moving. These internal company people must combine their own efforts with

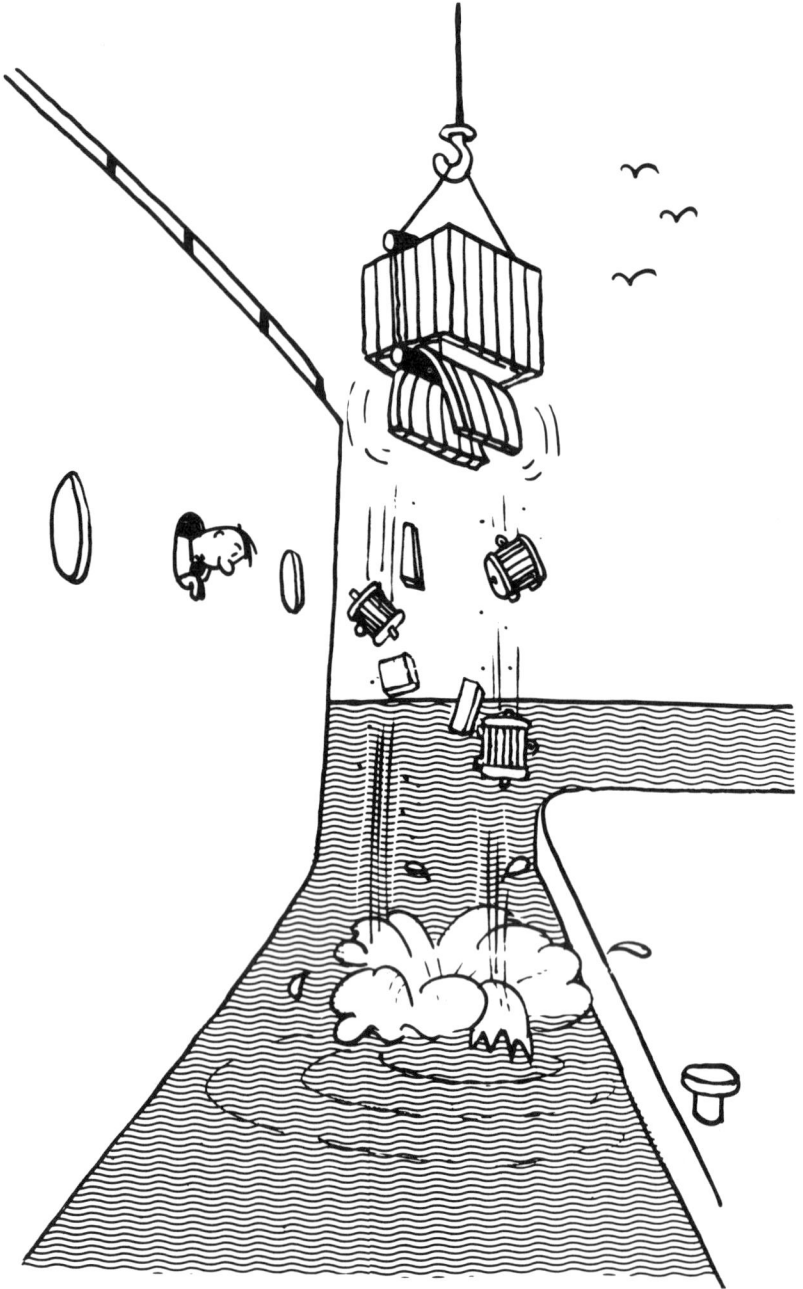

Not every carpenter knows how to make seaworthy boxing and crating.

those of the best forwarding agent they can find at the exporting end, and the best customs broker they can find at the importing end.

A new company starting out with a substantial amount of international work that involves surface shipments had better hire an experienced international shipping and documentation clerk who is capable of giving good advice on such matters as containerization and consolidattion at export ports.

If the company is not able to justify hiring such a person while the international volume is still small, then it had better rely heavily on a good forwarding agent. American inland cities have very few good international forwarding agents, so it may be preferable for a company located in a small inland city to use one of the best forwarding agents it can find in another major city and somehow try to get him to pay extra attention to the company's shipments and watch out for the company's best interests.

Air Freight vs. Surface Freight

International air freight is considerably simpler to handle than international surface freight, so if the product can be shipped more cheaply by air than by surface, the international shipping operation becomes much simpler. Air shipments do not require nearly as much follow-up work as surface shipments to insure that they are not forgotten somewhere along the route. And many companies can take advantage of the different special commodity air freight rates, which are much lower than the general cargo rates.

In most countries, moreover, air freighted goods pass customs clearance much faster than steamer freighted shipments. (But in some countries—for example, Italy—the only way to get something through customs quickly is by trucking, provided that you have the goods cleared at the border without changing trucks.)

Never believe the transit times quoted by a forwarding agent, whether they are for air or surface shipments. It seems that no matter how you ask, they all quote the minimum times, which are seldom achieved, instead of the maximum times, which are what you really need to know to calculate your shipping date for meeting an overseas delivery date.

For this reason, it is not uncommon that a forwarder will quote, say, two days by air and three weeks by surface, door-to-door from an inland U.S. city to an inland European city. (My rule of thumb for the same shipments would be one week by air and two months by surface.)

For shipments from the United States to Europe and northern Latin America, air freight is sometimes cheaper than surface freight, even for goods that would normally be shipped only by surface within the United States. A typical cost comparison of air freight to surface freight for fairly light and expensive industrial equipment is given in Table 2.

Often additional factors should be considered when making a comparison of costs, such as interest rate on the value of the goods in transit and on the larger stock that is necessary to keep overseas when utilizing the slower and much more uncertain means of transportation.

The smaller the shipment is, the larger is the disadvantage of shipping by surface (provided the shipment is above parcel post size). As a rule, no international nonconsolidated maritime freight shipment, no matter how small, costs less than $100, and no transoceanic air freight shipment less than $30, counting all costs at both export and import sides.

Table 2   Comparison of air and surface shipping costs.

COSTS BY AIR

Air freight, inland U.S. city to New York	$ 89.50
Air freight, New York to inland European city	315.00
Total air freight	$404.50
Insurance over and above that included with the air freight	12.20
Average telex and long-distance telephone cost for follow-up	5.00
Total cost by air	$421.70

COSTS BY SURFACE

Surface freight, inland U.S. city to New York	$ 53.50
Maritime freight, New York to European port	149.00
Surface freight, European port to inland European city	41.00
Total surface freight	$243.50
Cost of seaworthy crating material*	40.00
Cost of seaworthy crating labor	74.40
Ocean bill of lading	15.00
Pier delivery charge, New York	16.00
Other handling charges	40.00
Martime insurance	89.50
Average telex and long-distance telephone cost for follow-up	20.00
Total cost by surface	$538.40

*Over and above the cost of standard inland packing, which is usually satisfactory for air shipment.

Distance makes little difference to the cost of maritime shipments of most goods other than the cheapest commodities. Thus, total costs for a maritime shipment of machinery from the United States will be about the same to Singapore as to Venezuela.

Containerization is already radically changing maritime freight and is saving time and packing costs; but much remains to be done, especially in improved consolidation facilities, including inland consolidation points, on both the North American and European continents.

Suppose we had fast, frequent, scheduled, consolidated, and direct container shipments between many inland U.S. cities and many inland European cities, rather than mainly between port cities on both sides. This would be the only new development in surface freight that could hope to slow down the increasing conversion to air freight for goods of high value per pound.

FREE TRADE ZONES

If your goods have a high value per pound, and if your sales volume warrants it, you might consider using:

The Colón free trade zone in Panama for supplying part of the Caribbean, Central America, and at least the northern part of South America by air;

The Schiphol (Netherlands) airport or Rotterdam free trade zone for supplying distributors in Europe; and

Either Hong Kong or Singapore for supplying part of Southeast Asia by air.

Doing so will cut down considerably the stock that each distributor needs to keep. The goods can be shipped by steamer to the different free trade zones and forwarded from there to each distributor by air or truck as required.

A Few Fundamentals About Shipping Documents

The shipping documents that are always needed, usually in many copies, are the *invoice* and the *packing list*.

The invoice not only concerns the payment from the customer, but also (in most cases) forms the basis for the customs duty assessment.

The packing list indicates to the customer as well as to the customs inspector which box contains what part of the shipment. Thus, it facilitates customs inspection through sampling. To gain the confidence of the customs people, you must make certain that the packing list is correct.

Ocean freight needs a *bill of lading,* which in the United States is prepared by the forwarding agent. Air freight needs instead an *air waybill,* which experienced companies cut themselves, while the less experienced companies have them prepared by the airline, the air freight consolidator, or a forwarding agent.

The bill of lading and the air waybill give instructions on matters such as how the shipment should be made, to whom the goods should be consigned (important), and by whom the freight should be paid.

Exports from the United States always require an *export declaration,* which is very easy to prepare.

Some countries require in addition other import documents, such as a consular invoice, a certificate of origin, or a coy of the import license. Some less industrialized countries require rather accurate net and gross weights for each category of items.

If the shipping documents are not prepared with precision and care, the shipments may be seriously delayed, subjected to fines, or in some countries even confiscated.

The customers' shipping instructions must be followed carefully, unless they are quite illegal—and this is not too infrequent.

Small differences in wording can mean serious difficulties for importers in many less industrialized countries, where one name for a product may mean that it pays 15 percent duty and another, equally good name for the same product may mean that it falls into a category of 100 percent duty, or even one of prohibited imports.

There must be separate invoices and packing lists for each shipment to each customer.

Invoices must show only net prices, never gross prices less discount; otherwise, the customs officers will probably charge duty on the gross prices.

For several countries, you can have no variation in prices to different customers within each country, because the customs authorities may compare and charge customs duty on the highest prices to all the customers. This means that for these countries you cannot ship to both wholesalers and retailers.

If you are shipping between related companies, some countries will require that you open your books and correspondence files in the importing country to inspection by customs authorities just as freely as you open them to income tax authorities.

A foreign company exporting to the United States may also be required to open its books and files in the exporting country to inspection by U.S. import authorities, particularly if there is any doubt regarding the fairness of the invoice values, or if the company is suspected of dumping.

A U.S. conviction of dumping is a hazard that can be very serious and costly. U.S. antidumping regulations have been severely criticized as unfair by our major trading partners. Some companies go to the extreme of making certain models available only for the United States in order to decrease the risk of a dumping charge.

For air freight shipments, the exporter should always telex the importer, stating the air waybill number and date and, if possible, the transoceanic flight number and date. This practice, combined with a good follow-up on both sides, can cut days and even weeks off the total door-to-door transit time.

For both steamer and air freight, it is always the practice to send the consignee and the ultimate importer copies of the main shipping documents. For steamer shipments send also advice regarding which steamer the goods are aboard. Following up steamer shipments from both sides reduces the likelihood that they will be forgotten, possibly for months, in such a place as a warehouse or, even worse, on a dock, where they are subject to rain, sun, snow, salt-water spray, and pilferage.

16

Some Practical
Travel Hints

HERE are some ways you can make business travel more effective through better preparation and scheduling.

Stay Independent

Even some experienced businessmen often succumb to the friendly offers from foreign affiliates to be picked up at the airport upon arrival. They further compound this mistake when they agree to talk business on the way from the airport to the hotel right after a long flight. None of us is able to think sharply after a night or a full day on an airplane. Also, the person who picks us up is often the wrong man to discuss the subject with, or he represents only one side of the situation. Others are not available for consultation or questions.

You don't do your company any good if you work when you are exhausted, so you shouldn't hesitate to adjourn the business discussion until later at the office, breakfast the following morning, or some other time and place more suitable than a car ride from the airport. This can be done in a friendly but firm manner.

If you are not firm in establishing your independence from the beginning, certain licensees, subsidiary managers, or distributors will snap a collar around your neck upon your arrival, attach a leash, and guide you around "their" territory; they will show you only what they want you to see, discuss only what they want you to hear, deposit you in your hotel late at night, pick you up in the morning, snap on the leash again, guide you to the airport, and let out a deep sigh of relief when you take off. It is up to you to refuse this kind of guidance, whether the affiliate likes your refusal or not. You must be free to talk with whomever you wish and see the situation from every angle.

Normally, I refuse to tell affiliates my exact arrival time. This saves valuable people many hours of waiting in airports for delayed flights and missed connections, hours that they can spend on useful work instead.

In most cities, I rent a car at the airport. Thus, I am free to go and see a banker, lawyer, auditor, customer, or anyone else independently, without being a burden to local affiliates, and more importantly, without becoming obligated to them. Because I have been doing this for years, I now find it easy to drive alone in most of the important cities of the world without referring to the map too frequently. This helps me feel at home anywhere.

Since I have a car, employees, distributors, and customers can easily invite me out or ask me to their homes, just as they would invite any local person who has his own wheels. And with a rented car, I can skip away when I am too tired to think about business, or when I want to see a show at the theater, visit personal friends, or just be alone.

I much prefer dictating memos and letters about matters that need action at one location before going on to the next one. But in order to be able to do this, I have to be firm with affiliates and distributors about deciding at least part of my own schedule. Frequently, the best place to do this homework without interruption is the hotel room.

Staying on top of correspondence and homework while traveling is a real challenge, and it takes many working nights. A small, battery-operated dictating machine is a great help in accomplishing this work. (Philips-Norelco and IBM make two that are good.)

Unless you are a banker or a government employee, one type of foreign travel to stay away from is official trade mission trips, which spend time on far too general matters for the specialized needs of each company.

Maintain the Balance Between Business and Private Life

Every hour a man spends on a long business trips is expensive to his company. Therefore, he naturally wants to use every hour for his company's benefit.

But I must warn you against overdoing the work, as many do. Not that anyone should loaf on a business trip; but don't work, work, work every moment. If you do, you will become dull and tired and you will start snapping at colleagues and making bum decisions.

This is especially dangerous if you are on a long trip and you are going from country to country on a tight schedule, visiting subsidiaries, licensees, and distributors. In each country, people have lots of problems to discuss; they meet you for breakfast at your hotel, arrange lunches with customers, and tend to entertain you till late in the evening, discussing business most of the time. After a while, you are saturated with these problems. Unless you change the schedule, you will get very little time alone to recharge your batteries.

Usually, your wife, children, or girlfriend should be left at home. On most overseas business trips, they are a hindrance. This is not the time for togetherness. You had better keep vacation travel separate from business travel, and, if you are on a vacation trip, conscientiously avoid making any customers, distributors, or colleagues feel they have to meet you or entertain you.

Unless you have some special reason to take pictures in your work (Polaroid cameras are usually best for that), leave your camera at home as well, or at least keep it hidden in your suitcase until weekends.

Try to get enough sleep on your trips. Nobody can be sharp in the office after spending several nights in a row "inspecting" night spots with customers. The other customers you see the next day don't appreciate dealing with bleary-eyed representatives.

Preparing for the Trip

Most businessmen read in advance a travel guide on any country they are going to visit for the first time. But in addition, you really should try to read up more thoroughly on the country you are going to visit. It will be well worth your while to look it up in some good history book, or at least in an encyclopedia.

Furthermore, on my way, I usually try to get hold of a newspaper from the country I am going to. Even if the newspaper is a day old, it makes me feel at home upon arrival, and it often contains items that you can use as springboards for interesting small talk at cocktails or dinner with local businessmen.

Don't change money on the black market for traveling expenses, at least not for India and the East Bloc. It is not worth the risk of getting caught.

Take along plenty of business cards, especially for Japan. If you are going there or to the Soviet Union, consider having the back of your American cards printed in Japanese or Russian. Other languages might also be helpful if you are staying long enough in a country to warrant it. For continental Europe, your title on your business card should include any doctorate or other high degrees, even if this is not the custom in the United States.

Bring plenty of small but nice business gifts when you go to Japan, and find out from your Japanese advisors when and how to present them (for instance, they should always be nicely wrapped).

For most of the less industrialized countries, it is better to get a tourist visa instead of a business visa, unless you personally will earn money in the country.

I always put all irreplaceable papers in my briefcase, rather than with the checked baggage. If the checked baggage then gets lost, never mind—it's only a matter of money.

Scheduling Your Stops

If you are going to have long, tough negotiations in one of the countries on your itinerary, it is useful to allow for two alternative departure dates from that country. Tell your associates there about only the earlier date. Many negotiations won't get serious until the eve of your departure. Then everyone may try to rush the business deals through and get the best out of you by the exhaustion method. In that event, you are better off if you can delay your departure at the last minute and finish up the business meticulously.

On the other hand, if you are planning a regular business trip through a continent like South America, without any such tough negotiations, then it is much better not to schedule firm dates along your way. In this manner, you can tell your distributor that you will stay in his country as long as necessary. Then he has only himself to blame if he discovers after you've left that everything was not finished by the time you departed. You can stay longer on a moment's notice wherever it is beneficial, and you can always go quickly through the places where there is little business for the moment. The minimum time for a business trip around an area as complex as South America is six weeks, as a rule of thumb.

In northwestern Europe and northern Italy it is best to take evening flights rather than morning ones in order to avoid the frequent morning fogs, which can cause interminable delays.

If you live in the United States and you have many stops to make in a continent like Europe, it is much more practical to tell somebody in Europe your objectives and let him make the appointments (scheduling them into a logical round trip), rather than trying to do it all from the United States and finding that half the people cannot see you on the dates you had thought of visiting them.

Above all, I have two cardinal rules for international business travelers:

> 1. *Allow sufficient time to see each person long enough to nurture mutual trust.*
> 2. *Don't see any more people than you can talk to long enough to comply with rule 1.*

This subject is covered more thoroughly in the chapter on Operation Europe.

ADJUSTING TO DIFFERENT TIME ZONES

Always try to schedule some rest immediately after any long East–West trip that puts you in a substantially different time zone. Be particularly moderate in drinking and eating during and after such a trip. (Eat only easily digestible foods.)

I find it far better to take daytime flights from the United States to Europe. Many people try to save time by using night flights, but they pay for it by being tired during business hours for several days following the trip.

For a few days after going from the United States to Europe, it is preferable to try to schedule the most important conferences in the afternoons. After going from an extended stay in Europe back to the United States, it is preferable for a few days to try to schedule the most important conferences in the mornings. This is because you are most alert during the daylight hours of the time zone you have just left.

It is false economy to disregard the fact that the body takes days to adjust to a new time zone. You cannot compensate simply by determination and will power. A person's mental capacity depends on his physical well-being, whether he realizes it or not.

Pan American makes the following recommendations: Try to avoid eating much during those hours when your stomach would be unaccustomed to getting food in the time zone you left. In flight, don't eat or drink too much. On long flights, move around occasionally instead of staying in one position in the seat. On night flights, loosen your tie, belt, and other tight clothing, take off your shoes and put on slipper socks, use the pillow and blanket, and try to sleep.

In the chapter on East Bloc business, some hints are given about travel in that part of the world.

17

Seeking Advice on Legal, Tax, and International Management Matters

DO not ever assume that the laws, the ethical rules, or the business procedures in a foreign country are the same as in the United States.

The more different the country is, the more you must constantly depend on advice from a local lawyer, auditor, or management consultant, or on international experts within your own firm. It is amazing to see what troubles even experienced multinational firms of American origin get into when they forget to consider and reconsider the legal, moral, and management differences at all times, even in routine matters such as local legal screening of advertising.

Even in a country as similar to the United States as West Germany, for instance, you would not be allowed to make many of the claims in advertising that are made daily in American business. You would not be allowed to advertise, for example, that your product is better than all others in the world, even if that happens to be true.

Your Choice of Lawyers

Before you choose a lawyer in a foreign country, as a matter of course you ask advice, get references, and choose a good one, despite the high cost. In many matters, you may not want to consult the young man who has learned all the rules about what you may not do, but rather the old fox who knows how to do these things anyway—perfectly legally, of course.

If the legal problem on which you want advice involves more than one country, then you must obviously choose a good local lawyer in each country or the local branch of a good international law firm.

The local foreign branch of a U.S. law firm that has many foreign branches, Baker & McKenzie, may not always know all the local tricks and shortcuts, but it offers you an advantage in that you can call on their closest office in the United States for further clarification of a foreign legal point if need be.

Often the local branch of a U.S. or international law firm is more expensive; but this is not always so, because most U.S. firms in corporate practice charge on a straight per-hour basis, while many foreign lawyers do not charge in proportion to the hours they spend, but ask a certain percentage of the business deal they assist in. Where this is the normal manner of calculating the legal fee, you can often negotiate a different basis of payment, say an hourly or monthly rate, provided that you do so in advance.

YOUR LAWYER'S FIRST THOUGHTS

Suppose for a moment that your problem in a foreign country is to get some necessary governmental permission. Suppose, furthermore, that you have just outlined the problem to your lawyer in that country. Before he answers you, here is what might run through *his* head.

If the lawyer is an *expatriate American,* he may think, "How can I present this case to the government so that it gives the *impression* that it is within the regulations?"

The *German* lawyer, on the other hand, may think, "This client must change his approach to get within the regulations."

A *French* lawyer I once consulted with assessed the situation this way: "That ministry goes on vacation in two weeks, so I can probably slip the application by the officials, who will only notice it enough to approve it when they clear their desks. It's less work to approve it than to decline it, and they are very busy right now."

Your *Brazilian* lawyer may say to himself, "My cousin Pedro used to work in that section of the ministry. I wonder if he is still there."

Your *Mexican* lawyer might figure, "Señor Sanchez usually charges 20,000 pesos for such a permit, but 15,000 really should be enough."

Your *Kenyan* lawyer might think, "I'll have to get a Kikuyo to handle this matter for me, because I wouldn't have a chance in that government department."

And your *Indian* lawyer might think, "These matters average eight years in the government before they are rejected, so if he wants to try anyway, I had better get a small quarterly retainer."

Keep your lawyer's first thoughts in mind when you choose one.

DON'T USE MORE THAN ONE ADVISOR IN EACH FIELD

In theory, a foreign subsidiary could save money by using a very capable, but expensive, lawyer for its major, important questions, and a small, neighborhood lawyer for its minor day-to-day questions. Long ago, a very capable lawyer advised me against doing that, and this has proven to be good advice.

The reason is that the small day-to-day matters have a way of becoming part of the larger, important questions. If you have two advisors in the same field, you easily end up paying two fees and spending twice the time for advice on the same subjects.

Furthermore, if you ask two different lawyers for advice on the same complex subject, you are bound to get two different answers. This expense in time and money is, of course, warranted only for very important matters.

SEEK STRAIGHT ADVICE

I value any advisor nearly as much for what he does not say as for what he says.

Assume, for example, that I am starting a subsidiary in a country, and I ask a lawyer what legal form it should have. If the lawyer tells me the legal forms it *could* have and mentions that it could be a branch as well as a couple of other forms, explaining the advantages and disadvantages of each one at length, then I know that I should switch lawyers and find one who doesn't spend his and my time on useless legal education for me, but guides me straight to the route I should follow. In reply to such a question, the lawyer I would choose would state at once: "You should have a—."*

I am not complaining about the advisor who spends time educating me on useful topics and pitfalls I should look out for; but I shun the one who, in reply to a simple question, goes into long, needless dissertations, reading aloud paragraphs of law, regulations, and so on. I prefer

---

* For Japan, he would probably recommend a KK (*Kabushiki Kaisha*). For Germany, normally he would recommend a G.m.b.H. (*Gesellschaft mit beschränkter Haftung*); but for a large corporation, of which shares were to be sold to the public, he would advise an A.G. (*Aktiengesellschaft*) instead. In France and in Venezuela, the lawyer would probably recommend the S.A. (*société anonyme*) and the C.A. (*compañia anónima*), respectively. And so forth.

the one who replies without mumbo-jumbo, "Yes, you can do it, provided that you . . . ," or "No, you cannot do it, unless you are willing to sacrifice . . . ." That kind of lawyer may be well worth his additional hourly charge.

Management consultants and tax consultants usually also present their answers to your questions in one of these two ways, and again, your preference for straight, clear answers should be obvious.

In addition, management consulting firms and major accounting firms often have a third answer: a proposal that they make a special study to reply to your question. In many such cases, it is preferable to ask for their preliminary, off-the-cuff answer instead, because your company may be under time pressure or may not be willing to spend the money to let consultants study each question in great detail.

Your Choice of Accounting Advisors and Management Consultants

Many foreign subsidiaries are given little, if any, choice in selecting their tax and accounting advisors. If the parent company uses a large, internationally oriented auditing firm, the foreign affiliates of that auditing firm are frequently the only auditors the subsidiaries are allowed to use, as far as the treasurer of the parent company is concerned (barring unusual circumstances). If each of the foreign subsidiaries is a small company, it is often most practical for it to get its accounting advice, tax advice, and intercompany pricing advice from the accounting firm that is also its auditor.

If the parent company has used a small, purely domestic auditing firm in the past, it may well become more practical, when going global, to change to an accounting firm with the ability to give advice on international matters. The main international accounting firms have highly valuable human resources when it comes to complex tax and accounting questions, such as minimization of global taxes and customs duties.

But don't go to your lawyer or auditor for management advice. This is the field of the management consultant. Some auditors have a separate management consulting department, which is fine if it is staffed with capable people. Another possibility is to go to the outside, independent management consultant.

Antitrust Law

The field of antitrust law has become so complex and so filled with pitfalls that it is impossible for anyone but the experts to keep up with it—and even for them it is hard. For that reason you must frequently ask legal advice in this area. Not being a lawyer, I am very careful never to give legal advice; here I will just make a few simple remarks from the viewpoint of a nonlawyer.

European companies used to have "exclusive" distributors, meaning that nobody could sell in anyone else's territory. Instead, many now work with "sole" distributors. The term means that you may not appoint any additional distributor within a given territory, but it leaves open the possibility for you and your other distributors to export into the territory thus assigned. The sole distributor there may also export to customers outside his own territory, even into other sole distributors' territories. In some fields, such as industrial equipment, this possibility is only a theoretical one because of the organization and after-sales service back-up needed, in practice, for a real sales effort.

The right to have sole distributorships in the Common Market was granted by an EEC regulation following the Grundig-Consten case (1964) that confirmed the outlawing of exclusive distributorships in the EEC.

To further confuse matters, the word "exclusive" is still used in distributorship agreements, but the new meaning is what used to be called sole.

The lawyers are most emphatic that there be no gentlemen's understanding that the distributors stay away from each other's territories or that they follow each other's pricing. I agree that such verbal understandings are wrong, even though they are very common among foreign companies. In the long run, it pays to keep actual business practice corresponding to that written into the legal agreements, even though the antitrust laws, especially in the area of licensing, make it very difficult for American businessmen to remain competitive with those foreign businessmen who do not have to labor under the severe restraints of the Sherman and Clayton acts.

What bothers me most is that some antitrust regulations are so vague and diffuse, with so many large gray areas that have no clear black or white answers, that even if a company tries hard to comply with the regulations, some employee may well do or write something illegal now and then. Also, foreign distributors who don't know U.S. antitrust regulations will often write letters that seem to imply that some illegal understanding is in effect, even though it is not. If a company is attacked for alleged antitrust violations and several such letters are taken out of context and presented in court, it can be difficult to prove that everything was done legally.

In antitrust matters, companies today sometimes find themselves in the same position as the mailman who sued the owner of a dog that had bitten him; he lost because the lawyers of the dog's owner proved in court that the mailman had bitten the dog.

Thus, the international businessman is constantly under the obligation not only to act in a legal manner, but also to insure that all his company's files positively confirm that everything was above-board. In a company that is sensitive to antitrust attacks, it is necessary to educate innocent foreign distributors not only about their rights to charge what they wish and sell where they wish, but also about refraining from writing the company and asking about what price they may charge and where they may sell. Such letters can be embarrassing if uncovered.

Some lawyers even prefer that instructions on such matters be given verbally and not in a letter, so that none of the files can later be taken out of context and presented in court to give the impression that a law had been broken.

As a matter of fact, some antitrust advisors virtually sound as if they advise not to exchange any information, not to sign anything, not to write anything, not to say anything, and not to sell anything—at any price.

We are concerned with three main groups of antitrust provisions:

1. The local antitrust regulations in each foreign country. In most countries these are not severe, but care must be exercised, especially in West Germany and (in the case of licensing) in Japan.
2. U.S. antitrust regulations. Even foreign subsidiaries of U.S. companies are subject to most of these, except the Robinson-Patman Act, which does not apply overseas. Also, the Federal Trade Commission Act is not used on behalf of foreign competitors.
3. The European Common Market Treaty, Articles 85 and 86.

These two Common Market Treaty articles are modeled after the U.S. antitrust laws and are directed against price fixing, undue control over making, selling, and developing goods, applying unequal conditions to different customers, and tie-in sales.

Article 85 prohibits agreements on the above matters between enterprises. It also prohibits agreements about division of territories. Thus, at least two enterprises must be involved to violate Article 85. Article 86, on the other hand, can be violated by a single enterprise, but only if it has a dominant position.

Both articles apply only within the Common Market. They are very easy to read, but you must use a lawyer to interpret them. On the surface, they are not at all as difficult to understand as the U.S. antitrust legislation.

Incorporation

In every country where a company is "deemed to do business" for income tax purposes for more than a year, it is usually a good policy to incorporate rather than work through a branch.

You are usually deemed to do business in a country if you sign acceptance of orders there, write contracts there, and so forth. On the other hand, you are not deemed to do business there if your employees travel only temporarily into the country for sales negotiations without signing sales contracts inside the country, or if your service personnel travel there only to execute repairs under warranty or to supervise installation of equipment. Thus, for income tax purposes, you are not deemed to do business in a country if you only sell from outside the country to distributors in the country.

Some people may tell you that you can conduct business in a foreign country through a branch, but unless you are a bank or other financial institution, unless it is only a paper or administrative operation, or unless you want to pay high fees later to international tax advisors, don't normally use a branch for conducting active trading or manufacturing in a foreign country. Governmental tax authorities of many countries are especially fond of branches, and you may end up paying income taxes to two countries on the same income—with no recourse.

Most governmental tax authorities consider that the incorporation of a subsidiary helps divide the income between countries in a somewhat clearer manner.

Patent Protection

Since there is no such thing as international patent protection, it is necessary to file for a patent in each of the countries where you want protection. The foreign filing in most countries must be done within one year after you have filed at home. For some Latin countries, however, notably France and Italy, you will sometimes need to file earlier. The Paris patent convention, which includes nearly all industrialized countries and some of the less industrialized ones, details some of the international patent relationships.

You can list the countries of the world in order of decreasing importance for your invention and stop wherever the potential benefits of patent protection don't seem to justify the costs. Don't forget to include the U.S.S.R. (See Chapter 19, which deals with East Bloc business.)

If you apply for foreign patents at the lowest possible expense to yourself, you will not get much more than mediocre translations of your U.S. patent application. You get really good applications only through working with a good patent agent in each country, a man who makes sure that your applications are in shape to give you the best possible protection under the local laws in his country.

This additional care is usually worth the additional cost, because not only patent laws, but the whole fundamental thinking behind patents varies widely from country to country. In most European countries, except the United Kingdom, a patent court will look at what is the basic, inventive idea, somewhat independently of the descriptive words. In the United States and the United Kingdom, on the other hand, the courts will generally look more closely at the precise words that define the idea. This fundamental difference becomes very important in many patent cases.

Whereas in the United States the date of priority is the date of the first provable disclosure, in most other countries the date of priority is the date of application to the patent authorities. Thus, there is no hurry in applying for a patent in the United States if you are interested only in U.S. protection.

But if you wish patent protection in other countries as well, and if there is risk that somebody else might be applying in another country, then you had better prepare your U.S. application fairly quickly and get it in, so that you don't lose out on the date of priority outside the United States to somebody applying there.

In some countries, a less expensive, weaker protection than that of a full patent is also available. It is valid for a shorter time. The most important of these is the German *Gebrauchsmuster*.

In the United States, the duration of a patent is 17 years *from the date of grant,* but in most other countries it is 17 years (or another number of years varying from 15 to 20) *from the date of application.* Since there may be quite a few years between the date of application and the date of grant, this difference actually means that the effective life of a patent is shorter in many countries than in the United States.

Japan is one important country with excellent patent protection— contrary to common belief in the United States and Europe.

Also contrary to common belief in the United States, most industrialized countries will grant rights and protection to foreign patent owners fully equal to those granted nationals, and the courts of industrialized countries will not discriminate unduly against foreigners in favor of nationals in patent matters—at least not in the vast majority of cases.

Some countries have a certain amount of discrimination officially built into their patent law, in that they require "working" of the patent within the country. What is meant by "working" varies from country to country, but it is usually some type of manufacturing of the patented device within the country.

Italy is such a country, but that particular Italian law has now been invalidated by the Common Market regulations against discrimination. Thus, we have in Italy the illogical situation where a foreign patent holder who has not "worked" his patent in Italy may lose patent suits in all courts up to the Supreme Court of Italy, but win there because the Supreme Court of Italy must obey the Common Market regulations, which are above the national laws of each member state.

Many countries, such as France and Spain, are referred to as *nonexamination countries*. In such countries, patents are issued easily and quickly without investigation, as a form of registration. Whether these patents have any validity or novelty are matters to be defended once they are challenged.

Other countries, for example, the United States and the United Kingdom, are referred to as *examination countries*. In these countries, patents are issued only after a thorough search of prior art and investigation of the patent claims for correctness, inventive character, and technical advance.

Since this investigation is a time-consuming process, new patents are likely to be published first in a nonexamination country. For this reason, at least one such country should be included among those in which a company is studying all new patents within its field of interest.

In the middle 1960s, the Netherlands started a new procedure that to some extent combines the advantages of both systems and thus puts the Netherlands in a separate group between the examination and the nonexamination countries. A similar new procedure was later adopted by West Germany and Japan. Since it is likely to spread to additional countries, I will describe briefly the three-step procedure to obtain such a patent.

Assume that you file only an initial patent application (Step 1) in the Netherlands, without filing at the same time a request for examination of novelty. Within one month, you will be notified in case there are any formal deficiencies in your application, but there will be no examination at this stage of the novelty, or patentability, of the invention. Eighteen months after your initial application, the application and any changes in it that you have requested are laid open to public inspection.

So far, the procedure is similar to that of nonexamination countries.

Then, if you or a third party files a petition for novelty examination (Step 2) and pays the fees for it, after some months you will receive an official letter stating the results of the novelty examination, but not stating whether the invention is otherwise patentable. Thereafter, you may "petition for grant"* of the patent (Step 3), provided that you do it within seven years from the initial application date. This last petition starts the lengthy procedure required before your patent is granted. Should your petition for grant not be filed within the seven-year period, then the initial application will lapse automatically.

If you have a device that is patented in the United States, and if you are bothered by a flood of infringing imports, then the U.S. customs authorities will under certain circumstances cooperate with the patent courts and stop the infringing devices from entering the country.

The customs authorities may even go one step further. Even if the patent applies not to the device itself, but only to a process used in manufacturing it, you may still under some circumstances be able to stop the importation of the device into the United States.

In foreign countries, as in the United States, a patent is worth nothing unless defended. But in each country, the cost of defending the patent must be weighed against the benefits. The cost of defending a patent is largely independent of the country's size, but the benefits are not. If the country is small, the benefits are usually small, so you may not want to defend the patent there. Thus, even though patent protection in small countries is, in theory, just as good as in large countries, the practical effect is that many patents are not worth defending in the small countries because the cost is bigger than the benefits. We therefore conclude:

Patent protection is in practice much better in the world's dozen largest industrial nations than in all the smaller countries.

SOME COMMENTS ON TRADEMARKS

The company that wishes to avoid future conflict between its new trademarks and those already owned by others should survey not only the similar trademarks existing in the United States, but also those in a

---

* In the Netherlands, a patent is in theory a favor granted by the Queen, not a right that an inventor can demand.

few other key countries, such as Germany, France, Japan (although such a survey is difficult there), and the United Kingdom. Compu-Mark, a Belgian firm,* offers international computerized trademark searches.

As I mentioned before, when licensing foreign factories, it is important to exercise quality control on all goods sold under your trademarks and to insist on the required quality. Word of bad quality spreads quickly today, even from the remotest corner of the earth to your biggest customers at home. (At least this is true in the field of industrial equipment.)

As mentioned in Chapter 4, never sell in any country the rights for a trademark that you intend to continue using at home, no matter what attractive tax and other advantages are offered. A sold trademark can leave you without rights for quality control. It might also be misused so that it becomes a generic term that anyone may use.

Contrary to the situation with patents, it is possible to obtain an "international trademark," provided that you have a resident business establishment in one of the following countries:

Austria	Italy	Rumania
Belgium	Liechtenstein	Spain
Czechoslovakia	Luxembourg	Switzerland
East Germany	Monaco	Tunisia
Egypt	Morocco	Vietnam
France	Netherlands	West Germany
Hungary	Portugal	Yugoslavia

Such an international trademark is valid only within these countries (notice that the United States is not included). I hope the United States and other industrialized countries will one day join this group.

Arbitration

Disputes on contracts covering matters that are international and commercial can be settled more conveniently and with less publicity by arbitration than through slow and expensive court procedures.

To prepare the way for arbitration, I recommend including in most international commercial contracts the following standard clause: "All disputes arising in connection with the present contract shall be finally settled under the Rules of Conciliation and Arbitration of the Interna-

* The firm's address is Aalmoezenierstraat 68, B-2000 Antwerp, Belgium. Telex: 31093.

tional Chamber of Commerce by one or more arbitrators appointed in accordance with the Rules."

Some may prefer to state instead a definite number of arbitrators, usually one or three. I prefer to add the national law applicable to the contract and the location of arbitration. This location should be within the territory of the national law applicable.

All parties entering into such a contract must, of course, consider that the arbitration is binding on both parties and that no appeal is possible for any reason.

Certain governmental agencies or public corporate bodies in some countries may have to state in advance that they waive their rights under national law to refuse to submit to arbitration.

Certain bankruptcy and patent matters, however, are specifically excluded from arbitration by the national laws of some countries, for example, matters of patent validity in France.

18

Operation Europe

TO most companies, Western Europe is by far the most important market outside the United States. Western Europe, of course, is geographically compact. The main industrial area is within some 500 miles of any logical European headquarters location. Yet, in each of the three largest West European countries, business must be handled in ways that are characteristic of that single country and different from the ways business is handled in other European countries.

Among some of the smaller European countries, however, there are certain similarities in the way business should be transacted. Thus, in this chapter I can make a few generalizations about West European business. (Some general comments about East European business appear in the next chapter.)

Three European Views of Americans

Any businessman worth his salt considers a piece of business from the other party's point of view during his preparations. Similarly, before going into Europe, we should spend some time looking at Americans from the viewpoint of many Europeans.

A lot of West Europeans consider Americans *naive, wealthy,* and *lacking in culture.* Why? Let's look at how each of these characteristics arose in the European mind, so that we in turn can understand the Europeans better.

"AMERICANS ARE NAIVE"

Broadly speaking, in the European view, the world is changing for the worse, or at least for something equally bad. True, the standard of living is improving, but that is a superficial matter; someone who thinks this means that the world is improving "must be naive." The world is more complex than that.

Take the European view of medicine, for instance. Certainly it is good that we can now operate for appendicitis, but consider all the poor old creatures who are being kept alive by fantastic modern machines and drugs although they suffer severely. They would be better off dead.

The European learns at school and at home that things are probably not as they seem on the surface, and are possibly the very opposite. The American attitude is to take things the way they appear, until and unless proved otherwise. This attitude the Europeans find incredibly naive. Frenchmen especially delight in showing their sophistication by approaching matters in exactly the opposite way.

How often has it happened to American executives traveling in Europe that we are asked about some perfectly simple, straightforward memo from the United States, "What is behind this?" We answer, "There is nothing behind it. The matter is simple; we have just decided to do it this way in the future."

But this answer never satisfies the European mind. Surely, the European thinks, there must be more behind this change—perhaps a sinister plot, perhaps a power struggle. If the traveling American doesn't reveal the real cause, he must have some reason—perhaps distrust in us? Although this American is naive, he could hardly be so naive as to believe that there is nothing beneath the surface!

The experienced American businessman, in this situation, will not sweep the question aside and go on discussing more "useful" things. He will sense that mutual trust and credibility are at stake, so he will take the time to describe all the considerations that went into the memo, what each American involved thought about the subject; he will ask the European whether he has any different viewpoints to put forth and whether the Americans in the company perhaps had forgotten some considerations. Thus, and only thus, will he reestablish trust.

But this takes time. Inexperienced American businessmen schedule too short stops and too little time with each person they see on their overseas trips, leaving no time for these "piddling details." The experienced manager schedules fewer stops and ample time with each person to nurture mutual trust, which is so important when the day-to-day dealings have to be by telex instead of in person.

Particularly in negotiations, Frenchmen consider Americans naive. An American, after figuring out a complex deal, will, as a general rule, back off a little to his own advantage for bargaining purposes, then present the whole deal to the other party on a take-it-or-leave-it basis. The American abhors losing time on lengthy negotiations, wanting eagerly to get them over with, so he can go on to the next deal.

To the Frenchman, this is silly and misses the whole fun of negotiating—dropping a hint here, making a large concession there in return for something substantial from the other party. If you want a concession on a certain point from a Frenchman, he will sometimes bluff unwillingness to even discuss that point. A Frenchman will tend to wear out an American at innumerable lunches and dinners, the finer points of which the Frenchman enjoys thoroughly. The American, on the other hand, feels only guilt about the adverse effects on his waistline.

Furthermore, the American feels under considerable pressure, trying to find his way in the seemingly Byzantine channels of the Frenchman's mind. In reality, this French mind is quite straightforward. It is made to appear more complex so that the Frenchman can come out of the negotiation with a better deal.

Typically, the Frenchman will be convinced that he has, in fact, come out better through long bargaining, and the American will be convinced that he is losing an inordinate amount of time. The American may be too afraid to call the Frenchman's bluff, thinking that he would be hurting his feelings.

Many French businessmen consider that their raison d'être is to negotiate deals, whereas Americans typically want to get things done as fast as possible.

How does the experienced American businessman get around all this? He does not deprive the Frenchman of his fun, but he designates another employee, whose time and waistline can be spared, to handle most of the negotiation. For this purpose, it is necessary that the Frenchman be given the impression that the other party is fully authorized to act on behalf of the American corporation and to make all concessions necessary. If the negotiator for the American side is not fully authorized, that fact must remain hidden from French ears, or the negotiations will halt quickly, until a truly authorized executive arrives on the scene and starts "wasting his time."

To operate the same way in Japan is often impossible, because the Japanese pay too much attention to the title of the person negotiating.

What has been stated about Frenchmen is true in varying degrees, and with some differences, about businessmen of nearly all the countries around the Mediterranean. For instance, the Italian will generally find the American attitude toward taxes incredibly naive—and ruinous financially.

"AMERICANS ARE WEALTHY"

Because of the large size of cars in the United States and because many American tourists in Europe have blue-collar jobs at home, Europeans are under the misconception that it is very expensive to live in the United States, and that American are much wealthier than they are. Let's look at why this is so.

Cars in Europe are generally still bought in accordance with status or wealth. Europeans forget that a full-sized, six-passenger, 350-horsepower American sedan costs less to buy and run in the United States than a small, four-passenger, 100-horsepower car in most of Europe, considering taxes, gasoline, and the like.

Few blue-collar Europeans can afford transoceanic tourism, and when they go on a trip in Europe, they often stay in inexpensive hotels without private bathrooms. Europeans do not know that many American blue-collar workers earn more than many American white-collar workers. Therefore, because some American blue-collar workers "do" Europe, many Europeans think that all Americans must be wealthy.

It is often difficult to negotiate salary with a European being transferred to the United States for the first time, because he is often under the impression that virtually all Americans earn over $30,000 a year. He discovers only slowly that this is not the case, and that it is vastly cheaper to buy food in the supermarket than his U.S. restaurant bills would seem to indicate. Also, Europeans do not realize that home appliances, many industrial products, and other goods are much less expensive in the United States than in Europe.

Even though Americans are not as wealthy as the Europeans think they are, they are still comparatively wealthy—and that fact causes resentment.

"AMERICANS LACK CULTURE"

The Americans most Europeans see in Europe are the tourists, who represent a good cross-section of the American people, including, as I said, many blue-collar workers and many self-made men with little schooling.

The Latin Americans, South Africans, and Japanese, on the other hand, whom most Europeans see visiting Europe are a select group of university-educated people from the top layer of their society. Most Europeans do not realize this difference, so they conclude that as a whole Americans are less educated or less cultured.

Europeans are generally very surprised when they see statistics showing that the percentage of university enrollment is over twice as high in the United States as in France, Germany, England, Denmark, Japan, and most other developed countries.

Other American traits showing "lack of culture" to Europeans include holding the fork in the "wrong" hand, not shaking hands with all the ladies at a party, and talking too loud.

Some people think that the lack of a Leonardo da Vinci, a Vivaldi, or a Bach in the United States clearly indicates a lack of culture. They disregard the fact that the United States did not even exist during the times of these men. Most Europeans do not stop to consider where the bulk of today's music comes from, or that *the* place to exhibit and study for most painters and sculptors is no longer Paris but New York.

Regarding the sciences, the high percentage of American Nobel prize winners is almost embarrassing.

If you should really want to put the needle into some cocky young European acquaintance filled with a vast sense of superiority, you can discuss the new "science" of management. (Sometimes I think it is more an art, though.) It is so American that most of the fundamental management words have not yet become known in their own local translation. Examples of words that are used in their American version in Germany, France, Sweden, and other countries overseas are such basic terms as "marketing" and "public relations."

But, of course, you are not so tactless with your French friend. Instead you prefer to ask him whether he thinks that today's youth movement has roots similar to those of Jean Jacques Rousseau's call for a return to nature.

Even so, you will hardly shake him in his firm belief that you must be naive, wealthy, and lacking in culture—after all, you are an American citizen, aren't you?

Deeply rooted wrong ideas are not held only by Europeans. There are quite a number of American tourists coming to Singapore, Hong Kong, and Taipei who discover to their amazement that all Chinese are not laundrymen.

Step by Step into Europe

When an American company's export business to Europe has grown (or perhaps failed to grow as much as it should) through independent distributors or licensees, the day may come when the American company is ready to start its own venture in Europe.

We are concerned here with setting up business in Europe according to a logical, step-by-step procedure in which the final objective is visualized from the start. Each step should be thoroughly prepared and smoothly executed, so that the European customers maintain their confidence in the parent company and feel only that distribution and service are getting better and better as the execution of "Operation Europe" progresses.

We assume that the suitability of the products has been thoroughly checked in advance, that the U.S. company has an astute international manager, and that the market in at least one European country is large enough to support a subsidiary. Usually, if the German, French, or British market is large enough, the other two markets are also, because these three markets are not too different in size for most products.

We will assume here that business will continue to be carried out through independent distributors in the smaller European countries.

We will also assume that no unusual circumstances make a joint venture more attractive than a subsidiary.

Usually, it is most logical to start in Europe by establishing a subsidiary in the largest market—West Germany or France perhaps, but rarely England first, despite the advantage of the language and despite England's entry into the EEC. This is because of England's physical and mental separation from the remainder of Europe (described later). Many American companies have made the mistake of putting the bulk of their European investments into England, simply because their executives understand the language.

When the first subsidiary has proven itself successful, the second one can be added in the next country, and when that one is also successful, the third logical subsidiary is started in another country, unless special circumstances or an unusually good distributor or licensee in one of the countries allows you to have only two subsidiaries. The second and third subsidiaries must in no way be made to feel that they are directed by or from the first one. Each must get its direction from the parent company in the United States or its resident representative in Europe.

If there is such a resident representative, coordinator, or European manager, he must be scrupulously careful to be neutral in his dealings with the subsidiaries. The personnel of any of the three major subsidiaries will resent it deeply if that company is considered secondary to another European subsidiary.

With the smaller European countries, this problem usually does not exist, but among the three leading countries one must thoroughly guard against it. Otherwise, this jealousy could seriously decrease efficiency. Thus, if a European manager or coordinator is to be appointed, he must be chosen very carefully, particularly if he should be German, French, or British.

As we saw in other chapters, most of the capital needed, except for seed investment, can be borrowed locally, and all the management and personnel should be European, except for those people doing the initial training, people who might be sent over on a strictly temporary basis, and executives involved with several countries.

Since little money and few, if any, employees leave the United States permanently for the European operations, the benefit that the U.S. parent company should give generously to the subsidiaries is training— not only technical product training, but also the management training that is so important.

Frequent and not too hurried travel by several key people from the United States to Europe and by several key Europeans to the United States should be encouraged. Their face-to-face exchange of ideas could give the European subsidiaries a great advantage over their European competitors.

It has been mentioned that in most cases it is better if building space is rented, at least during the first few years of European operations. When hunting for building space, some of the major considerations to keep in mind are the expansion possibilities, parking, and access to super-highways, airports, and, for some companies, railway stations.

We have seen in the chapter on staffing that it is advisable to have German management in Germany, French management in France, and British management in the United Kingdom. I also mentioned in the chapter on financing that most companies would do well also to present a German corporate face in Germany, a French one in France, and so on. The U.S. parentage need not be any secret, but for most companies it should be played down in these three major countries.

Usually it is better if even the corporate name seems to be of local origin. Names such as Cleveland Tool & Die G.m.b.H. or Globe Equipment S.A. do not help sales in Germany or France one bit. There are exceptions, of course. Any very well known company, such as Caterpillar, maintains its corporate identity around the world. Some companies can make their names easier to pronounce in many languages by abbreviating them, as IBM did. In certain industries, an American-sounding name can be a definite asset—particularly in many of the smaller European countries, and even in Italy.

An essential part of Operation Europe is to transfer the work of serving and supervising the distributors in the smaller European countries to one or two new centers. It is preferable to transfer such services for one distributor at a time to insure that he will be cared for better, and not worse, than before. Good preparations and capable international personnel are necessary requirements for a successful transfer.

If at any point in the Operation Europe time-plan the success of any step should not measure up to expectations, it should be possible to delay later major steps. Some companies have rushed through their plans too fast, or with inadequate personnel, and thereby damaged distributor and customer relations.

While one can slow down the steps of entering Europe (or Japan) with business ventures, one can never reverse them (unless you should discover some fundamental reason why you cannot make a profit in Europe—but you should have discovered that before you decided to proceed).

Entering Europe (or Japan) is not like entering Colombia: If the political or business situation in Colombia deteriorates, you can pick up your bag and leave. On the other hand, when entering Europe, you must do it wholeheartedly. If reverses are experienced, they must be worked out just as you would solve any problems you might have, for instance, in the Midwest.

The reason for this is that once you enter Europe or Japan with subsidiaries or joint ventures, you must stop thinking of the world as the United States plus some other areas. Europe and Japan are important, essential parts of the commercial–industrial globe, just as the Midwest and the East Coast are essential parts of the United States commercial market. Thus, once you enter Europe or Japan, you must start thinking globally.

Choice of a Distribution Center for Europe's Smaller Countries

Most medium-sized or small manufacturers would want to have one or more distributors in each of the smaller European countries where the market usually does not justify a distributing subsidiary.

One or two centers must then be chosen somewhere in Europe to provide these distributors with the necessary push, assistance, supervision, supplies, and service. Since it is important to have good travel connections and communications between the center and the remainder of Europe, only the suburban areas of a few cities can be considered: Brussels, Amsterdam, Frankfurt, or Paris. Usually, I would not consider London, Milan, Rome, Copenhagen, Düsseldorf, Hamburg, Munich, or Zurich, for various reasons.

London (and the remainder of England for that matter) is not Europe. It is a wonderful place to visit, with fine, honest people who even have the endearing habit of speaking a language you understand; but they are separated from Europe by much more than the Channel.

Mentally, they are removed from the mainstream of European attitudes. Although the English have been world traders since before the United States even existed, today you will find most international businessmen on the Continent thinking that the English somehow have lost the touch. On the Continent, deliveries and replies from Great Britain are expected to arrive late, while the English have their cup of tea.

The British customs authorities are worse than one would expect in an industrialized country, in terms of delays, red tape, uplifting the value of goods, and the like.

There is a big difference between the American and the Continental views of England: Americans (myself included) view England with love. It is a country of democracy, fair play, tolerance, good temper, and common sense. However, in Northern and Central Europe, outside the United Kingdom, England is viewed as the one industrialized country that has remained behind in development, a country plagued with wildcat strikes and impeded by more dedication to leisure than to work. A Continental industrial buyer is in a pickle if a British factory is the lowest bidder. The buyer worries: "Will they deliver on time? Will we get service when needed? Will they train our operators? If so, will they train them in our language?" Perhaps he has had too many bad experiences buying from England in the past. He prefers not to do it again if he can avoid it. This Continental attitude about England weighs heavily against deciding to place either an international sales office or a factory in the United Kingdom.

Milan is a place to which you had better not try to travel by air in fall and winter, when its two airports are closed by fog for extended periods.

Zurich and other Swiss cities used to be excellent locations for European centers until Switzerland closed down on foreign residence permits in a harsh and shortsighted move.

Rome and *Copenhagen* are too far from the geographic center of Europe; but if one center had to serve only Finland, Scandinavia, and the Benelux countries, then Copenhagen is well located. Danish personal income taxes, however, will be a barrier if you try to attract international executives to live there.

Düsseldorf, Hamburg, and *Munich* lack the excellent air connections of Frankfurt.

Either *Frankfurt* or *Paris* is, of course, a logical location for your European center—if you want it combined with the subsidiary serving either Germany or France. In the long run, of the two cities, Frankfurt will be the less expensive location for most companies. It will probably also be politically and economically more stable, and suffer fewer interruptions due to strikes.

But a location in Germany, France, or Great Britain has a major disadvantage as a center for European operations, because of the attitude of the people in these three countries. This attitude disadvantage is little understood in Germany, France, and Great Britain, and even less understood in the United States, which is even less international-trade-minded. Therefore, I will explain it:

The smaller countries in Western Europe comprise over 40 percent of the West European market. Their attitudes, interests, and desires are quite different from those of the three big countries. International trade is so much more important to the smaller countries than to Germany and France that all the people in the smaller countries—from secretaries and postal clerks to executives—have a more positive attitude to foreign trade than Germans and Frenchmen.

Customers in the small countries feel this difference. When they deal with a German or a French company, they are usually shunted to an export department often staffed with the least experienced people (who are the least unwilling to travel). On the other hand, when these same customers deal with a Belgian, Dutch, Scandinavian, or Swiss firm, they are treated as the prime customers.

Try telephoning an internationally active company in Germany, France, or the United Kingdom. Chances are that its telephone operator will speak only the language of her own country. Telephone instead an internationally active company in any of the smaller countries, and you can be fairly certain that the first girl you talk to speaks some English, German, and French in addition to her own language.

To be international-trade-minded is important, not only for your salesmen and executives, but also for your shipping clerks, secretaries, billing clerks, telephone operators, and other personnel. Englishmen, Germans, and Frenchmen do not grow up with as much international orientation in their everyday lives as people in the smaller countries.

If you don't believe me, ask any experienced Scandinavian, Benelux, or Swiss international businessman, and he will generally confirm that for the best and smoothest interpersonal relations with customers and distributors in the smaller European countries, you should also put your European center in one of the smaller countries.

Italians, Spaniards, and Portuguese have a certain brotherly understanding of each other and for Frenchmen. This understanding goes beyond the close relationship of their languages. For that reason, customers in these countries do not object to dealing with a European center in France as much as Dutch or Swedish customers would object to dealing with a European center in England, Germany, or France.

Many North Europeans, including most Germans, have little understanding of Mediterranean people, so you would generally do best to have international staff of South European origin looking after the smaller countries around the Mediterranean, and international staff of Scandinavian, Dutch, Belgian, or Swiss origin looking after the remaining small countries of Western Europe.

Brussels and *Amsterdam* remain at the top of the list as a choice for a center to serve all the smaller countries of Europe. Whether Brussels or Amsterdam is chosen depends on where you can get the best sum of advantages.

Belgium has the lowest corporate taxes and a very favorable tax treatment of non-Belgian international staff that travels a lot. This advantage may substantially hold down your payroll costs. A Belgian location, with its personal tax advantage, may enable you to attract some of the most qualified Europeans in your business. No other EEC country offers as good tax advantages as Belgium.

Amsterdam's airport, Schiphol, has one of the best free trade zones in the world for air freighted goods. Other countries will state that they have just as good facilities, but with the exception of the Colón free trade zone in Panama, I have not seen any zone as free from red tape and governmental interference as the one in Schiphol. Rotterdam is equally excellent for surface shipments.

In either place, you can receive goods from abroad, check them, make minor changes, stock them, repackage them, and ship them elsewhere by air or surface transportation without interference from Dutch authorities.

If you don't wish to tackle these duties with your own staff, a dozen private, competing firms stand ready to do it all for you on a contract basis and for very reasonable charges. As a matter of fact, if your products do not require too specialized know-how, chances are that these professional stocking–forwarding firms can carry out the physical distribution more cheaply and better than your own personnel.

To summarize, then, unless special conditions apply to your company, the ideal home base for a multilingual, expensive European traveling staff is Brussels, and the best European physical distribution center is Schiphol for air freighted goods and Rotterdam for surface freighted goods. Because of excellent telephone and telex communications, the two locations can be combined, so that the central office and home base is near Brussels, but packing, stocking, and shipping are centered some 120 miles away in Schiphol or 85 miles away in Rotterdam. (Both cities will be connected to Brussels by superhighway shortly after this book goes to press.)

Roughly half the European market is within a good half-day's drive of Brussels, and over three-quarters of the European market is within one day's drive of Brussels.

European Manufacturing

The first question of a newcomer to Europe is whether to manufacture in Europe at all.

West European businessmen and Japanese businessmen often take it for granted that most things made in the United States have cost too much to manufacture. This is quite wrong. Much manufacturing is done at a lower cost per unit in the United States than in Europe or even Japan, despite the higher hourly wages in the United States. And it is amazing how often raw materials, components, and subassemblies can be purchased more cheaply in the United States than anywhere else.

I state these facts to point out that manufacturing in Europe (or Japan) is not always as self-evident an advantage as many otherwise experienced European (or Japanese) executives think.

Yet, in a large market like that of Western Europe, most manufacturers will not be really strong until they have located a substantial part of the whole business cycle for the European business within Europe. Of course there are many exceptions to this rule, but let's look at the situation a little further.

Refer to Figure 1 on page 15, which shows the whole business cycle: product development, manufacturing, and sales. The company that only markets in Europe, without manufacturing there, may well earn money for the time being; but it is not built on solid European foundations that will enable it to weather technological changes and competitive onslaughts.

In some companies, however, such as those in the heavy industrial equipment field, part of the product development function should remain *central* for the whole world, for reasons outlined elsewhere in this book. It is equally important for some companies dealing in consumer products that part of the product development function be *decentralized* in order to stay physically close to the different markets.

Considerations regarding the choice of country for manufacturing in Europe were discussed in Chapter 14.

Barriers Between European Countries

Believe me, barriers exist; and between some European countries they are high. They even tower between some countries that have belonged to the EEC for years, and even between those that speak the same or similar languages. Don't believe that a Frenchman in Lille, France, can sell well in Belgium, 20 miles away, across a border with no customs duty and in areas where they speak French.

If they are totally honest, Germans and Frenchmen will admit that they really don't like to do business with Englishmen. As a matter of fact, Germans and Frenchmen don't even like to do business with each other, despite the length of time they have been together in the Common Market. Germans and Frenchmen wish their countries were self-sufficient, though they will not, of course, admit it in polite conversations.

Emotional barriers between European countries are so formidable that many American parent companies have found their various European subsidiaries embarking on quite divergent roads, often conflicting with each other.

An inexperienced American parent company manager might think that a little healthy competition between the European subsidiaries would be good. But he is inviting trouble. Before long, the subsidiaries might well be competing with each other so relentlessly that they forget to compete with outsiders.

In technical matters as well, subsidiaries tend to pull in opposing directions instead of in the same way. Sometimes the worst mistake an industrial salesman in Europe can make when he wants to sell equipment to an American subsidiary is to tell the company that its sister company in a neighboring country bought his product. This may well invite the prospect to find every excuse for buying the product of a competitor instead of what was chosen by "those dumb bastards on the other side of the border."

The same salesman would have been much safer if he had mentioned that his product had been bought by the local competitor of the American subsidiary.

It is impossible to completely avoid this attitude of competition, slight, and scoffing between European subsidiaries; but it is obviously necessary to minimize it and to put strong management efforts, time, and expense into doing so.

There are various ways of easing the problem. You can try to select internationally oriented top and middle managers, preferably multilingual men. You can sometimes temporarily interchange two middle managers between two countries or have one man help out in a sister company for several months. You can form international steering committees of middle managers within the same field, such as a marketing committee or an engineering committee. (These committees may not accomplish much in relation to the time spent, but at least the members get to see things from one another's viewpoints.) You can also appoint a European coordinator if you can find a good man for the job; but such men are rare indeed.

At the same time, you must also avoid allowing a European manager, or even a European headquarters, to become too strong and to try to tell each subsidiary how to run its business.

You may need a European manager, but he must be careful not to usurp the power that rightfully belongs to each subsidiary in order to ensure maximum efficiency. This manager may be either a European or an American. If he is a European, he must be somebody other than a manager of one of the subsidiaries. (Otherwise the other subsidiaries would feel themselves to be at a severe disadvantage.)

An exception to this general rule can be made if the management of one of the subsidiaries is weak. Then the European manager can step in and temporarily run the company that is faltering. But he should also step out again as soon as possible after finding a permanent solution, preferably a good manager for the company.

Caution: Europe Will Change You!

Do not consider Europe as just another market to be exploited for the company's products. Having this attitude will rob you of much of the benefits European operations can give a company.

Say you want to market in a small Latin American or African country. You organize the distribution of your products there, you ship the products to the country, and you take home your profits. The small country has given you nothing but additional profits and sales volume.

Europe is another matter. You go there, you make a small seed investment and nurse its growth with European capital and European executives and employees. But above all, you should make sure that your domestic and worldwide operations are enriched by ideas from your European subsidiaries and from your European competitors, suppliers, and customers.

For most American companies that undergo this expansion into Europe, the results are much more than increased net profits and gross volume. Europe changes the view of central top management from the concept of the United States plus various export markets to the concept of a global theater of operations with new ideas and new developments coming back to the parent company from the different countries, just as they might come in from California and New England to a parent company in New York. Thus, Europe widens the company's horizon.

What has been said above about Europe can be repeated about Japan.

Conversely, the same is even more true about European and Japanese companies expanding into the United States. Any European company that considers the United States (or Japan) as just another export market, only bigger, makes a tremendous mistake. A U.S. subsidiary will profoundly affect the very core of any European or Japanese company. If this should not be the case, then the company has not utilized the benefits of operating in the United States.

In the same manner, the rare American company that does not find its fundamental central management thinking changed by its operation in Europe has missed one of the main benefits of global operations. Such a company should consider letting key men from several parts of the company—management, research, engineering, manufacturing, and marketing—spend more time in Europe with orders not only to talk but also to listen.

If the communications barrier with Japan were not so high, the same guideline would undoubtedly be useful there too.

As I said before, key European employees should also spend time at the U.S. headquarters. The visitors from both sides of the ocean always find that they discuss many more matters than they had planned. True communication will considerably enrich both parties. This, however, requires that an atmosphere for good cross-pollination of ideas has already been established by top management.

19

East Bloc Business

IN his 1965 State of the Union Message, President John F. Kennedy urged American businesses to increase trade with the Soviet Union and the East European satellites. Every administration since then has continued to encourage this trade expansion, and the Bureau of Export Control has repeatedly eased its regulations setting forth what constitutes goods for peaceful purposes, which may be exported to the East Bloc, and what constitutes goods for military purposes, which may not.

After having conducted business in most of the East European countries since 1965, I am convinced that trade in peaceful goods builds bridges to the East and does more good than harm for the United States.

Presently, the greatest barrier to increased East–West trade is the East Bloc's total inexperience in marketing in the West. If they acquire this experience, they will undoubtedly multiply their present sales to the West and earn enough hard currency to be able to purchase the products they so dearly want from the West.

Lately, there have been indications that the East Bloc countries are slowly starting to improve their marketing in the West through joint ventures with Western firms—a very sensible approach.

However, since they are learning Western marketing methods so slowly, it seems unrealistic to expect convertibility of the ruble in the foreseeable future. Their import restrictions will continue to be the main barrier to be hurdled by Western salesmen.

Prior to beginning any sales efforts from the United States to the East Bloc, you should find out from the Bureau of Export Control of the U.S. Department of Commerce whether your products may be sold to the East Bloc. For exports from a foreign affiliate to the East Bloc, a similar clearance should first be obtained from the Office of Foreign Assets Control, U.S. Department of the Treasury. (Any attempts to export to Rhodesia and Cuba should be cleared in the same manner.)

In this chapter, we will first consider traveling to the U.S.S.R., then selling to the U.S.S.R., and finally the differences between selling to the U.S.S.R. and selling to the satellite countries. In the next chapter I will make some guesses about future developments in Eastern Europe.

Some U.S.S.R. Travel Hints

Visa requirements vary from time to time, but the only European East Bloc countries that have usually required much red tape before issuing visas are the U.S.S.R. and Poland.

It is best to try to get an official invitation from the organization in the U.S.S.R that you are dealing with. You can then apply to the U.S.S.R. Embassy in Washington for a service visa as an official visitor. This visa affords you a more comfortable, more pleasant, and cheaper trip than a tourist visa, which requires you to make arrangements through Intourist, forcing you to pay a large daily fee for room, board, guide, and transportation. I much prefer having neither the guide nor prepaid transportation.

If you are going to the East Bloc for the first time, I advise you to spend an hour in advance learning the Cyrillic alphabet (and the few letters in the Polish alphabet that are different from ours). Then, even if you don't speak the language, you can read street signs and find a restaurant or a business office. I find this knowledge indispensable for driving in Soviet cities. (You can look up these alphabets in good travel handbooks and even in some American dictionaries.)

Don't get upset over the horribly slow service in the restaurants. Just keep telling yourself that the personnel has not really singled you out personally to receive extra slow service. Incredible as it may seem, they are giving the same slow service to everybody else, and no shouting or pleading will make them change for anyone.

Tipping is customary only in the one single excellent restaurant in Moscow, the Aragvi. It is so good that you nearly always have to invent some gimmick just to get in. (I won't tell my gimmick, because then I'll have to invent a new one.)

Don't be disappointed in your Moscow hotel. The other hotels there are no better, so don't complain.

Don't mail home any dictated belts, tapes, or similar nonwritten material from the Soviet Union or from any other country that has censorship. Some businessmen advise not to leave any highly confidential material (such as papers stating your lowest price) in your hotel room or anywhere else. They feel that you should carry confidential figures preferably only in your head, or possibly on your person. However, I doubt that anyone would touch your documents or tape the conversations in your room. On the other hand, you will never know for sure.

It is highly unlikely that you will be drawn into any political discussion by Soviet business executives, but if you are, you can usually make them laugh by describing yourself as "only a capitalist" and then quickly change the subject.

If, despite serious efforts, you should fail to get out of a political discussion, remember that words mean different things over there. The word "democratic" often means to them what "communist" means to you. "Socialist" is the word you should use in most cases when you would say "communist" at home. The opposite is "capitalist," but that word has quite a different shade of meaning there, a criticizing, derogatory one. If you want to avoid that connotation, you can use other words, such as "Western." The expression "free enterprise" is often not understood at all. "Freedom" to them usually means "freedom from capitalist oppression" or other evils of which you have never even heard. A "Russian" is a person from only one specific country in the U.S.S.R., one of their republics. Many of the people you meet in Moscow are not Russians, although they are citizens of the Union of Soviet Socialist Republics. The nationalism of the different countries or republics in the U.S.S.R. is strong. Many Soviet citizens, speaking different languages, are proud that they are not Russians but rather, say, Ukrainians, Lithuanians, or Kazakhs.

The Western businessman who travels in the East Bloc does so to conduct business there, not to spread any political beliefs, no matter how strongly felt. He should stay away from any political proselytizing, just as much as any communist businessman traveling in the West should avoid all political activity. Political propagandizing on either side never promotes good business deals.

There would be no more point in criticizing Soviet standards of living or shortcomings than there would be in talking to your host at a party about the cracking paint in his living room and the dirt on his worn rug. Such criticism is just as rude in the U.S.S.R. as in the West. The Soviet people have made achievements in health, education, welfare, and many other areas, so there are plenty of subjects to discuss and learn about, other than their obvious shortcomings.

Frederick Dewhurst of the Twentieth Century Fund points out: "Of all the great industrial nations, the one which clings most tenaciously to the capitalist system has come the closest to the socialist goal of abundance for all in a classless society." Of the Soviet citizens who talk to Westerners, travel abroad, or read and hear about the West, many will draw this same conclusion without being prodded in any way by Westerners.

When you finally do get to talk to the actual Soviet decision-makers you have gone to see, you will find them very capable, very pleasant, and amazingly similar to intelligent decision-makers in the West.

Selling to the U.S.S.R.

Your foremost consideration is to have available what the Soviet side wants to buy. Consumer goods are usually not salable in quantity to the Soviet Union. Equipment for industry, especially sophisticated equipment for mass production industry, is what they want. And if you sell industrial equipment, you will find Soviet buyers eager to get the most highly automated models, despite the additional cost.

The Soviet buyers much prefer dealing with the leading company in each industry. Khrushchev once said, "I like much better dealing with a fat capitalist than with a thin capitalist." (But don't ever quote Khrushchev over there!)

No matter what your field is, you will encounter Soviet specialists in your field who have thoroughly studied the best Western trade magazines and technical books. If they do not already know your company's standing in relation to your Western competitors, you can usually explain this to the specialists. It would be well worth your while to try to convince them of the superiority of your products. Even though you see no immediate results, you may find years later that your products have been singled out and specified in some large Soviet purchases. At that stage, your competitors may find that their efforts to change the specifications fall on deaf ears.

While it is all right to invite to lunch or dinner several of the Soviet people you are dealing with (not just one alone), it is, on the other hand, pointless to try to establish a personal friendship with the Soviet buyers. They are bureaucratic employees, and you should never put them in a position where they could possibly be criticized for buying from you. Personal friendships in the U.S.S.R. can be very useful, but only if they are at the very highest levels.

Soviet organizations are sometimes eager to buy technology through a license agreement, whenever this is the better solution for them. This was not formerly the case. Years ago, they often bought some units of equipment, copied them, and then ended up with yesterdays' technology after having spent a lot of engineering time on the effort. Now, they often prefer to buy today's and tomorrow's technology in the form of drawings, samples, and licenses, rather than going through all the work by themselves.

The U.S.S.R. is a member of the Paris convention on patents. Therefore,

> *It is now worthwhile to apply for Soviet patents on major new industrial processes and devices that you are patenting in other major countries.*

Some businessmen don't agree with this policy because patents cannot be policed in the U.S.S.R, but I doubt that there is any more violation of patent rights going on in the Soviet Union than in Western Europe, and there may well be less, provided you pay attention to your Soviet patent rights. No Soviet executive likes to be caught cheating.

Thus, having Soviet patents greatly strengthens your position as a prospective licensor to the Soviet Union.

All non-Soviet technology is bought by Licensintorg, one of some 40 foreign trade organizations (here called FTOs) in the Soviet Ministry of Foreign Trade. Licensintorg acts as a capable, tough purchasing agent. But Licensintorg does not normally decide what to buy or how much the U.S.S.R. can pay for it. These decisions are usually made by the State Committee for Coordination of Scientific Research (SCCR), and approved by the All Union ("Federal") Planning Committee, Gosplan. Both these organizations report to the Supreme Economic Council (VSNKH), which in turn reports directly to the lofty Council of Ministers of the U.S.S.R.

Together, the FTOs handle all foreign trade of the Soviet Union. Certain classes of articles are assigned to each FTO. The one that buys your product has a monopoly position for that product, and the same one buys from your competitors around the world. There is no way for you to sell to the Soviet Union except through that FTO. You cannot go around it.

I emphasize this because the first reaction of any red-blooded American salesman, although very well aware that the FTO is the only purchasing agent, will be to try to find a way around it and contact the ultimate decision-makers. He will discover that this is difficult to accomplish, almost impossible, and in any case, dangerous to your good relations with the FTO—unless you first ask their permission, or at least keep them fully informed of what you are doing.

Even if you tell them verbally about your plans to contact someone else, you should also confirm this in writing, so that your file at the FTO is complete when the personnel changes.

Western salesmen are accustomed to first creating a desire for their products among the ultimate users and then contacting purchasing agents to get the sales contracts signed. But in the Soviet Union, it is often pointless to contact the ultimate users because they want your product anyway. So you need only go back to the FTO, which will actually buy the products—with approval from Gosplan, SCCR, or other agencies.

As a salesman in the U.S.S.R., you are in a position similar to that of a salesman for children's candy: Do you really need to give a sales talk to the children? If you can convince their dad to untie the purse strings, then you've got it made!

Use only *very soft selling* in the U.S.S.R., and be prepared to give many facts about your products and to answer very detailed technical questions.

If you can illustrate your sales pitch with an overhead projector, slides, movies, samples, or other visual aids, you will increase its impact. (Bring your own equipment. Only 220 v., 50 Hz. will work on the European and Asian continents.) It is difficult to find projection equipment in Moscow.)

Because of the need for a highly technical presentation, normally I would not use an export sales agent traveling from the United States, even if he specializes in East Bloc trade. The main exceptions—the times when it is advantageous to use an American export agent—are cases where the prospective volume and profit are small, or when the U.S. exporter can combine the products with those of other manufacturers in a logical package.

In other instances, if you do want outside help for your U.S.S.R. sales, you might try to be represented by one of the Western-owned trading offices, which are located either in hotel suites in Moscow or in the only Moscow building for such offices. Being permanently on the spot, they may be of greater use to you than someone located in New York or San Francisco. So might a West European agent, in some cases.

Another possibility, probably better if your products are at all complex, is to let one of your wholly owned West European subsidiaries handle the East Bloc, as agent for the U.S. parent company. This is assuming, of course, that the subsidiaries have someone available who is experienced in East Bloc trade.

Soviet buyers much prefer dealing directly with the principal seller, rather than with middlemen, but they don't quite consider a West European wholly owned subsidiary a middleman, particularly not if your representatives are highly qualified in technical matters and are given full authority to negotiate concessions without having to ask the U.S. parent company. Also, Soviet buyers like to deal with a combination of an inside company man, who is a technical expert on the product, and an outside advisor who can guide an East–West trade deal to a successful conclusion.

Normally, you should try to stay away from Amtorg in New York and other Soviet trading posts in the West, unless they contact you. Dealing directly with the appropriate FTO in Moscow is best, and you can find out which one is for you simply by writing and asking the Ministry of Foreign Trade* or the Chamber of Commerce of the U.S.S.R. (The latter also arranges expositions.) But don't expect quick replies to any letter.

Don't travel to Moscow unprepared, with no appointments or concrete information on procedures, thinking that you can find out everything there in person. If you are unlucky, you may not get to see anyone for weeks. Make your appointments long in advance, by mail or telex. When you do arrive, *arm yourself with lots of patience.* As traders with the East Bloc know from long and bitter experience, the need for patience is enormous.

Many experts state that it is necessary to wait at least two years before you can reap the first benefits of any sales efforts toward the East Bloc, but I have found that this is not the case. An intelligent sales effort may bear fruit in less than a year, though it may sometimes take longer, particularly if the products must first be entered into the five-year import plan of the Soviet Union.

For most industries, advertising in the U.S.S.R. is of questionable value, particularly advertising in media other than specialized magazines. Vneshtorgreklama is the Soviet organization you must use if you nevertheless want to try advertising in the U.S.S.R. They will furnish advice on media, direct mail, and so forth.

Your well-planned, well-executed participation in the right trade

* The address is 32/34 Smolenskaya, Moscow G-200.

exhibition in the U.S.S.R. can be a good door-opener. It can also be very costly, so get a positive statement of serious interest in your products prior to participating in a trade show.

Such statements of buying interest cannot be taken sufficiently seriously to justify a decision to invest in a trade exhibition if the statements come from organizations merely specializing in mounting exhibitions in the East Bloc, or from anyone else who has an ax to grind. But if you hear these same statements directly from high-level executives in the FTO serving you, or even better, in the organizations with the power of decision behind the FTO, then it may pay you to participate in a trade show on a substantial basis.

Ship over everything you need for the exhibition and make sure it is extremely well packed. A large supply of cheap give-away lapel buttons is extremely popular at such East Bloc exhibitions, especially if the origin, U.S.A., is plainly visible.

Have capable personnel available to answer the technical questions and to spend lots of time there before, during, and especially after the exhibition. Interpreters can be hired locally for very low fees. (Some little knowledge of the Russian language is nevertheless very useful for getting around alone in Moscow.)

If you are serious about your sales efforts to the U.S.S.R, then your main quotations, letters of transmittal, and main brochures should be in Russian, just like the give-away lapel buttons.

Unless you have perfect understanding not only of the Russian language but also of the Soviet way of thinking, you should sign only the English copy of any contract, not the Russian copy.

In a big negotiation, when presented with the standard Soviet purchase contract, the proper reaction is to pull out immediately your own "standard" sales contract and to be willing to discuss a few concessions from it, rather than irritate the buyers by wanting to change nearly everything in their contract.

Don't be surprised if the buyers are uninterested in getting spare parts, service, or training in how to use your products.

In the U.S.S.R., American industrial equipment is often considered to be of the highest quality in the world, probably followed by West German, other West European, Japanese, Czech, East German, and—far down the line—Soviet equipment. Of course, this is a wild generalization, and it has many exceptions. Nevertheless, major American manufacturers of industrial equipment are starting out with an excellent reputation in the U.S.S.R., even before they start selling in the East Bloc.

Usually, it is best for these American companies to offer their American-made products, rather than products made by their subsidiaries in other countries. The buyers often have more confidence in the "original" products.

On the other hand, if long credit terms are required, then it is better to provide the goods from a subsidiary's factory in France, Japan, the United Kingdom, Belgium, or some other country that gives excellent government help in providing the necessary credit at low interest rates.

Credit terms are usually requested for orders of durable goods of over $100,000. For larger orders, those of over half a million dollars' worth of heavy equipment, the credit requirements are long-term. For the largest orders, several years may be specified.

For long-term credit, you may want to insist on a State Bank (Gosbank) guarantee on major promissory notes, even though this is illogical from the U.S.S.R. viewpoint, because the State Bank is just another branch of the same employer, the government. Nevertheless, you can explain that the State Bank guarantee will make it easier to discount the notes in the West, "where people don't understand the Soviet system."

The notes can usually be discounted without trouble in several West European banks, including the Soviet-owned Moscow Narodny Bank in London. Gosbank controls the policy of the Foreign Trade Bank, Vneshtorgbank.

The FTO will agree only to certain maximum interest rates. Often the FTO will state in advance that the purchase will be for cash and ask you to quote only cash terms. Once you have done this, they may ask you for the credit terms, and you are then presumably stuck with the low maximum interest rate that Soviet buyers will allow.

Western firms, however, know this buying technique well. Therefore, when quoting cash in the first place, they include in the cash price an allowance for the present value of the difference between the interest they want and the interest they can get, both calculated over the expected period of credit required.

More importantly, they also include other types of allowances that they have found necessary. Some of these may be for special higher costs incurred to satisfy unusual requirements in packing or installation.

The two largest allowances are usually made for the final bargaining session and (more often in satellite countries than in the U.S.S.R.) for barter or switch deals. The allowance for final bargaining gives the Western firm the valuable opportunity to come down in price several percentage points, once the FTO has been given orders to close the deal at the lowest price they can bargain down to.

Of course, the FTO is the main beneficiary of this bargaining allowance. Afterwards, they can boast how much money they have "saved the U.S.S.R." The FTO shuns companies that quote firm prices and that have no margin for bargaining.

The allowance for *barter deals* makes it possible for the seller to accept payment in goods from the country he is selling to, in lieu of Western currency. The alternative allowance for *switch deals* makes it possible for the seller to accept payment in goods from a third country, often a less industrialized country, in lieu of Western currency.

Of course, the seller does not actually take possession of the goods in such barter or switch deals, but converts the rights to them to hard currency at one of the Zurich or Vienna banks or other firms specializing in barter and switch deals. These firms will accept the barter goods for a fee, the size of which diminishes, the more easily salable the goods are. The fee may range from 5 percent to several times that figure; the percentage will usually be higher for a small deal than for a large one.

Prepare for your negotiations in satellite countries by finding out in advance what export goods the customer might have that can be easily converted to dollars. Some of the main banks that handle barter and switch deals are, in Zurich, Bank für Handel und Effecten, Bank Hoffman, and Bank Cantrade; and in Vienna, Bank Winter & Co.

The bargaining sessions in Moscow can be long and arduous. Executives sent there to go through them must have not only tremendous patience, but also lots of plain old stamina, an even temper, a good sense of humor, and a fair capacity for vodka.

These executives must pay careful attention to every word and dot in the contract. If they want room for future variance from the contract, such provisions must be clearly spelled out from the beginning, because otherwise it may later be totally impossible to get permission for any variance, even if it seems perfectly reasonable to the Western mind. But it may be impossible for a communist bureaucrat to allow it.

On the other hand, once the contract is signed, the Soviet party will fulfill its obligations down to the last iota, and the credit risk is nil. I do not think there is any known commercial case of an unwarranted delay in payment from the U.S.S.R. (Lend-lease was political, not commercial.)

When the final deal is negotiated, don't be surprised if there are some 15 people on the other side of the table. Everything you say will be translated, even though most of them will understand English. Only parts of their conversations will be translated back to you by their interpreter.

An acquaintance of mine went through two days of negotiations noticing that one of the many people on the other side never opened his mouth—that is, not until they reached the arbitration clause of the contract. Then this person came alive; he did all the talking and was most difficult to deal with, at that. Apparently, he was their arbitration clause expert.

Speaking of that, you might as well use the standard arbitration clause of the International Chamber of Commerce in Paris, but use Sweden (or Switzerland) as the location of arbitration and have Swedish (or Swiss) law govern the agreement. This is much more acceptable to Soviet buyers than U.S. law. It should also be acceptable to you, because Swedish and Swiss legal thinking is quite logical to American international lawyers.

The Soviet side often wants a U.S. or Soviet location for arbitration, depending on which party raises the complaint. This will not provide the best protection for the type of misunderstandings that may well come up. The Soviet side will usually back away from having a disagreement arbitrated in any Western country.

If you choose Sweden, you may want to use Sweden's Technical Industrial Arbitration Institute, Sveriges Tekniska Industriella Skiljedomsinstitut.

The only lack of performance you can expect from Soviet buyers is caused by differences between their thinking and ours. An example will illustrate this difference.

A large mill was being built at a remote location in the U.S.S.R. The Soviet buyers were to provide deluxe housing, food, and transportation for the American equipment installation supervisors, who had to stay several months.

The "deluxe" housing was far from luxurious and did not even approach Howard Johnson standards, but it was accepted willingly by the Americans. Between the housing and the site of the mill, however, there was a distance of a couple of miles. Consequently, the Americans stated to the Russians that they needed daily transportation.

To the Soviet people, it was quite natural to walk this distance, and they maintained that transportation was "clearly understood" to mean from the U.S. to the place of housing, and return. So the Americans walked to work.

In a contract, it is important to spell out the maximum time you will allow for each step, and the maximum time a man can be kept in the U.S.S.R. without allowing him to return home to see his family. Soviet thought on such matters is quite different from ours.

The man, or men, you do send over must be instructed not to sign any paper that contains unclear phrases he does not fully understand and agree with, which might later obligate his company.

Normally, a daily written record is kept of what happens on a Soviet installation site. It is presented daily to both parties for signature. Called the *protocol,* it may become a very important document in case of a dispute on some borderline subject.

While people in the Soviet Union have little regard for time in many instances, they do take delivery times seriously, and they require Western suppliers to be just as meticulous in keeping to promised delivery times as they would be themselves. Consequently, Western firms are well advised to quote ample delivery times and to make doubly certain that they do not deliver late—both to avoid costly penalties and to avoid damaging their own name as a trusted supplier.

One of the basic differences between Soviet and American legal thinking in the writing of an agreement is that the American puts much thought into his possibilities of recourse in case of noncompliance, whereas the Soviet executive takes compliance for granted and finds the American preoccupation with noncompliance irritating, useless, and even insulting.

Differences in Selling to the East European Satellite Countries

All European communist countries except Yugoslavia (and Albania, which is not discussed here at all) have their society and governmental organization patterned after the U.S.S.R. model. Therefore, trading with the satellites should in theory be identical to trading with the Soviet Union.

In fact, a few similarities do indeed exist: These countries all have their FTOs and their science academies. It is also important to build your reputation with these organizations.

But otherwise, business in East European satellite countries varies widely from country to country. In Yugoslavia, where you deal directly with major industries, conditions for doing business are in some respects quite similar to those in some West European countries. In most of the other satellite countries, it is usually preferable at least to start out with the appropriate FTO.

I hesitate to outline in which countries you should deal with the FTOs and in which you should deal directly with the ultimate customers, because this would vary from industry to industry and from circumstance to circumstance. In all satellite countries, certain major companies have permission to buy directly from abroad, without going through an FTO.

If goods similar to yours are produced in a satellite country, you can of course consider the organization producing them as a local competitor. But the problem is that "your" FTO in that country will be acting as a sister organization of your competitor, protecting them at every step. Such an FTO may call in a representative of your local competitor and ask him to be present at all negotiations. The ultimate customers for your goods may not necessarily have the same protective attitude as the FTO, even though their organizations have the same "owner" as your local competitor: the government.

Thus, you may want to deal as little as possible with the FTOs in some satellite countries.

The FTO may invite you to speak at a conference on your field and your type of products. Before agreeing to do so, it is wise to ascertain exactly who will be present. Obviously, if it is mainly personnel of your local competitor, you can either refuse to speak, or tailor your talk to the competitor.

The local competitor may try to obtain a licensing agreement. In many cases, this is not to your advantage. Thus, you may want to be prepared from the beginning to avoid your East Bloc competitors.

These competitors will often tell you how they cover the whole East Bloc through the Comecon trade association. For a few products, this is true, but for most industrial products, Comecon has been a flop, and East Bloc countries have become sick and tired of the sloppy quality of the products they have bought from each other.

Thus, if you should have, say, a Bulgarian licensee for some industrial equipment, his products will very likely meet more buyer resistance than your own in most of the other East Bloc countries, because experience has taught them that they should buy wine from Bulgaria, but not industrial products. Even if the other countries have plenty of Bulgarian leva and few dollars available, they may still prefer your industrial equipment to that of your East Bloc licensee.

If you are going to license someone in the East Bloc, it makes the best sense, of course, to license someone in your largest market there. For nearly all products, this is the Soviet Union. You may still reserve the right to continue to sell directly to the satellite countries, or alternatively, to license someone in one of the major satellite countries, except East Germany. (The other satellite countries ostracize East Germany to some extent, at least emotionally.)

A major deterrent to licensing an East Bloc producer is the impossibility of exercising quality control. For that reason you will probably refuse to license your trademark.

It is always difficult for an East Bloc licensee to pay the royalty in Western currency. Therefore, the East Bloc countries have devised all sorts of coproduction agreements that they propose to Westerners. Such agreements usually provide that the Eastern organizations pay for components purchased from the West, as well as their license fee, with subassemblies and other components made by them to Western specifications.

The difficulties of such agreements are usually in getting acceptable quality and sufficient quantity to pay for the know-how and components furnished to the Eastern supplier. For that reason, the agreements must provide for payment in Western money in case of failure of payment in components. (Such a clause may have to be approved by the local central bank.)

In satellite countries, it is not difficult to get appointments quickly, particularly not for high-level American businessmen. Thus, a round trip to these countries can yield a lot of information and many good connections, without necessitating extremely thorough preparations.

Just as in the Soviet Union, your efforts in a satellite country may not seem to produce results for a long time; then suddenly you will get a big order through the mail, or at least an invitation to come over and discuss a deal.

Advertising may not have quite as questionable value in some of the satellite countries as in the Soviet Union, if you can find just the right media for your products. In some cases, direct mail may be better than advertising in the local media. Both direct mail and other advertising are handled by the local monopoly advertising organization—Rapid in Czechoslovakia, Publicom in Rumania, Agpol in Poland, and Magyar Hirdeto in Hungary, to name a few.

In some of the satellite countries, you are likely to be approached by local persons or organizations that call themselves agencies for foreign firms. Their work often proves to be useless, but you may be lucky and find an agency that has a man who will take a personal interest in promoting your product. Even so, he will probably not be authorized to spend any money for the sale of your product, so you should be prepared to help him along at every step in order to make him effective, if you choose to deal with him at all.

Before deciding to use such an agent, you would be well advised to go *alone* to your main buyer or FTO and ask their opinion of him. Make certain that you get their true feelings, not just what they are supposed to reply.

Decentralization in the satellite countries is progressing, but there have been some reverses. These countries seem to go four steps forward, then three steps backward, then forward again. When one country is going backward, another one is progressing. The decentralization affects foreign trade, planning, production, and many other elements in the life of the country.

Since the independence movement in the satellite countries is very strong, it is not always advisable to take Russian-language brochures to them. Here is a list of the latest language preferences of most people under forty. I have assumed that you have brochures available only in English, German, French, and Russian.

Country	First Choice	Second Choice
U.S.S.R.	Russian	English
Yugoslavia*	English	German
Poland*	English	German
Rumania*	English	French
Czechoslovakia*	English	German
Hungary*	English	German
East Germany	German	English
Bulgaria	Russian	English

Several years ago, the countries marked with an asterisk used to prefer the language shown as second choice over the one shown as first. Many people over forty in these countries are still likely to know the language shown as second choice better. In the countries that have English as first choice, the second choice language is nearly equally well known.

In the above list, the countries have been arranged in the order of their volume of imports from the West. These imports are not proportional to the GNP of these countries. East Germany has over three times the GNP of Yugoslavia, yet it is next to last on the list, and Yugoslavia is second from the top. East Germany is low on the list because it is the only satellite country that follows the rule laid down by Moscow to import as little as possible from the West.

For many products, a very good entry to the satellite countries can be made at one of the three spring fairs. These fairs are located in Poznan, Poland; Brno, Czechoslovakia; and Leipzig, East Germany. Historically, the Leipzig fair is the most important one, but since East Germany has been somewhat ostracized by the other satellite countries, the Leipzig fair is not necessarily the best one if you want to reach all the satellite countries.

20

Future Trends
in International Business

PETER Drucker pointed out in his excellent book *The Effective Executive** that the truly important events in the business world are not the trends. They are the *changes in the trends*. To perceive these changes in trends early may mean the difference between success and failure for a business.

The ability to see the changes in trends will in the future be doubly important, because

> *Changes in trends will reach deeper and occur more rapidly than in the past.*

Political Trends

LESS INDUSTRIALIZED COUNTRIES

What will happen in the less industrialized countries? Take Peru, for instance. It would seem that the political outlook, import restrictions, customs difficulties, personal safety hazards, and other conditions have become less favorable there. Is this the future trend for less industrialized countries in general?

I do not think so—at least not in the less industrialized world as

---

* New York: Harper & Row, 1967.

a whole. Some countries that are going downhill now will perhaps go uphill later. Others have their trends reversed. Declines are noticed more than improvements; the improvements come more slowly but more steadily. On the average, the future trend for less industrialized countries will more likely be mixed than all downhill.

One important trend that is often forgotten, although it has been going on during the entire industrial revolution, is the decreasing relative economic importance of the less industrialized countries.

Today we are often told that we would be unable to get along without the less industrialized nations. These statements are misleading. If the industrialized nations were cut off from the less industrialized world for a number of years, they would take compensatory actions. More oil wells would be drilled; synthetic coffee, tea, and cocoa and some other imitation products would be developed amazingly quickly; substitutes for certain minerals and rare metals would be found; and new sources would be opened up to cover part of the needs for iron ore, copper, palm oil, and some other commodities.

Whereas the industrialized world, after a difficult period of adjustment, would continue without a great change in its standard of living, the isolation would cause such an incredible disaster in the less industrialized world that it could never really occur.

This theory is quite contrary to the statements by communist agitators in the less industrialized free-enterprise countries. These agitators claim that the standard of living in these countries is as low as it is because the countries are exploited by the industrialized nations, and that the less industrialized countries are paid too little in exchange for their commodities. The agitators charge that their countries have to pay too much for what they buy, and therefore are contributing to our well-being while we keep them in slavery and misery.

Nothing could be further from the truth. Today, if a less industrialized country is in the immediate zone of influence of an industrialized one, the former normally constitutes a burden, not an asset, to the industrialized country.

England, France, and Belgium discovered this many years ago and got rid of their colonies. Portugal still suffers the drain of her African territories. The daily expense to the Soviet Union of keeping countries like Cuba alive is very large. Our own foreign aid is a well-known burden, but the official foreign aid is by far not all that Americans pay to help less industrialized countries.

Much of the remaining aid is hidden in coffee price maintenance agreements and other similar agreements; certain taxes; subsidized governmental investment and trade guarantees; regulations regarding direct foreign investment that discriminate in favor of less industrialized countries; and other significant forms of preference.

Despite the cost of all this direct and indirect aid, we should not isolate ourselves from these less industrialized countries, but continue to help them. We should, however, give them less direct political and military assistance than we have in the past—as should the Soviet Union. I would hope that the United States and the U.S.S.R. will come to this conclusion at the same time, so that they can agree on an eventual hands-off policy for military supplies and direct interference.

OTHER POLITICAL SPECULATIONS

The French thinker about the future Bertrand de Jouvenel states: "I would willingly say that forecasting would be an absurd enterprise were it not inevitable. We have to make wagers about the future; we have no choice in the matter."

As businessmen, we are forced to make guesses about very uncertain matters of the future. Here are some of my guesses for the next fifteen years:

1. Dangers resulting from the availability of atomic weapons to irresponsible and unstable governments will increase sharply.
2. A few of the less industrialized countries will turn communist.
3. A few of the East European satellite countries will move away from Moscow-directed international communism and toward a less rigid and less centrally directed economy, which would, nevertheless, remain what they call socialistic.
4. Many Western industrialized countries, including the United States, will move toward more governmental controls and welfare programs. These controls may approach those that exist today in Sweden.
5. The Soviet Union will follow a liberalizing trend away from strong, central direction and toward more economic and personal freedoms. The United States and the U.S.S.R. will thus move slightly toward each other.

Trend No. 5 goes in the opposite direction of the recent trend in the Soviet Union, which has been toward harsher, more Stalinistic attitudes. After much traveling in the Soviet Union, I am nevertheless convinced that among the Soviet people, strong pressures are brewing toward liberalization. Although the Soviet government is not what we call democratic, it is still subject to pressures from public opinion.

The Soviet military–industrial complex (and I mean exactly that) will not be as concerned in the future with the capitalistic countries because of the deepening split with the emerging China. Therefore, this complex will not be adamantly opposed to an internal liberalization in the U.S.S.R.

6. There will be a deepening of the Sino-Soviet split. Despite all the shrill ideological arguments between China and the U.S.S.R., the Sino-Soviet split also has, to a large extent, economic causes. It is based on the natural conflicts between the partly industrialized and the less industrialized major communist countries.
7. Relations between the United States and the Soviet Union will continue to improve, probably even reaching something like a rapprochement. This is really a consequence of trends 1, 3, 4, 5, and 6, as well as a consequence of a very strong desire for change felt by people under 35 in the Soviet Union. This desire seems to be shared by many Americans under 30.
8. In the West, serious political danger will be caused by the increasing gap between the industrialized and the less industrialized nations. This trend could be considered a part of trend No. 1 on the preceding page.

It will be interesting to see in fifteen years whether and to what extent my guesses about these trends actually proved correct.

Trends in Foreign Markets and International Trade

MARKET SIZES OF INDIVIDUAL COUNTRIES

In Chapter 11 I gave some hints about how to forecast future market sizes for individual countries. It is important that we, as business managers, separate our own thinking from the loose and misleading talk about changes in market sizes. In the United Nations, for instance, they have talked for years about how the "developing" nations should catch up with the others. As far as I can see, most of this is political double talk, or perhaps just wishful thinking (wishful for the United States, too, because better distribution of wealth is in the interest of the United States).

Wishing for something, however, doesn't mean that it will happen, and businessmen should concentrate on the concrete facts, which indicate that the less industrialized countries are likely to improve their standard of living at a slower rate than the industrialized countries. Thus, these countries in general will unfortunately slide further and further behind the industrialized nations, and the differences between the "have's" and the "have-not's" will continue to increase.

CONGLOMERATION OF THE MARKETS OF INDUSTRIALIZED COUNTRIES

The future trend of greatest significance will not be the changes in the sizes of individual national markets, but the coming together of the markets of the industrialized nations into regional markets, some of which may become more than just trade blocs.

I would hope all the industrialized trade blocs could combine one day to form a single, huge market of all industrialized countries; but there is no evidence that politicians and voters will rise to the occasion and make these sensible arrangements within the next fifteen years. As businessmen, we have to be realistic and count out even having a fully integrated Atlantic community within that period of time.

On the other hand, as a trade bloc the EEC has already been highly successful. The political integration of the EEC was more difficult to achieve than we had all hoped when the community started in 1957. The very failure to integrate politically, though, became one of the keys to enlarging the membership of the EEC. In the more distant future, I hope that additional countries inside and outside the boundaries of Western Europe will be able to enter the EEC.

I would hope that someday an Atlantic free trade area could be formed between the EEC, the United States, and Canada, although, as I said, I am pessimistic about the prospects of this happening within the next fifteen years, and I am even more pessimistic about the possibility of Australia, South Africa, and Japan ever joining such a trade bloc.

Australia and South Africa would have serious difficulties integrating their small industrialized economies into that of an Atlantic community that would be so much more efficient through size alone.

Efficiencies of scale are of much greater importance than most people realize. Take as an example goods produced in moderate quantities in Australia and South Africa, such as cars. They end up being considerably more expensive there than in the United States or West Germany, although they are made by the same company, General Motors, in all four locations. The main reason, of course, is that the production runs in Australia and South Africa are smaller. The lack of local competing suppliers of subassemblies and industrial equipment also constitutes a serious handicap for small markets such as theirs.

For the foreseeable future, the less industrialized countries (with a few spectacularly successful exceptions) are likely to choose to stay out of the industrialized trade blocs, even though by doing so they will hurt rather than help themselves with their misplaced protectionism.

Since the birth of LAFTA and similar associations of less industrialized countries, I have been saying that these trade blocs would fail to achieve the integration of markets that their politicians had discussed. This prediction has turned out to be right in the past, and I see insufficient reason to change that generalized prediction for the next fifteen years, despite some slow improvements in the outlook.

I conclude, however, that:

> *The conglomeration of Western Europe, the growth of Japan as a market, and increased international trade are three factors that will greatly decrease the relative advantages that American companies have enjoyed in the past in terms of large home market size and efficiency of large-scale production.*

Nationalistic countertrends. Of course, there will be sharp and noisy countermovements against the conglomeration trend for industrialized countries. These countermovements, caused by fear of competition, nationalism, discrimination, protectionism, isolationism, and other shortsighted reasoning, may reverse the general trend, but only temporarily.

EAST–WEST TRADE

Despite the East European's spectacular lack of know-how about selling in the West, East–West trade is bound to grow tremendously. If the independence movements among several East European satellites should gain force, and if the West should come to some political rapprochement with the East, then East–West trade will, of course, spurt ahead even more.

International businessmen have been many years ahead of politicians in integrating the economies of the private-enterprise industrialized nations. In the future, these businessmen will also build more bridges to the communist countries.

Our globe is too small and our means of destruction are too great for old-fashioned nationalism and rivalries between different ideologies. International businessmen must continue to make our small world a better and safer place to live.

INTERNATIONAL COMPETITION IN THE UNITED STATES

We have seen how U.S. corporations will be able to extend their operations to other industrialized countries in the future. Foreign corporations are going to be able to extend their operations into the United States with increased ease. Consequently, there will be a rapid increase in imports into the United States and in foreign-owned subsidiaries operating in this country. I will explain why.

In the past, the sheer size of the U.S. market was a major barrier to European and Japanese companies. Today, since they have already penetrated several other national markets, the United States no longer looms so formidable.

Take, as an example, the case of a French manufacturer who formerly sold mainly in France, which has about one-seventh the market size of the United States. If he should expand into the United States and be as successful as in France, he would have to add something like seven times his former production capacity during the start-up period in the U.S. market. This would require an unreasonable expansion.

But now suppose that as a result of the increased European integration, the French manufacturer has already become dominant in his field in all of Europe, which in 1978 will have around four-fifths the market size of the United States. If this larger French manufacturer now expands into the U.S. market and is successful, he needs to add only 1.2 times his former production capacity, a much more reasonable rate of expansion.

You might ask why the company couldn't start in one corner of the United States, say in New England, and attempt to sell only there. This approach has been attempted repeatedly and has worked for a few products; but for most imported products it has failed, mainly because of the impossibility of advertising economically in only one region. As soon as a product is advertised in specialized trade magazines whose readership is nationwide, inquiries come in from all over the country, and a nationwide sales and service network becomes a necessity.

For these and sometimes for other reasons, entrance into the U.S. market is usually an all-or-nothing proposition for foreign corporations.

Many European and Japanese companies have discovered—sometimes painfully—that the U.S. market is not only larger, but also quite different from their own. For example, Renault found out, after a couple of years in the United States, that the electric generators in its cars were inadequate for U.S. habits and had to be replaced.

Foreign corporations have also discovered—again, often painfully—that not only must they have American managers to run their U.S. subsidiaries, but they also have to listen carefully to what their managers advise them to do, even when it sounds strange to them. Thus, in the future, foreign-owned operations in the United States will generally be stronger.

JAPAN

Perhaps it is because Japan will undergo the greatest changes, the largest improvement in standard of living during the next fifteen years, that I have real difficulties trying to make any forecasts for that country.

How can one predict what will happen politically in a country that is undergoing such enormous economic change? Certainly, Japan will become quite independent of the United States, but will Japan continue as a Western ally? I believe so, but nobody can be certain. Japan will probably go her own way even more obstinately than France did under de Gaulle.

Far behind the healthy leaps and bounds of Japan's present economy, her economic policies are being improved very slowly and very reluctantly. To be frank, Japan's present trade policies seem, from the outside, to be recalcitrant, isolationist, and antiquated; but if viewed from inside Japan, they seem more understandable.

In general, whenever a country's policies seem strange from the U.S. point of view, you should study the matter instead from the point of view of that country, taking into consideration its cultural background and the inside reasons that eventually led to the formulation of the "strange" policies. In nearly all cases, these policies are then much more understandable.*

Since the bombing of Hiroshima, Japan has tended to be antimilitaristic, but this trend may not continue, and Japan might well become quite militaristic. Military discipline goes well with the Japanese character. The Japanese in civilian life regard their superiors with awe and are quick to obey. I said ten years ago that there probably will be both internal and external pressures on the United States to decrease military presence in and around Japan. We see it now, and these pressures will continue to increase. The U.S. forces there will have to be replaced by young Japanese from a generation that has grown up long after Hiroshima, a generation that is extremely (and justly) proud of the power and independence of Japan.

From now on, we had better acknowledge that whatever happens in Japan is going to be more important to the world as a whole than what happens in West Germany, France, or the United Kingdom.

---

* As has been previously mentioned, the same should be done for company policies: If your foreign subsidiary manager insists on doing something his way, you cannot sit in Cleveland or New York and tell him he is wrong. Instead, you need to go to him and make sure that you know what led to his decision. It is more than likely that you will discover that he was right. And in those instances when he is wrong, you will have the opportunity to persuade him that your way will be better.

When Japan's standard of living and labor costs pass those of several West European countries during the next 15 years, it is likely that Japan will no longer be able to maintain her past real growth rate of around 10 percent. It is encouraging that enlightened Japanese economists have recognized this. A diminution of the growth rate is already well in progress. Even so, I would guess that Japan's growth rate will continue to be higher, even in the early 1980s, than that of other industrialized countries.

Part of the reason for the higher growth rate is the Japanese willingness to work hard and to forgo immediate benefits in favor of saving capital for the future or investing in education.

It should be noted that the above comments refer to average growth rates over a period of years. Individual future years probably will have violent up-and-down swings in Japan because of the basic instability of her business economy, which is built so much on extended credit.

INFLATION

Inflation probably will continue to plague most of the industrialized world, primarily because full employment and business expansion are very tempting objectives for the politicians. Few countries will enforce the fiscal discipline that West Germany has imposed on itself so successfully.

With increased foreign trade, inflation will tend to spread beyond the borders of the country where it is most prevalent at the time and therefore become more international.

We businessmen could hope for inflation to become *more equal from country to country,* so that we could avoid one of the reasons for currency devaluations and revaluations, but this may prove to be a vain hope.

We could also hope for the rate of inflation to become *more constant in relation to time,* so that we could avoid the unsettling increases and decreases in the inflation rate, but even this probably will not happen, considering the general irresponsibility of politicians and the lack of knowledge and patience of their constituents.

INTERNATIONAL TRADE IN INTELLECTUAL SERVICES

For many years, world trade in concrete, physical objects has grown, partly because of international differences in physical skills. For example, the United States imported watches from Switzerland and women's dresses from France and exported earth-moving equipment and passenger aircraft. This was because people in the respective countries were either exceptionally good at designing or making these items, or they put a greater effort into production or organization of production, as the case may be.

I predict that another commodity will enjoy a rapidly increasing import–export trade: intellectual services, the product of mental rather than physical skills. The results of research, consulting engineering work, and many other services will be traded internationally in vastly expanded quantities. As an explanation, consider the following examples from the research field.

Basic research can often be performed in several West European countries at a lower cost than in the United States. Some American-paid basic research is already being done in Europe for that reason. This importation by the United States of the results of basic research is bound to increase.

Applied research, on the other hand, seems in many fields to be yielding more practical products per dollar spent in the United States than in Europe, despite the higher salaries.*

Perhaps the reason is the difference in attitude that exists among American researchers, research directors, and management in general. Americans often want to try something new to see if it is better, whereas many Europeans consider the new and untried as probably worse. Europeans often know all the reasons why "it cannot be done."

At present, there would be too much vested executive interest and misguided pride for the British ICI to have an applied research center in New Jersey or for the German AEG to have one on the outskirts of Boston. But if the top managements of those fine companies† were to analyze the situation factually, they would probably conclude that such American applied research centers are exactly what they should have.

Instead, many European companies find themselves dependent on licensing—which is another form of paid intellectual import—and on copying—which is an unpaid intellectual import.

Competitive pressures and eventual realization of the facts will one day force companies to expand international trade in intellectual services, despite local pride.

Finally, there is likely to be a substantial increase in an old type of intellectual import that is now coming from new directions: emigra-

* This is, of course, a gross generalization, and there are many exceptions. In some industries, foreign applied research has been more productive. The Swedish and Austrian steel industries are examples; they are now consulted by U.S. steel companies.

† Both companies are usually referred to by their initials; their complete titles are Imperial Chemical Industries Ltd. and Allgemeine Elektricitäts-Gesellschaft. —*Editor's note.*

tion of some of the best-educated and most energetic people from less industrialized countries to industrialized nations with higher standards of living.

This is sad for the less industrialized countries, because these emigrants are the people they need to keep at home most, and they are more scarce in those countries than in the industrialized countries.

Trends Toward Globalization

NEED FOR BIGGER PRODUCTION UNITS

We have noted that technological change is occurring more and more rapidly in most industries. Research and development will become increasingly costly. A leading company will have to run faster and faster to stay ahead. It will have to budget for more research each year to do that.

As noted above, in order to pay for this research a company would have to make its sales volume so big that the percentage of sales spent on research remains reasonable. The only way to do this is to sell in the world market.

Obviously, this imperative applies to foreign companies just as much as to U.S. corporations. Thus, successful foreign companies cannot afford to leave the big, rich U.S. market to their American competitors to play in as they wish and harvest all alone.

The internationalization of production is progressing rapidly. Although reliable figures are hard to obtain, it seems that somewhere between 11 and 13 percent of the American GNP comes from foreign-owned enterprises. In the noncommunist world outside the United States, the percentage of foreign-owned production should be about twice as high. Whatever these percentages actually are, they are rising rapidly, both inside and outside the United States.

It is obvious (and regrettable) that it will be increasingly difficult under these circumstances for small manufacturers to find a geographic market area that is covered inadequately by the large firms. Therefore, small manufacturing companies will have an even tougher time just staying alive.

For these reasons, the competitive battle will occur more and more among the larger companies that operate globally.

INTERNATIONAL DISTRIBUTION OF COMMON STOCK

In terms of distribution of stockholders, a truly global company does not exist today.

In the future, an increasing number of companies will feel that if they produce dividends for stockholders in only one or two countries, they will not succeed in the long run as truly global companies. Despite all the barriers against it now, these companies will strive to internationalize stock ownership and even the boards of directors of the parent companies.

ANTITRUST AND NATIONALISTIC COUNTERTRENDS

Against this general trend toward larger global companies, there will be two countertrends:

1. Increased antitrust activity and legislation.
2. Nationalism, protectionism, isolationism, and xenophobia. (As mentioned earlier, nationalism is also a countertrend against the conglomeration of industrialized markets.)

I believe that the general trend toward larger global companies will win out over these two countertrends in most industrialized countries, or at least in those of North America and Europe. Even so, international top managers had better prepare for the future strength of the two countertrends with one or two steps.

First, they must ensure that all future international line managers get some grounding both in U.S. antitrust legislation and in the antitrust regulations of the countries and market blocs where they operate. Many of the foreign regulations were written recently, others are being written right now, and several will be added in the near future.

Future international line managers must know enough about antitrust regulations to know when they have to ask lawyers for further advice before plunging their companies into needless trouble. This step is particularly important for companies that dominate their industry.

On the other hand, companies that are not well known should try to present the appearance of being of local nationality in countries such as Germany, France, the United Kingdom, and Japan. This can well be done without directly making the American parentage any secret, as we noted earlier.

We also noted, however, that in most smaller countries, the American parentage can well be shown. In many, it is even an outright advantage.

Here again, Japan is a special case, but for most industries, it can be stated that if you succeed in getting majority ownership in a Japanese company, it is preferable to let that fact be known to as few people in Japan as possible, and to have Japanese managers run the company virtually as if it were Japanese-owned.

Advances in Communications and Transportation

It is much easier to make predictions in the field of communications than in the field of politics; but have you considered what a few days in the life of a company's international operations manager might be like in, say, 1988?

Let's call our manager Jim and suppose that he works for Acme, Inc. We will follow Jim as he enters his office on January 2, 1988, in a New York suburb.

On his desk are the telexed monthly statements and financial analyses of Acme Pty. Ltd. from Australia and Nihon Acme KK from Japan. It is too early for the European statements to be in, because it is still only 14:30 local time in Western Europe, so there is plenty of time for Jim to sit down and think about the Japanese and Australian situations. Meanwhile, the Business International wire news service comes by telex—a very expensive news service, but it is computer controlled to include only items of likely interest to Acme.

After a while, Acme's German *Geschäftsführer* telephones. This man happens to be in a real mess. Jim pushes some buttons on his phone and thereby connects Acme's outside antitrust lawyer to the same line for a three-way conversation. Could they please both come over right away, the German asks. Jim scans his calendar and replies that he can take the flight at 18:00. (Back in '73 it was called 6:00 P.M.) The lawyer cannot go but promises to be available by phone. (He always prefers not to use telex for antitrust advice.)

Two and a half hours after take-off, Jim's flight lands in Frankfurt. The next day, Jim gets up at 5:00 New York time (which is 11:00 German time) and joins the German Acme managers at their lunch table, but Jim eats breakfast. (During his short stay in Europe, it is not worthwhile to change over completely to local time. By working noon to late evenings local time, Jim gets in more sharp working hours than if he had changed to local working hours.)

Whenever Jim needs the advice of a specialist at the home office, he pushes the buttons on the nearest office or hotel phone, reaching the person he wants directly, without going through any manual switchboard anywhere.

A few days later, after Jim has helped solve the Germans' problems, he eats lunch while the Germans have dinner. He then flies back to

New York, dictating a report on the way. He arrives home well in time to have dinner with his family.

Later, Jim reflects on the marvels of communications in 1988:

"International air freight now has taken over many categories of freight from steamer transportation. In fact, cargo ships now handle mainly commodities and heavy shipments, but no light or highly intricate industrial goods. Telephone, high-speed telex, and facsimile are so cheap now that they are used to an extent that was totally unimagined back in 1973. In those days, businessmen wrote letters—now letters have been nearly totally replaced by high-speed telex, and we use mail for long, involved reports that have no urgency. Can you imagine waiting a whole week for a reply to a letter? People really must have had lots of time back in those leisurely days. And sometimes those letters were delayed even further, because they had to go to somebody for translation. It's sure different now—we just dial the telex message through a computer center that automatically sends a rough machine translation immediately after the message in the original language."

It might be technically possible to achieve most of the advances in travel and communications described above in the late 1970s, but businessmen probably will be mentally behind the technical advances, just as today the procedures for foreign travel of many American companies remain what would have been appropriate back in the days of piston-engine aircraft. (A few American companies are even still in the steamer era.)

Improved communications will profoundly affect both business attitudes and the manner of working. Let's look at what changes improved

A few American companies are still in the steamer era.

communications and travel will produce in the typical corporate organization.

New York export offices or New York overseas operations offices of Midwestern companies are bound to continue disappearing, because Cleveland and St. Louis are getting closer to Cologne and São Paulo through communications and travel improvements.

In 1988, a subsidiary manager in Brazil or Germany will not be any farther away from a New York head office than is a branch manager in St. Louis in 1973. The foreigners may have different laws, taxes, languages, and attitudes, but in *transmission* of communications they will be just as close as the St. Louis branch is today.

Within the U.S. head offices of companies with substantial international activities, I would guess there will also come a trend away from the separate international division and toward integration of international work into the whole head office. For such international companies, it will not be appropriate to have a head office concerned with domestic operations and an appendage concerned with international operations. That is only satisfactory for those companies with limited international activities, or with international activities in a field that is different from the field of the domestic part of the companies.

A U.S. corporation with substantial international interests must in the future have all its top corporate officers familiar with the international aspects of their daily work, whether they are involved in marketing, manufacturing, finance, legal aspects, research, or engineering. They must consider the corporation from a worldwide viewpoint.

Trends in Management

NEED FOR INTERNATIONAL-PEOPLE-MANAGEMENT ABILITY

International-people-management ability is something we'll need far more of in the future. We'll need to acquire a thorough understanding of the differences in cultural background, outlook, reactions, and attitudes, as well as a thorough understanding of the best ways to motivate people of different nationalities and help them to work well together with a minimum of conflict.

Anyone who has tried to get German, French, and British subsidiary managers to cooperate and pull in the same direction, instead of in three different directions, knows only too well the need for international-people-management ability. Those three nationalities are all European. Had the managers been from three different continents, building a more cohesive unit could have been even more difficult.

Although international-people-management ability is much needed now, the rapid growth of international business operations will make it even more necessary in the future.

FOREIGN MANAGEMENT METHODS

It is incredible to me that modern American management methods have not penetrated more into Europe. The thoughts and ideas have reached the colleges and some advanced firms, but not European business in general. When they do, we will see stronger management in Europe and elsewhere in industrialized countries.

Japan is here again a special case. The Japanese probably will go their own way even in management methods. Americans might do well to study the Japanese methods, because the Japanese certainly are successful. However, their success might be more the result of other factors than management progress.

Improvements in management are coming much more slowly and will appear later in the less industrialized countries.

HOW THE PROSPECTIVE INTERNATIONAL BUSINESSMAN CAN
PREPARE HIMSELF FOR 1988

Suppose a young man just entering college comes to you tomorrow and asks what he should study in order to become a good international business executive in 1988. What would you tell him?

Here are my suggestions for allocating his study time, both for his college years and for his home study program during the first ten years following college:

40% Studies conducive to understanding how to manage, motivate, and influence people in many countries.
25% Languages: Either German, Spanish, and Russian; or Japanese.
10% Antitrust laws and regulations, including the new ones that will come up later in the 1970s.
25% Other business administration subjects such as marketing, sales, accounting, economics, business law (other than antitrust), and general trade and business practice.

These subjects, of course, are in addition to his study in the specific field of the company he joins.

If possible, the aspiring international executive should ask his company to send him for a few years each to Europe, Japan, and a less industrialized country. This foreign experience, coupled with the first 65 percent of his studies as shown above, should afford him good international-people-management ability, provided he has what it takes to begin with.

21

Underdevelopment: A Mission for Businessmen?

A famous visitor to Brazil, after traveling around there for several months, exclaimed enthusiastically, "This is the land of the future!" A man who had lived most of his life in Brazil replied sadly, "Yes, Brazil has always been the land of the future, and Brazil will always remain the land of the future."

This happened a few generations ago. Unfortunately, today it is equally true, as it is of most of the less industrialized countries.

I may as well confess it right away: I love Brazil. And Venezuela. And some other countries in the less industrialized world. I love their people. Therefore I feel so terribly sorry for them, because their progress is too slow in relation to that of industrialized countries.

Climate

There are various causes for underdevelopment; but it would take another book to discuss them, so I will mention only that climate is one of the foremost causes. Many fine people have argued vehemently that this could not be one of the prime causes for underdevelopment, but I believe they are wrong.

Both tropical and severe arctic climates tend to retard progress. Nearly all the less industrialized countries are within 30 to 35 degrees latitude of the equator. Apparently they lack the invigorating influence of winter, which supports the spirit of hard work that helped countries like West Germany and Japan to rise quickly from the ashes of World War II to their great prosperity only 25 years later.

Of course, the tropical countries also lack the need to plan ahead for winter; but it seems that this lack of need for planning is less important than the direct languishing effects of a tropical climate.

Politics

One of the immediate problems of the less industrialized countries is that the expectations of their people advance at a much more rapid rate than that at which the people themselves are able to advance their standard of living.

This causes a fervent desire among the poor people to get out of their rut—quickly. Only the communists are cynical enough to promise them quick remedies. The communists' problem, however, is that they cannot deliver, either. This is quite apparent in Cuba and in other countries.

The socialist parliamentary system in India has also tried to deliver the better life and has also failed. The Indian government's detailed controls of private enterprise have had a severe hampering effect on the standard of living—precisely what the controls were supposed to help.

The effects have been equally negative for other types of governmental efforts, such as most protectionist measures, currency controls, and excessive welfare requiring nearly confiscatory taxation of incentives.

In summary, it can be said that barring a few exceptional areas, such as parts of Puerto Rico, the free enterprise system and democracy have failed to deliver even a medium standard of living to the average person in the less industrialized countries; and yet, so have all other economic and political systems.

In this unfortunate situation, investments are subjected to political and economic risks, whether they are made by private industry in free enterprise countries or by communist governments in less industrialized communist countries.

Governments can aid the national development of these countries by working on the infrastructure in areas such as education, health services, sanitation, and road building. But when governments become involved in business, they hinder more than they help.

Doing Business in Less Industrialized Countries

Many companies find that their exports to some less industrialized countries are being replaced by goods manufactured locally. Thus, these companies are faced with three disagreeable alternatives:

1. To go into a sole or joint venture in these countries and risk the capital.
2. To license somebody there and risk creating a more efficient competitor.
3. To try to continue exporting and risk being locked out.

Each case is different, and little can be generalized about how to solve the dilemma, or even about how to do business in the less industrialized countries.

These nations are all so different from one another. In one country the main difficulty might be living with a wild inflation; in another one it might be the intricacies of a highly developed system of graft, like the *mordida;* in a third, the government interference in all aspects of business and private life; in a fourth, the personal insecurity that makes the life of expatriates difficult and risky; in a fifth one it might be sensitive government relations and excessive nationalism that scares away foreign investors and ruins the chances of industrial development.

In most of the less industrialized countries, friendly and close government relations are highly recommended for all relatively successful corporations. Companies must identify with the host country. All successful expatriates will do the same and cultivate personal relationships with local nationals.

Despite the hardships, some countries are making headway in some areas. Mass-produced consumer goods have been made in many of the less industrialized countries for some time. Industrial equipment used in quantity is beginning to be manufactured in some countries (although usually at very high cost). Still, sophisticated industrial equipment used only in small quantities normally cannot be made economically in less industrialized countries.

Underdevelopment: A Mission for Businessmen?

What can we as international businessmen do about underdevelopment? The industrialized nations can and should do little in the area of politics to aid the less industrialized countries—except be sympathetic neighbors.

Direct interference with the politics of other countries causes more harm than good. So does a direct give-away welfare program, whether from private-enterprise countries or from communist countries.

To be effective, aid must work as a catalyst. We must help these countries help themselves rather than help them directly. We must teach their teachers rather than teach the people directly.

Our help should be primarily in education—not only education in the three Rs, but more importantly, education in the responsibility and attitudes needed for a complex industrial society. This aid benefits people of industrialized countries as well, because in the long run the growing gap between the less industrialized world and our world will be dangerous to our welfare.

The less industrialized countries offer plenty of challenges for the energetic, creative, innovative young businessman—and plenty of difficulties, risks, and disappointments. Let us now see how businessmen can—and do—help these countries.

Let's assume that you are successful in the world market, including the less industrialized countries, and that you earn lots of profit for your company. What effect does your success have beyond your financial statements? Was it all worthwhile?

It has been shown during recent years that one of the main needs of the less industrialized countries is not capital but change in people's attitudes and work habits. Professor Hans B. Thorelli, of Indiana University, pointed out as early as 1966 that multinational corporations are among the principal agents promoting these changes.* They thereby make a much more important contribution to the less industrialized host countries than the capital they invest.

Edward F. Denison, of the Brookings Institution, estimated that advances in knowledge and education in the 1950s created four times more growth in GNP than did investment in plants and equipment.

We saw in the beginning of this book that expanding your company's market to include the whole world gives your company increased profits and the opportunity to invest more in research and in the development of more know-how, which in turn benefits your stockholders, foreign customers, and foreign employees.

But at the same time, your company will be demonstrating better management and better operating policies to foreign competitors. These other companies will then grudgingly begin to improve their management and operating procedures. As a result, their profits may increase, their employees may receive better pay, and the economic condition of their

---

* *Southern Journal of Business,* Vol. I, No. 3, pp. 1–9.

country may improve toward more stability and growth. Thus, excellent management of multinational corporations has a multiplying effect far beyond the perimeters of the multinational companies themselves.

The Peace Corps and some other efforts in foreign aid are admirable and well worthwhile. But by working efficiently, honestly, and straightforwardly in their companies' self-interest, international businessmen do more to improve the standard of living around the world than all the Peace Corps and foreign-aid people put together.

Recommended
Information Sources

THE best information available in this field is principally found in periodicals. The following are outstanding.

PERIODICALS

Business Asia (weekly), *Business International* (weekly), *Business Latin America* (weekly), *Financing Foreign Operations* (monthly updating), and *Investing, Licensing & Trading Conditions Abroad* (monthly updating). These excellent periodicals are published by Business International Corp., 757 Third Avenue, New York, New York 10017.

Business Europe (weekly) and *Eastern Europe Report* (bimonthly). Published by Business International S.A., 12–14 Chemin Rieu, CH-1211 Geneva 17, Switzerland.

International Management. Published monthly by McGraw-Hill Publishing Co., Ltd., Maidenhead, England.

BOOKS AND ARTICLES

The Challenge of World Poverty, by Gunnar Myrdal. New York: Random House, 1970.

Creative Management, by Shigeru Kobayashi. AMA, 1971.

Doing Business with Australia. Management Bulletin 87. AMA, 1966.

"How to Negotiate in Japan," by Howard F. van Zandt. *Harvard Business Review,* November–December 1970.
How to Profit in the Far East, by Worth Wade and Toshio Shimizo. Ardmore, Pa.: Advance House, 1967.
The International Businessman in Japan, by Herbert Glazer. Rutland, Vt.: Charles E. Tuttle Co., 1969.
Japan: Meeting the Challenge of Asia's Richest Market. Research Report. New York: Business International Corp., 1966.
"The Multinationals Ride a Rougher Road." *Business Week,* December 19, 1970.
Organizing for Asia/Pacific Operations. Research Report. Hong Kong: Business International, Asia/Pacific Ltd., 1972. Available from Business International Corp., 757 Third Avenue, New York, New York 10017.
Organizing the Worldwide Corporation. Research Report. New York: Business International Corp., 1970.
Penetrating the International Market, by Robert Douglass Stuart. Management Report 84. AMA, 1965.

HANDBOOKS AND GUIDES

The Businessman's Guide to Europe, by Paul B. Finney. New York: McGraw-Hill, 1965.
Electric Current Abroad. (Lists voltages and frequencies available in foreign countries.) Published by Bureau of International Commerce, U.S. Department of Commerce. Available from U.S. Government Printing Office, Washington, D.C.
Exporters' Encyclopaedia. Published annually by Dun & Bradstreet Publications Corp., 99 Church Street, New York, New York 10007
Foreign Commerce Handbook. Washington, D.C.: Chamber of Commerce of the United States, 1967.
International Trade Handbook, edited by Leslie L. Lewis. 2nd ed. Chicago: Dartnell, 1967.
International Trade Reporter Export Shipping Manual. Updated weekly. Published by Bureau of National Affairs, Inc., 1231 25th Street, N.W., Washington, D.C. 20037.
International Yellow Pages. Published annually by Reuben H. Donnelly Corp., 235 East 45th Street, New York, New York 10017.
Living Abroad, by Eleanor B. Pierce. New York: Pan Am Publications, 1965.

MISCELLANEOUS SOURCES

Bureau of International Commerce, U.S. Department of Commerce, Washington, D.C.
Her Majesty's Stationery Office, Atlantic House, Holborn Viaduct, London EC1P 1BN, England.

La Documentation Française, Sécrétariat Géneral du Gouvernement, 29-31 q. Voltaire, Paris 7e, France.

United Nations, United Nations Plaza, New York, New York 10017.

Most embassies.

Various large banks and major auditing firms with offices around the world. These have excellent, periodically updated publications. I have particularly used the Foreign Information Service of First National City Bank, 399 Park Avenue, New York, New York 10022; and the International Business Series of Ernst & Ernst (certified accountants), 140 Broadway, New York, New York 10005. The latter is a series of booklets on the most important countries, giving a general profile and describing their tax system, their legal system as it affects corporations, and their major accounting regulations.

SOURCES FOR SPECIFIC CHAPTERS

Chapter 3 (On distributors)
Improving Foreign Distributor Performance. Management Monograph 22. New York: Business International Corp., 1965.

Chapter 4 (On licensees)
Appraising Foreign Licensing Performance. New York: National Industrial Conference Board, 1969.

International Licensing Agreements, edited by Gotz M. Polzien and George B. Bronfen. Indianapolis: Bobbs-Merrill, 1965.

Licensing in Foreign and Domestic Operations, by Lawrence J. Eckstrom. 3rd ed. 2 vols. New York: Clark Boardman Co., Ltd., 1971.

Licensing Know-how, Patents, and Trademarks Abroad, by Lajos Schmidt. Reprints available from Baker & McKenzie, Prudential Plaza, Chicago, Illinois 60601.

Public Law Considerations in Common Market Licensing, by Klaus Newes. Speech presented at the annual meeting of the Licensing Executives Society, October 1968. Reprints available from Baker & McKenzie, Prudential Plaza, Chicago, Illinois 60601.

Chapter 5 (On subsidiaries)
"After the Acquisition: Continuing Challenge," by Charles M. Leighton and G. Robert Todd. *Harvard Business Review,* March–April 1969.

"Corporate Surgery: How Disinvestment Can Boost Profits by Cutting Sales," by James C. Lobb and Charles D. Ellis. *Corporate Financing,* May–June 1970.

"How to Play the Acquisition Game," by Lawrence T. Peifer. *Management Review,* January 1969.

"How to Size Up a Merger Candidate," by Robert E. Healy. *Business Management,* December 1968.

"Master Plan for Merger Negotiations," by Gary E. MacDougal and Fred V. Malek. *Harvard Business Review,* January–February 1970.

Measuring the Profitability of Foreign Operations. Management Monograph 39. New York: Business International Corp., 1970.

"Why Mergers Don't Jell," by Alan N. Schoonmaker. *Personnel,* September–October 1969.

Chapter 6   (On joint ventures)

Joint International Business Ventures, by W. G. Friedman and G. Kalmanoff. New York: Columbia University Press, 1961.

"Joint Venture Troubles." *Fortune,* February 1966.

"Les fusions d'entreprises." *La revue fiduciaire,* July 1969. (Address: 51 rue de la Chaussée d'Antin, Paris 9e, France.)

Mergers, published by Department of Trade and Industry. London: Her Majesty's Stationery Office, 1969. (Address: Atlantic House, Holborn Viaduct, London EC1P 1BN.)

"The Perilous, Problematic, and Profitable Business of Joint Ventures." *Business Management,* May 1967.

"Problems in Joint Ventures." *International Management,* December 1966.

Chapter 8   (On staffing)

Compensation of Overseas Managers: Trends and Guidelines. New York: National Industrial Conference Board, 1969.

Developing the International Executive, by Dimitris N. Chorafas. AMA Research Study 83. AMA, 1967.

"The Problem of International Executive Compensation," by S. David Stoner. In *Compensating Executive Worth,* edited by Russell F. Moore. AMA, 1968.

Chapter 9   (On cultural barriers)

The Communication Barrier in International Management, by Dimitris N. Chorafas. AMA Research Study 100. AMA, 1969.

The Silent Language, by Edward T. Hall. New York: Doubleday, 1959.

"The Silent Language in Overseas Business," by Edward T. Hall. *Harvard Business Review,* May–June 1960.

Chapter 10   (On financing, pricing, and economics)

Applying Financial Controls in Foreign Operations, edited by Elizabeth Marting. IMA Special Report 2. New York: International Management Association, 1957.

A Banker's Guide to Financing Exports. New York: American Bankers Association, 1964.

"The Euro-Dollar Market: Some First Principles," by Milton Friedman. *Morgan Guaranty Survey,* October 1969. (Reprinted by University of Chicago Graduate School of Business, Selected Paper No. 34.)

"Financial Management in Multinational Corporations," by Merwin H. Waterman. *Michigan Business Review,* January 1968.

Financing International Operations, edited by William D. Falcon. AMA Management Report 82. AMA, 1965.

The Gnomes of Zürich, by T. R. Fehrenbach. London: Leslie Frewin Publishers Ltd., 1966.

International Financing: Tapping the Entrepôt Capital Market, edited by John H. Hickman. Management Bulletin 95. AMA, 1967.

International Money Management, by Max J. Wasserman, Andreas R. Prindl, and Charles C. Townsend, Jr. AMA, 1972.

"Re-evaluating ROI for Foreign Operations," by Rolf M. Treuherz. *Financial Executive,* May 1968.

Solving International Pricing Problems. Research Report. New York: Business International Corp., 1966.

Chapter 11 (On market statistics)

International Financial Statistics. Published monthly by International Monetary Fund, 19th & H Streets, N.W., Washington, D.C. 20431.

Statistical Yearbook. Published annually by United Nations, United Nations Plaza, New York, New York 10017.

The World's Telephones. Published annually by American Telephone & Telegraph Co., 195 Broadway, New York, New York 10007.

Yearbook of International Trade Statistics for Imports and Exports. Published annually by United Nations, United Nations Plaza, New York, New York 10017.

Chapter 13 (On planning)

Multinational Corporate Planning, by George A. Steiner and Warren M. Cannon. New York: Macmillan, 1965.

Planning for Profits. Research Report. New York: Business International Corp., 1967.

"The Special Problems of International Long Range Planning," by Irwin Goldman. *Management Review,* April 1965.

"Technological Forecasting," by James Brian Quinn. *Harvard Business Review,* March–April 1967.

Top Management Planning, by George A. Steiner. New York: Macmillan, 1969.

The Workbook for Corporate Planning, by Edward J. Green, AMA, 1970.

"Your Company Can Gain from International Long Range Planning." *Business Abroad,* May 1, 1967.

Chapter 17 (On general legal matters)

Contracts and Agreements I through *Contracts and Agreements V.* Series of reprints of contracts and agreements used by major U.S. corporations. Essex, Conn.: Foreign Operations Service, 1958–1971. (Address: Gates Road, P.O. Box 185, Essex, Connecticut 06426.)

Guide to I.C.C. Arbitration. Paris: International Chamber of Commerce, 1963. (Address: 38 Cours Albert Premier, Paris 8e, France.)

The International Business Environment, by Harold J. Heck. AMA, 1968.

A Lawyer's Guide to International Business Transactions, edited by Walter Sterling Surrey and Crawford Shaw. Philadelphia: Joint Committee on Continuing Legal Education, 1963.

"Overseas Distributorship Agreements," by Marcellus R. Meek. *Business Lawyer,* April 1966.

Rules of Conciliation and Arbitration. Paris: International Chamber of Commerce, 1967. (Address: 38 Cours Albert Premier, Paris 8e, France.)

On industrial property rights:

"International Patent Planning," by John R. Shipman. *Harvard Business Review,* March–April 1967.

Patent Cooperation Treaty. July 11, 1969. Available from U.S. Patent Office, U.S. Department of Commerce, Washington, D.C.

"Protecting Industrial Property Rights Abroad," by Andrew W. Brainerd. *Business Abroad,* January 11, 1965, and January 25, 1965.

On antitrust laws:

The Common Market and American Antitrust: Overlap and Conflict, edited by James A. Rahl. New York: McGraw-Hill, 1970.

On taxation:

Company Taxation in Western Europe. Amsterdam: Bank Mees & Hope N.V., 1971. (Address: 548 Herengracht, Amsterdam, Netherlands.)

"Tax Considerations for International Operations," by Walter A. Slowinski. University of Missouri at Kansas City *Law Review,* Winter 1966.

"United States Taxation of Foreign Income: The Increasing Role of the Foreign Tax Credit," by Walter A. Slowinski and Thomas M. Haderlein. University of Illinois *Law Forum,* Vol. 1965, Fall Number.

Chapter 18 (On European markets)

The American Challenge, by Jean Jacques Servan-Schreiber. New York: Atheneum, 1968.

EEC on the Move. Research Report. New York: Business International Corp., 1972.

France Enters the 70's. Research Report. New York: Business International Corp., 1970.

How to Profit in Europe, by Worth Wade. Ardmore, Pa.: Advance House, 1968.

Le pari européen, by Louis Armand and Michel Drancourt. Paris: Réalités, Entreprise/Fayard, 1968. (Address: 6, rue Casimir-Delavigne, Paris, France.)

Researching the European Markets, by Robert J. Alsegg. AMA, 1969.

Chapter 19 (On East Bloc countries)

Coexistence and Commerce: Guidelines for Transactions Between East and West, by Samuel Pisar. New York: McGraw-Hill, 1970.

Doing Business with Eastern Europe. Research Report. New York: Business International Corp., 1972.

Doing Business with the U.S.S.R. Research Report. New York: Business International Corp., 1971.

The New Yugoslavia. Research Report. New York: Business International Corp., 1968.

The Unperfect Society, by Milovan Djilas. New York: Harcourt, Brace & World, 1969.

Chapter 20   (On future trends)

The Age of Discontinuity, by Peter F. Drucker. New York: Harper & Row, 1969.

Future Shock, by Alvin Toffler. New York: Random House, 1970.

1985: Corporate Planning Today for Tomorrow's World Market. Research Report. New York: Business International Corp., 1967.

Winning the Markets of the 1970s. Research Report. New York: Business International Corp., 1970.

The Year 2000, by Herman Kahn and Anthony J. Wiener. New York: Macmillan, 1967.

Index

124105